"*Voices from the Spectrum* is a symphony of rich den[...]
contributors who graciously share their myriad [...]
struggles, hopes, and thoughts on life mingled with autism spectrum disorders. At times easy to read and at times the kind of reading that leaves lumps in the throat and thuds in the heart, *Voices from the Spectrum* is always honest and genuine. I whole-heartedly recommend it."

—*Liane Holliday Willey, Ed.D.*
Author of Pretending to be Normal *and* Asperger Syndrome in the Family

"This is a masterful collection of essays describing the various personal experiences of autism—it is uniformly poignant, often brutally honest, and always uplifting. Many of the selections were penned by parents who relive the anger, sadness, struggle, and either the gradual resolution of the condition or acceptance of their child's unique weaknesses and talents. Just as compelling are the voices of other members of the autistic community including siblings, grandparents and caring professionals. Most surprising and welcome are the contributions of affected adults who can directly offer insights into the inner reality of autism. These include those who relate the sensory issues, social myopia, and learning differences that define Asperger syndrome as well as one of the lucky ones with classical autism whose language and cognitive abilities returned fully after severe regression in early childhood.

There are many other places to find definitions of the autistic spectrum, discussions of scientific advances, and resources for supporting the educational, therapeutic or emotional needs of the autistic child. But *Voices from the Spectrum* is the first comprehensive collection of personal experiences that encompasses the tragedy, the mystery, and the gifts of autism.

Thank you for the opportunity for an early look at this fascinating volume."

—*Lawrence W. Brown, M.D., Associate Professor of Neurology & Pediatrics*
Co-Director Pediatric Neuropsychiatry Program
The Children's Hospital of Philadelphia

"Drs. Ariel and Naseef have edited a gem of a book. Intended for families of children with autism, *Voices from the Spectrum* includes poignant essays from parents, grandparents, siblings, and professionals—all of whom have been touched by this vexing condition. Depending on severity, autism spectrum disorders challenge families emotionally, behaviorally, and socially.

These carefully edited essays present a rich portrait of families as they come to grips with the vicissitudes of autism. They reflect a kaleidoscope of perspectives, emotions, and coping mechanisms that will help readers sort out their path as they come to grips with the challenges of this disorder."

—Milton Seligman, Ph.D., Professor Emeritus, University of Pittsburgh
Co-author of Ordinary Families, Special Children

"Cindy Ariel and Robert Naseef have put together a unique collection of first-hand accounts of the autistic spectrum, providing a voice for parents, grandparents, siblings, as well as people with Asperger Syndrome. These voices complement the professional perspective and teach us how autism feels to each of these observers. A rare anthology."

—Simon Baron-Cohen, Professor
Autism Research Centre, Cambridge, UK

"It is with great pleasure that I endorse this collection of essays written by families and professionals who live with and care for children with Autism Spectrum Disorders. This book gave me the unique experience of seeing 'behind the scenes' with a view of the impact on families of the diagnosis, treatment, and interactions with treating professionals.

I recommend that you put this book on your list of required reading for family, friends, colleagues, and trainees to improve care of children and families with autistic spectrum disorder."

—Susan E. Levy, M.D.
Director, Regional Autism Center
The Children's Seashore House of The Children's Hospital of Philadelphia

"*Voices from the Spectrum* is a beautiful collection of personal essays. A must read for any parent struggling to accept and embrace the diagnosis. This book gives you a rare and heartfelt glimpse of personal journeys of parents, grandparents, siblings, professionals, and adults affected by autism who have found peace of mind, joy in their life, and tremendous personal growth in the process."

—Nancy D. Wiseman, Founder and President of First Signs, Inc.
Author of Could It Be Autism?
A Parent's Guide to the First Signs and Next Steps

Voices from the Spectrum

of related interest

Asperger's Syndrome
A Guide for Parents and Professionals
Tony Attwood
Foreword by Lorna Wing
ISBN 1 85302 577 1

Everyday Heaven
Journeys Beyond the Stereotypes of Autism
Donna Williams
ISBN 1 84310 211 0

A Different Kind of Boy
A Father's Memoir About Raising a Gifted Child with Autism
Daniel Mont
ISBN 1 84310 715 5

Coming Out Asperger
Diagnosis, Disclosure and Self-Confidence
Edited by Dinah Murray
ISBN 1 84310 240 4

Asperger Syndrome in Adolescence
Living with the Ups, the Downs and Things in Between
Edited by Liane Holliday Willey
Foreword by Luke Jackson
ISBN 1 84310 742 2

Voices from the Spectrum

Parents, Grandparents, Siblings, People with Autism, and Professionals Share their Wisdom

Edited by Cindy N. Ariel and Robert A. Naseef

Jessica Kingsley Publishers
London and Philadelphia

First published in 2006
by Jessica Kingsley Publishers
116 Pentonville Road
London N1 9JB, UK
and
400 Market Street, Suite 400
Philadelphia, PA 19106, USA

www.jkp.com

Copyright © Jessica Kingsley Publishers 2006
Second impression 2006

The right of the contributors to be identified as author of this work has been asserted by
them in accordance with the Copyright, Designs and Patents Act 1988.

All rights reserved. No part of this publication may be reproduced in any material form (including photocopying or storing it in any medium by electronic means and whether or not
transiently or incidentally to some other use of this publication) without the written permission of the copyright owner except in accordance with the provisions of the Copyright, Designs and Patents Act 1988 or under the terms of a licence issued by the Copyright
Licensing Agency Ltd, 90 Tottenham Court Road, London, England W1T 4LP. Applications
for the copyright owner's written permission to reproduce any part of this publication
should be addressed to the publisher.

Warning: The doing of an unauthorised act in relation to a copyright work may result in
both a civil claim for damages and criminal prosecution.

Library of Congress Cataloging in Publication Data
Voices from the spectrum : parents, grandparents, siblings, people with autism, and professionals share their wisdom / edited by Cindy N. Ariel and Robert A. Naseef.— First American pbk. ed.
    p. cm.
Includes bibliographical references.
ISBN-13: 978-1-84310-786-6 (pbk. : alk. paper)
ISBN-10: 1-84310-786-4 (pbk. : alk. paper) 1. Autism in children. 2. Autistic children—Care. 3. Autistic children—Family relationships. I. Ariel, Cindy N. II. Naseef, Robert A.
RJ506.A9V65 2006
618.92'85882—dc22

                        2005028733

British Library Cataloguing in Publication Data
A CIP catalogue record for this book is available from the British Library

ISBN-13: 978 1 84310 786 6
ISBN-10: 1 84310 786 4

Printed and bound in the United States by Thomson-Shore, Inc.

We are dedicating this volume to the special needs of children around the globe.

After World War II, children in Europe faced famine and disease. The United Nations International Children's Emergency Fund (UNICEF) was created in December 1946 by the United Nations to provide food, clothing, and health care to over 8 million children in 12 countries ravaged by war. Today UNICEF (www.unicef.org) is the world's largest, most respected and widely recognized children's development organization with a presence in over 158 countries. UNICEF's work with children is non-political and non-controversial and provides opportunities for maximum support from the widest constituency. Current projects include tsunami relief efforts, HIV/AIDS, girls' education, and health care.

Autism is a global public health issue. UNICEF advocates for change on behalf of all the world's children and is the world's leading organization working specifically for children, including children with disabilities. Its global reach allows sharing knowledge across borders.

With an overarching vision of peace and social progress, UNICEF is committed to ensuring special protection for the most disadvantaged children—victims of war, disasters, extreme poverty, all forms of violence and exploitation, and those with disabilities. All of these programs are entirely dependent on voluntary contributions. With this in mind the editors of this volume are pledging all of the royalties of this volume to UNICEF—for our world's children, the future of the human spectrum.

Cindy N. Ariel and Robert A. Naseef

We are grateful to all the individuals who dedicated their time and efforts to voice their experiences and submit essays for this book. We regret that we could not publish all of them.

Contents

Part 2: The Grandparents' Connection   119

Part 3: The Sibling Experience   139

Part 4: Diagnosed on the Spectrum

Part 5: Working on the Spectrum

Introduction: Learning from Autism

Is a diagnosis on the autism spectrum a puzzle to be solved, or is the child with the diagnosis someone to be embraced and accepted just as she is? As the editors of this collection of essays, drawing upon our professional and personal experiences, we firmly believe that both are essential—with many lessons to be learned.

For this book, parents, people with autism, close relatives, and professionals of various disciplines were invited to write about their experiences. We wanted to hear lessons of mind and heart culled from life and professional practice. The contributors were asked to address how autism has changed their lives in love and/or work, what they have learned, and what they would want others to know that might help them. We were interested in situations from the most mild to the most severe—from classic autism to Asperger's. We were deluged with hundreds of essays from many countries including Australia, Canada, Ireland, Kuwait, the United Kingdom, South Africa, and many parts of the United States. We were faced with the unexpected and unwelcome task of rejecting many heartfelt and well-written accounts.

You will be reading 60 personal accounts of issues such as diagnosis, treatment options, and family relationships. While the journey of each person is unique, we wanted to pull together many accounts about individual turning points and personal evolution. As the number of new cases skyrockets around the world, the issues are many and complex including the causes of autism, the impact on families, the status of research, and the need for early diagnosis and intensive treatment. In 1980, the incidence of autism was 1 in 2000. In 2005, the incidence is in the vicinity of 1 in 200—a tenfold increase which experts agree cannot be accounted for by the changes in the diagnostic system alone.

As psychologists, we help families deal with the often treacherous emotional landscape once autism strikes. It's been called the "autism bomb." People often spontaneously describe how the diagnosis of their child's autism was a bomb that exploded their hopes and dreams. The calendar of their lives was ripped off the wall and replaced by an uncertain future as

they began intensive intervention to help their child, while they struggled
to find hope and to regain their footing in life. In our offices:

- A mother sobs as she talks about her 12-year-old son with
  Asperger's syndrome and remembers the time he said, "I wish my
  imaginary friends were real so that someone would play with me."

- Several teens with autism are learning how to control their temper
  and handle teasing.

- Another mother recounts how her life seems like "one long day."
  Her 8-year-old son rarely sleeps through the night. His autism
  includes seizures which have been difficult to control despite the
  excellent care of a neurologist.

- A 12-year-old boy is trying to understand why other students are
  tired of hearing him talk about one of his special interests, baseball
  and football statistics.

- In a group of fathers, a dad reiterates how not a day goes by that he
  wishes his son didn't have autism. Still, he never wishes he didn't
  have his son.

- Another man who has two boys with autism weeps as he recalls
  when his oldest son stopped talking.

- Young women and men in college with Asperger's syndrome try
  painstakingly to understand the complicated social rules of dating.

- Another mother tells her support group, "I wish the autism was a
  thing, and then I could drag it out of him and beat it to death. But it
  is a part of him and I love him."

- Couples come looking for help because they fear their marriage will
  break under the strain.

There are some things which we cannot change. As Josh Greenfeld wrote so
poignantly in *A Child Called Noah* in 1970, "There is a strain on any marriage whenever a baby is sick. And we always have a sick baby." Nonetheless, most families discover how to enjoy and celebrate everything their
beloved children learn to do. They find consolation and rewards in the reality that people with autism teach the rest of us profound and spiritual lessons in acceptance and in honoring the diversity of the human condition.

Yet there are also things we must change. Families are under siege. So many
children have been affected, and so many families have had their lives dis-
rupted. The money being spent on research is a tiny fraction of what is

needed. For example, we need more research about the vaccines and environmental toxins that may be harmful to children. We need answers about why certain parts of the United States, such as areas in California and New Jersey, have much higher incidences than other areas. We need to understand more of the neuroscience of autism, so that more effective drugs can be developed to help the condition when needed, regardless of the cause.

Even more immediately urgent is the need for state of the art services for children and their families who have been struck by autism. Research has demonstrated that early and vigorous treatment can make a huge difference in the outcome for individuals affected by autism and other developmental disorders. Alarmingly, a two-year-old child just diagnosed with autism in the United States gets only a few hours of home-based services per week, while experts recommend 30 to 40 hours of programing. In many parts of the world services are just beginning to be developed. Parents shouldn't have to beg and scream for services when their child enters school. Many of these schools are poorly funded, especially in the inner cities, and have inadequately trained staff and few or no opportunities for developing social skills by including children with autism with their same-aged peers. It is heartening to have the issues finally begin to be recognized more widely. We need to do our best to find solutions.

In this volume, we are pleased to bring you compelling voices from the lives of people and the work of professionals along the autism spectrum. The essays in this collection tell of the trials, the heartaches, and the emotionally charged path that individuals and families must travel in order to find peace of mind and joy in life as they grow and develop. The experiences and insights that you will read will make you laugh, make you cry, and help you to reflect upon your own experiences. Whether you are a family member, a person with autism, or someone who works along the spectrum of autism, we hope and trust that these voices will provide beacons of hope and positive models of acceptance and understanding.

Part 1: Raising a Child on the Autism Spectrum

Raising any child can be a daunting task. Given that each child and each family is unique, the emotional and practical challenges for parents seem endless. Learning along the way and fueled by the child's growth and development, the parent–child relationship flourishes. But what happens to the heart and soul when a child is diagnosed on the autism spectrum? The challenges can seem overwhelming and even harsh. Grief, worry, anger, and despair can drown out the hope and joy of daily life. Yet as the contributors to this volume demonstrate, love, endurance, courage, and acceptance are not in short supply.

Several themes emerge in the essays that comprise this first section. Initially parents struggle with the symptom clusters of autism: problems with speech and language, difficulties relating to others, and repetitive activities. Parents initially become very upset with their child's difficulties and struggle to accept their child's eventual diagnosis. They begin the protracted journey to put together the appropriate interventions. Through the heartache, in the passage to acceptance, they love their children passionately, they learn everything they can about their children, about autism, and they learn about themselves in the process. Some go on to create programs and services for others.

Just as the children fall along a spectrum from classic autism on one end through Pervasive Developmental Disorder to Asperger's syndrome on the other end, the parents also fall along a continuum. Their experiences do not sort out into discrete categories, for the journeys of mothers and fathers are as diverse as their children's. The children that parents describe can be extremely different from one another in terms of the severity of their symptoms. Undoubtedly, some situations are more trying than others. The stress levels of some families are certainly traumatic in nature, especially when severe behavior problems repeatedly trigger the reliving of intensely pain-ful emotions.

A reader may find that some essays do not sound at all like their child; nonetheless, the editors have found value in each journey chronicled here. Each story is authentic and deeply felt. We chose the essays for the models of insight and understanding that each one presents. We hope that each one has something to offer to every reader, but if not, take what helps you and leave the rest.

1. The Ride for Autism: A Community Gets in Gear to Help Solve the Puzzle

Andrew Abere

"Your son has a classic case of autism. I'm sorry, but there is nothing I can do for him." Those may not have been the doctor's exact words to my wife Lisa and me, but they are close. And they were almost as devastating as the original diagnosis of autism our son had received two years earlier at the age of 19 months. This time, we had flown to Chicago with our three-year-old son Spencer for an appointment with a prominent neurologist who had some success treating children with autism. But his words crushed any hopes of success we might have had for our son. It was a somber flight through gray skies back to our home in New Jersey.

We did not give up on seeking help for Spencer. We continued to visit other doctors. It seemed like we covered the whole pharmaceutical alphabet, from Anafranil to Zoloft. We attended conferences to learn more about autism. We enrolled Spencer in various therapeutic programs. He was already attending one of the top schools in the country for children with autism, but the pace of his progress seemed glacial compared to his classmates. He was nonverbal, and there was no sign he would ever gain language. Some of his behaviors were beginning to worsen, and new ones were beginning to emerge. Every morning when his school bus pulled away from the house, we could hear the echo of the words of that doctor in Chicago. Spencer was a "classic case." We began to resign ourselves to the fact that he was not going to be one of the miracle recovery stories we had read about in books and magazines.

Despite all the hours of therapy, numerous trips to doctors, and trials of medications, Spencer remained a happy child. In fact, one therapist described him as having "happy autism." When we related this comment at a parent support group meeting, the psychologist who led the meeting asked, "Why wouldn't he be happy?" He went on to explain that for Spencer, autism is the normal state of the world. He does not know that he is different and that we want him to change. In fact, he said, Spencer probably thinks it is the rest of us who are different and need to change! Yet, somehow, we could not tap into Spencer's happiness. The future seemed endless and bleak. Little did I know that Spencer's autism would soon become a source of inspiration and pleasure.

We strived to make his childhood as normal as possible. We tried to teach him to ride a tricycle, but he would not keep his feet on the pedals. Lisa, ever the resourceful mom, got some Velcro and put it on the pedals and on the bottom of his sneakers. Problem solved! But Spencer soon outgrew his tricycle. So, when he was seven, I set out to buy a larger tricycle, like the one you might see a senior citizen ride. I went to speak to the owner of the bicycle shop where I took my bicycle for repairs, hoping she could help me.

She was puzzled, and asked why I would possibly want such an item for my seven-year-old. Doesn't he want a cool bike like all the other kids his age? I explained that Spencer had autism and his problems with motor skills made a two-wheeler impractical. A smile of recognition came over her face. It turned out she had a nephew with autism, about the same age as my son. Our conversation turned from tricycles to autism. I steered it back a bit when I remarked that I had seen a number of brochures in her shop for charity bicycle rides for various diseases and disorders, but never one for autism. She told me that if I ever found one that she would ride in it with me.

I surfed the internet looking for such a ride but could not find one anywhere in the United States. Then it struck me. Why don't I start one? It seemed there was nothing I, or for that matter, anyone could do to cure Spencer. But I could sure try to raise money and raise awareness about autism to make his life, and the lives of others with autism and their families, better.

I had participated in charity bicycle rides, but I had never organized one. Where would I start? I returned to the bicycle shop to persuade the owner to help me. I told her that I had not found a ride for us but, before I could get the next word out of my mouth, she said, "Let's start one and my shop will help sponsor it." With that, the Ride for Autism was born.

We decided on a beneficiary for the ride, the New Jersey Center for Outreach and Services for the Autism Community (COSAC), a nonprofit agency founded in 1965. COSAC provides information and advocacy services along with family and professional education and consultation and had been very helpful to Lisa and me after Spencer was diagnosed.

While the shop owner was happy to sponsor, she did not have much time to help plan the ride. I realized quickly that I had a lot of hard work ahead of me. Here, though, Spencer became a source of inspiration. He was one of the hardest-working kids I knew, spending hours in therapy while most of his peers were playing. I got busy, sending emails to local bicycle clubs, asking for help. I received a response from only one club, but fortunately some of their members agreed to map out the routes. We were in business!

We would, however, need seed money to proceed. I decided to ask local businesses for sponsorship. My first visit was with the sales manager at a car dealership where I had purchased a couple of cars, thinking he might want to do something nice for a repeat customer. I began to explain the ride and to describe COSAC. He stopped me. I expected he was going to tell me that they would be unable to sponsor. Instead, he told me he knew the agency very well, because his son had recently been diagnosed with autism and sponsorship would not be a problem. Other sponsors came on board and we built a nest egg to bankroll the operation.

Next, we needed volunteers to help with the event. COSAC put the word out to their membership. Emails and phone calls came in from around the state, from parents, siblings, teachers, psychologists, therapists, and other professionals, wanting to help. We still, however, needed more warm bodies. One evening, I took Spencer to a meeting of the bicycle club that was helping us to try and get more of their members on board. When they got one look at my boy, with his rosy cheeks, chestnut eyes and warm smile, they could not resist!

The first Ride for Autism was held on June 16, 2001, which, coincidentally, was my fortieth birthday. I could not have asked for a better birthday gift. Over 400 people signed up to ride and we raised over $13,000. The success inspired us to make it an annual event. Despite the long hours and hard work, I find it to be a source of immense pleasure. My heart warms when I see all those cyclists and volunteers, knowing that they could have done something else on a Saturday in June, but they chose to come to the ride.

I have made many new friends as a result of the ride. I also have found a new side of myself. I built something from scratch, and helped draw a community together to raise money, raise awareness, and have a day of fun. Other organizations took note of our success and asked me to assist them with their fundraising events, which I was happy to do. Soon, I had something of a second career in the fundraising field.

Spencer, now 13, continues to be a source of inspiration. Lisa and I passed on that larger tricycle for him, opting instead for one of those cool kid's bikes, but with training wheels. After a few years we took off the training wheels to see how he would do. To our amazement, he took off like Lance Armstrong! His seven-year-old sister, Amanda, likes to ride around our neighborhood with him. Last year, Spencer and I raced as a father and son team on a tandem bicycle in the New Jersey State Special Olympics games. I was just happy to ride with him, but with his legs pumping furiously, we managed to take the silver medal! And as I stood on the podium with my son, I cried—not tears of sadness, but tears of joy.

Andrew Abere is President of Ride for Autism, Inc., a nonprofit corporation he founded in 2001. He also serves as Ride Director of the Ride for Autism charity bicycle tour. He and his wife Lisa live in central New Jersey with their son, Spencer, and daughter, Amanda. Andrew is a member of the Board of Trustees of the Eden Family of Services, a nonprofit organization founded to meet the lifespan needs of individuals with autism. He received the 2002 Development Achievement Award from the New Jersey Center for Outreach and Services for the Autism Community (COSAC). Oddly enough, he counts cycling among his hobbies. You can find out more about the Ride for Autism at www.ride4autism.org.

2. The Tree's on Fire: Voicing Experience

Marc Biondo

My precious son, Tony, I want you to know more than anything else how much I love you. I have yearned to express this from the beginning and still do now. I want the whole world to know how great you are. I love to explore the world with you, sharing the wonder and awe of consciousness. You are unique. There is no one like you; there has never been, nor will there ever be another you.

Be proud of your uniqueness; you are not a copy of anyone else. Celebrate yourself. I celebrate you and the miracle of your life. What a great joy it is sharing time with you. If only each day could be eternal so we could visit all the great places on earth together. That's why there were the big hugs, camping trips, amusement parks, water balloon battles, and pillow fights. I hope your memories of childhood are wonderful as you begin now to pass through adolescence and grow into manhood.

As a toddler you were always larger than other kids in nurseries and preschool classes. You were very friendly and would introduce yourself to everyone. You were happiness set loose upon humanity. Despite the occasional tantrum, you were the joy of each babysitter. Then something happened, something worse than the "terrible twos."

When you were two and a half years old we trusted your wise, experienced teacher who observed how you were in her class and brought it to our attention. She noticed that you did not talk or play with others. For unknown reasons you were not joining the other toddlers in group activity. You seemed not to hear when the teacher spoke, or when we spoke to you at home. And you did not speak.

We brought you to professionals to help you learn to speak, and to listen. I held onto the belief that you would speak in full sentences and learn to tell your mother and me what you needed and wanted. You did not disappoint me.

Early during this time you said something I will never forget. Arriving home one autumn afternoon you noticed bright red leaves on an ornamental bush. Expressing an incredible vision of your experience, you uttered, "The tree's on fire." My heart soared with joy. You not only spoke an entire sentence, you spoke imaginatively. You expressed a vision of your senses that told me volumes about the person you are. Not everyone sees a burning bush, son, so count yourself blessed.

All our time spent trying to teach you to say, "I want juice," or "cookie please," and your spontaneous expression was poetry about the world around you. Later came another utterance full of wonder and awe at the beauty of the clouds speeding across the sky. You said, "The moon is sailing." My heart nearly burst with joy and pride at those moments; even now remembering those times moves me deeply.

You worked hard with the staff at Abilities for Speech and Language. You learned to listen, attend to and follow directions, express your needs, socialize, and broaden your imaginary play. The triumph was beyond simply identifying needs, which itself is a miracle. You transcended mere survival to a higher level of self-expression.

You entered a different school as you turned three. Ignorant of educational laws, I argued unsuccessfully when you were separated from other "normal" children. Fortunately we all learned something very important anyway. We learned empathy and compassion for other people and learned to accept others with different human limitations. As my ideals moved from my head to my heart, I learned courage, tenacity, and advocacy. I also learned something significant: to take a stand for personal beliefs and values and defend them tirelessly. When you take a stand you discover who shares your values and who opposes them. It was not easy for us, but it was worth it.

When we decided to take a stand about your placement in school, the *battle for Tony* began. Some wanted to diminish you, deciding disability was more important than your ability. Some seemed to ignore the magnificent potential you have as a human being. They spoke in a strange language of professional jargon and acronyms while ironically criticizing your idiosyncratic unintelligible language. In their detachment some seemed to forget you are human, not just assessments, evaluations, and diagnoses. I fought and resisted with all my might, experiencing defeat and learning from the experience. I believed in you and you made me proud.

You had to learn our common language and I had to learn their jargon. I began to speak the languages and jargon of doctors, educators, and therapists. You loved dinosaurs, so I let you play with all the toys, books, videos, and whatever else helped you learn about them. You learned their names, eating habits, size, and everything else you could. You even learned to pronounce their scientific names, those Latin multi-syllabic descriptive words. You are amazing when you enjoy something. You amazed us when you went to the zoo and knew the names of all the animals, however exotic. You received the Presidential Award for Outstanding Educational Improvement.

One of our proudest times was the preschool year the teacher asked me, after the first week she spent with you, "What is your son doing in my class?" I was so glad she asked! I told her of the last two years of your education and the difficulty we had with the school system. She called together all those involved and moved you into the mainstream of school life. She simply did the right thing. I know you do your best and you make the effort it takes to learn. You exceeded everyone's expectations, even my most optimistic ones.

During this time I came to know other true allies. Parents for Exceptional Progress/Professionals for Exceptional Progress was a fellowship of parents and professionals who sought answers, shared resources, and provided moral support to one another. Thanks to the many wonderful people we met there, I became a better parent and a more knowledgeable advocate. Yet all I have learned from professional presentations, from books, newspaper articles, magazines, and the internet would have been useless without your brave spirit. You never quit, never give up. You may stumble but you rise again and keep going, just as you did learning to ride a bike.

The biggest surprise of my life came on your seventh birthday. Around midnight I awoke to you anxiously shouting, "What's the matter, Dad?" I saw myself covered in blood, unable to arise, stand or walk. A perforated ulcer was draining my life. You dashed for the telephone to call an ambulance. Returning relieved and certain of rescue, you declared confidently "Don't worry, Dad, everything is going to be all right. God is going to take care of you." How ironic that the once unintelligible boy would be the one whose faith and courage would save my life. You overcame fear and trusted in a positive outcome. Learn from this that negative experience need not obstruct your destiny.

Remember, my precious son, you can accomplish extraordinary things when you believe you can. There is no failure when you learn from your experience. Your fun-loving and flexible attitude will serve you. Many people will find your characteristics charming and appealing and become your friends, so be yourself and enjoy life. Know that you are brave, loving, and deeply loved. God loves you, and so do I.

Marc Biondo resides with his family in Baton Rouge, Louisiana. He has a B.A. in English from Louisiana State University. He is a child education advocate volunteering in his son's School Improvement Team, his local school district Special Education Advocacy Council, and with advocacy support groups throughout Louisiana. Marc's son, Tony, attends school and continues to achieve, still surprising skeptics, still inquisitive and enthusiastic. Active in the Boy Scouts of America, he enjoys computers and martial arts, and excels in music and spelling. Tony is being inducted into the Junior Beta Society.

3. Perspectives

Maribel Danta

A plate slipped from my hands and fell onto our cold tiled kitchen floor. It was so quick I couldn't hold on. It shattered into what seemed to be a hundred jagged pieces, like all the expectations I had for my son, Gabriel. I bent down to pick up the pieces only to catch a glimpse of my reflection on the oven door. I barely recognize myself anymore. As I gather the pieces one by one, my mind takes its usual tour through my mental to-do list, but always ends up thinking of a new way to banish our uninvited guest: Autism.

I think the cruelest thing about autism is that it's deceitful. While pregnant, you go through your series of tests. Everything is fine. You have your baby. You count ten fingers, ten toes, a healthy, perfect baby. You spend hours looking at your child, deeply in love with him. You wonder what he's thinking, what he's feeling, what he will be like, what his passions will be, and what kind of a life he will lead. You give yourself permission to imagine him playing with his siblings, cheering him on in his baseball game, taking his prom pictures, even attending his college graduation.

As I watched my son reach his milestones (rolling over, crawling, sitting up, walking), I drew sighs of relief with documented celebrations and stickers marking each event. One day though, I felt a shadow. My child was over a year and a half old, but he started to regress. He no longer motioned when he wanted something. He was not talking; no mama or dada. I knew something was very wrong, but no one seemed to be listening.

At first the professionals told me things like, "He is active, sometimes active children take longer to develop speech," and "He may be having problems adjusting to the newborn, there is always a bit of regression there." I was also told the ever popular, "Girls typically develop speech earlier than boys." But it got worse. Eye contact was gone, and there was no response when I called his name.

After a series of evaluations, an acknowledgement that there was something wrong, a placement in special education classes, and a team of therapists, I spent my days researching different ways to help my child. Although I did see some progress, my son was still not where a normal four-year-old should be. The final diagnosis came in; the culprit revealed itself. I remember the moment my fears were confirmed. I felt the words bounce off the walls and hit my hands, chest, spine, and face with their stinging bite. My Gabriel has autism. My special child has special needs. I tried to hold on to my dreams, but like the plate they fell to the floor and shattered into what seemed to be a hundred pieces. I began to pick up the pieces, catching a glimpse of what I thought to be true, who I was, and who I am becoming.

It would be fair to state that I have been developmentally delayed in grasping reality. Ironically, having to cope with my son's severe developmental delays has given me the opportunity to address my own dysfunctions. What has been my greatest challenge has been embracing the "one day at a time" mentality. I have three sons. Between my oldest and youngest there is only three years difference. Gabriel falls in between. Even though life is lived one moment at a time, I've taken it for granted, constantly getting ahead of myself, forgetting to enjoy the journey. The thing about rushing through every moment is that I missed out on not only the beauty around me, but, more importantly, the experience of nurturing and being nurtured by my surroundings. In the frantic pace to move ahead, I've never really learned how to let go, or the healthy way to hold on.

As an artist, I should have applied in life what I knew to be true on canvas: pay attention to the whole piece, plan, outline, rework, make sure there is symmetry in your composition, paint in layers to assure translucency, honor perspective, pay attention to details, study your subjects, their depth, their volume, light and dark are of equal importance, shed light on what you wish to bring out, work through your errors and learn from what doesn't feel right. Know your colors, their power and complement, don't fear using them. Seek balance, express yourself, challenge yourself, take time, be patient, know the limits of your medium, know when it's time to stop and acknowledge that it's done. But instead, I found myself silently lost in the extremities of anguished desperation. I read many books on autism, each with a different approach to treating it, all with the same conclusion: no cure.

Autism consumed me, haunting me while I went about daily routines. Late at night, I would hold private negotiations with God, offering different deals so that my son could be spared. It may sound silly and futile, but the truth is that I fear my son's tomorrows. I sometimes feel I am freefalling into an abyss of "what will happen," and "what if," because no one can tell me he'll be OK. No one can guarantee where my son will be developmentally in the future. I am relying on a big *if* he gets better, and I cannot always sleep through the night. Negotiation at that point seems like a worthwhile try, what would I have to lose? So somehow, right before the sunrise, I fall into a brief slumber lulled by my whispered mantra; my prayer "Please let him be OK."

While I know all my children are vulnerable, the undeniable vulnerability that drapes Gabriel suffocates me. I have many worries: the health and well-being of my family, my financial situation, my career; yet nothing compares to the worries I have for Gabriel, his present, and his future. I see these same worries in the eyes of my sorority sisters in the autism community. These women are my mirror images. Like me, they smile; they go on, somehow handling it. But the sadness that escapes through a shared glance is palpable, and immediately understood.

I've been completely humbled by a disorder that is incomprehensible. I've been humbled by the inner strength my husband possesses, the tenderness of my children, the support of my parents, but mostly by the profound love I have for them all. There is empowerment in that kind of love. I imagine it's that same love that has motivated grassroots efforts, initiated research, and built organizations. It's a love that drives a search for answers, for truth, for a better future, for a cure. I want to be a part of that. For starters, I will no longer dream for my children, I will give them the skills they need to dream their own dreams and set their own goals, whatever they may be. I will stop trying to work against time; instead, I will work with it, teaching my children to respect the rhythm a balanced life sets, savoring the sensory experience.

The dance between setting limits and going beyond them is performed on a fine line. I will continue to educate myself on everything that concerns all of my children. I will make sure that they have the best chances possible. Gabriel has many skills, but due to autism, his learning is splintered. We have to find a way to fill in the gaps so that one day he could have a fluent conversation, and he could answer "why" and "how." I know there is so much in him, so much in all these children. We can't give up. We are all a work in progress, with some good days and some bad. But we still live it one day at a time.

I stand up. I'm cradling all these broken pieces. It would be easy to throw them away, but I choose not to. There is potential in everything, we just have to allow ourselves to see beyond an altered state. I know that these broken pieces, arranged just so, with the right bonding, can come together once again to become a uniquely beautiful mosaic.

Maribel Danta, a native New Yorker, and her husband Carlos Rodriguez are raising their three sons, William, Gabriel, and Carlos, in Center Moriches, Long Island. Maribel has a degree in studio art and art history from New York University and runs her own business, Art by Maribel. Her artwork can be seen online at www.ArtbyMaribel.com. Maribel is also the Vice President of NAALI, Long Island's local chapter of the National Autism Association, and is the co-creator and co-director of the annual Autism Awareness Fair: see www.autismfair.com.

4. Facing the Pain of Autism—and Surviving

Nicholas Dixon

Ironically, a few days before Katie was diagnosed with autism, she had survived a nasty scare when we feared she was dying from a febrile seizure. Unlike the febrile seizure, though, the autism wouldn't go away. And indeed a child *did* die the day of her diagnosis: the daughter of our hopes and expectations, who would go on to a professional career using what we were sure would be her exceptional intelligence and abilities, who would marry and have children of her own, and with whom we would have endless conversations in which we would share our love of philosophy and life. On the contrary, we learned that Katie would have to defy the odds even to be capable of independent living at any time in her life.

My wife's irrepressible optimism was a great asset from the outset. She devoured the autism literature and focused quite sensibly on what we could do to help Katie. She pointed out that my moping and feeling depressed wouldn't help Katie and make her autism go away. I pointed out that grief isn't something you can turn off at will. My wife's family, thanks to their sincere religious beliefs, which give them remarkable strength in the face of adversity, were upbeat and remained thrilled with what a delightful girl Katie is (which is true). I felt like a character in a science fiction movie in which the world is endangered by a terrible threat, to which everyone is blind, except for one person. I wanted to yell (actually I did sometimes!), "Can't you see? I know Katie's wonderful and that we've got to do everything we can to help her, but why can't you admit that autism is a terrible disorder to have?"

I felt alienated by some of the books that I read and some of the presentations that I attended. The children with autism described in books by their parents and the adults with autism who speak at conferences are nearly always high functioning. This does not deny the enormous challenges that people with high-functioning autism or Asperger's (and their parents) face, or the inspirational nature of their triumphant stories of accommodation and success. It was just that little information contained in these stories seemed applicable to my own daughter, who wasn't speaking or displaying any remarkable intelligence. Moreover, I found the cheerful tone of several books as well as the upbeat Hollywood endings to be utterly divorced from the realities that I was confronting. If one half of people with autism never speak and the vast majority are never able to live independently, they and their parents need more realistic role models.

Nearly four years have passed since we learned that Katie has autism. She is now six years old. Just as when loved ones die, time really does help to heal the anguish of having a child with a severe disability. I've learned to let go of the dreams that I had for Katie before we learned of her condition. Besides, they always were *my* dreams. Katie herself never had any such dreams or expectations and she is perfectly happy with herself the way she is.

Even though I've let go of my inappropriate dreams, I'm still concerned about the *reality* of Katie's life. Life is difficult for a child with autism. Because she's still nonverbal, Katie sometimes can't communicate her desires and this can be very frustrating for all of us. She sometimes gets inconsolably upset for reasons that we can't discern. During some of her tantrums she bites herself and thrashes her body about wildly, risking injuries to herself and others. I fear terribly for her future. Because my wife and

I spend so much time with Katie, we can understand her needs remarkably well, despite her lack of language. And her preschool teacher and aides are wonderful, caring people. But as she grows older she will spend more and more time in school, away from the safe environment that we have created for her at home. What confidence can we have that her future teachers will be compassionate and understanding? I fear sadistic bullying at school from children without disabilities.

I anticipate that Katie will live with us for the rest of our lives, at least while we are physically able to care for her. My darkest, most painful thoughts pertain to Katie's life when we are no longer around. She will almost certainly need considerable assistance in living. Will we be able to leave sufficient funds to pay for decent care for the rest of her life? Regardless of how much money we leave, no one will love her as much as we do. I am tormented by the image of her being physically and sexually abused, unable to defend herself or report the unspeakable crime.

I'm also concerned for less noble, more self-interested reasons. Along with the joys that Katie brings us, caring for her can be draining and soul-destroying. Getting Katie to eat a decent diet is a constant struggle. Like many children with autism, she sleeps much less than other kids and sometimes wakes up for hours in the middle of the night. Because of her limited understanding of language, Katie isn't able to obey most of our commands and we usually have to simply grab her and carry her to where we want her to be—not so easy with a 45lb+ five-year-old. Watching your child suffer but being utterly incapable of helping her—which is sometimes the case when Katie has tantrums—is torture. It's worst of all when the tantrums occur in public. As I try to control my thrashing, screaming child, I feel the hostile, disapproving glare of strangers, convinced that I am guilty of poor parenting or even child abuse. I sometimes have the energy to explain to horrified onlookers that Katie has autism. This usually elicits sympathy and makes me feel good about doing my minor part toward raising awareness, but more often I just suffer in silence. I fear for my ability to control Katie during these tantrums as she gets older and stronger.

I fully understand and endorse the mantra that you have to stay calm when your child is having a tantrum. On those occasions when I manage to do so and Katie's tantrum quickly passes, my self-esteem as a parent gets a huge boost. When I lose my cool, though, it's easy to lose confidence in my ability to help Katie and hard to avoid descending into self-hatred. Parents of children with autism face moral challenges that many parents of "regular" kids can't begin to comprehend. We need to remind ourselves that finding these challenges difficult to meet is a sign of humanity, not failure.

I will never say that I'm glad my daughter has autism. I'm thrilled to be Katie's dad, I love her just the way she is, and I can't begin to imagine life without her, but I think it would be an act of self-deception for me to claim that autism has enhanced our lives. What I most certainly *would* claim is that several positive things have resulted from Katie's autism. We have met a whole cadre of dedicated, caring professionals who devote their careers to helping children with developmental disabilities. As an ethicist, I've long been aware of the importance of respecting the rights of people with disabilities in general, but my personal experience with autism has given me a much more visceral appreciation. When I see a person acting strangely in public, I no longer jump to judgment about how inappropriately he or she is acting, and I consider the very real possibility that she or he has a disability or is mentally ill.

Facing up to the anguish of the diagnosis and the difficulties it entails for the lifetime of both parents and child was for me an *essential* first step in accepting Katie's autism and reintegrating my life. While my wife and I have had very different reactions to our daughter's autism, one constant has been ongoing—open communication. I am confident that we will buck the high divorce rate and stay together for life, doing everything we can to help Katie.

The last four years have been a rough ride, but I sense that I've turned the corner toward acceptance. It's not just that I've let go my pre-autism hopes for Katie, but I'm also getting better at handling the everyday challenges that Katie presents to us. My anxieties about Katie's long-term future remain, but I hope they will diminish as she develops more living skills. I can easily imagine many parents of children with autism feeling alienated by tales of saintly parents cheerfully dealing with the cards they have been dealt. I hope that they will derive some comfort from the experiences of decidedly unsaintly people like me!

Nicholas Dixon is professor of philosophy at Alma College, Michigan. He specializes in applied ethics and has published papers on a variety of issues, including abortion, gun control, boxing, civil disobedience, physician-assisted suicide, and the adversary system in law. He is a past president of the International Association for the Philosophy of Sport and is currently editor of *Journal of the Philosophy of Sport.*

5. Happy with my Daughter

Sheryle Dixon

"It might be a good idea for you to take Katie to a child development specialist." With those words, our journey into the world of autism began. Katie had been diagnosed with a hearing impairment when she was 20 months old. The diagnosis had been made after a behavioral test showed Katie to have a profound loss in one ear and a severe loss in the other. It was Katie's speech therapist who, after a few months of working with Katie, had recommended the child development specialist. Since the speech therapist had had experience working with children with developmental disabilities as well as children with hearing loss, we took her words seriously. Although she had never used the "A" word, my husband Nick and I quickly sought out books on autism. The first books we read were fairly technical, looking at the diagnostic criteria for autism. It didn't take long before we realized that our daughter met the criteria in all three critical areas: lack of speech, minimal social interaction, and perseverative "play." By the time we had our appointment with the child development specialist, we were already expecting the worst. Although the specialist shared our concerns that Katie showed signs of autism, she said Katie was too young to make a prognosis as to what she would be able to achieve as she grew older.

Nick and I responded to the diagnosis quite differently. Perhaps it was my more religious upbringing or a more "cup half full" attitude than Nick's, but I chose to hope for the best and work with what we had. Nick found it more difficult to accept the situation. He had periods of depression where he focused on "shattered dreams" and "tragic losses." There were moments of tension between us when he thought I just didn't understand; that I was being unrealistic about what our life would now hold. I had trouble understanding why he didn't just accept our situation and "move on." I had to learn to let him grieve in his own way, although I thought he should grieve more quickly! Part of the urgency resulted from the reading we had done which emphasized the importance of early intervention.

The summer after Katie's diagnosis I spent frantically reading everything I could on autism and its treatment. We also attended a number of conferences and workshops on autism. It didn't take much reading to realize that there is a plethora of treatment suggestions for working with children with autism; options ranging from biomedical, behavioral, developmental, and more alternative options (e.g., swimming with dolphins, hippotherapy, etc.). Feeling the pressure to make a choice and start treating Katie, I started doing some Applied Behavioral Analysis (ABA) at home. I read some of the seminal work on ABA (e.g., Lovaas, Catherine Maurice, Leaf and McEachin) and attended an ABA conference and workshop. Advocates of ABA are very passionate and continually press the issue that ABA is the only "proven" treatment that works. Being a professor myself, I have a high regard for research. However, being a philosophy professor, I have a penchant for questioning the "logic" behind proposed treatment options. When using an ABA approach, we were able to get Katie to put rings on a pole and even eat beans (with a cookie "reinforcer"). However, I couldn't see how we could "train" Katie to want to be with us. So we turned to more developmental approaches.

Having read Greenspan, Wieder, and Simons' "floortime" approach and attended a "Play Project" workshop by Dr Solomon from the University of Michigan, I thought play therapy made the most sense for helping us connect with Katie. Although we kept in mind Greenspan's notion of "playful obstruction," we found it most helpful to just be with Katie. Sometimes she would let us engage briefly with what she was doing, but more often than not, we just sat in the same room with her. Since Nick and I are both academics, we would often read and mark papers by Katie's side. We would hang out wherever Katie was; even if that meant dinner in her bedroom! After a winter of this "togetherness," we began seeing a difference in Katie's attitude towards us. Where she used to take our hands and lead us out of the room she was in, she started leading us to the couch and wanting us to sit beside her. The first time she sat both Nick and me down and wouldn't let us stand up to go make dinner was a momentous occasion! Where most parents try to get their children to fall asleep on their own, the fact that Katie now wants us to lie down with her, with our arm around her, is something we will always cherish. (Even if it means many late nights—since like many children with autism, Katie has some strange sleep patterns!)

Although Katie has made some great strides on the social front, her language development has not seen as much improvement. Other than the odd word used inconsistently, Katie is still nonverbal. After the autism diagnosis, we had an Auditory Brainstem Response (ABR) test done on her hearing and it turns out that Katie has a severe loss in one ear, but only a mild loss in the other. Thus, the lack of language would seem to be a function of the autism rather than of hearing loss. Although Katie has been involved with speech therapy since her diagnosis, and the therapists have attempted to teach her sign language as well as Picture Exchange Communication System (PECS), she communicates mainly by leading us to what she wants, showing us what video cover she wants to watch, pointing to our pocket when she wants a pacifier, etc. Although Katie's life would be easier if she learned to speak, it never ceases to amaze me how much communication can occur without words.

Katie's lack of speech and odd behavior (including those inexplicable tantrums common to children with autism) has made me reflect on what we value as human beings. We often assume that because a person doesn't speak or act "normal" they have an impoverished life. Although I often wonder what goes on in my daughter's mind, I think she has a rich inner life. She does have moments of fear that we wish we could help ease her through, but she has many more moments of gleeful excitement—gales of laughter over something unbeknownst to us. Realizing that Katie is genuinely happy much of the time has made it easier for us to accept her situation. I am now at the point where I am perfectly happy with who Katie is, even during a tantrum. Nick and I will probably always have a different perspective on this, but I wouldn't want Katie to be anyone other than who she is. Coming to this place has been the result not only of living life with Katie, but also with having met adults with autism at conferences and through electronic mailing lists. Many of these adults are critical of people's attempts to cure autism. They see autism as part of who they are and attempts at "curing" them is, in a sense, saying that they are not good enough. Upon reflection, I realized that Katie is not only good enough the way she is, her unabashed happiness (which is the flipside to the tantrums), her excitement over little things, her lack of concern for personal possessions, her novel way of pursuing many activities, and her lack of concern for the way things are usually done, make an important contribution to the society that she is a part of.

Sheryle Dixon, Ph.D. is presently taking a hiatus from academia to stay home with Katie and twin infants Daniel and Adam. She is working towards increasing public awareness regarding autism, creating an inclusive situation for Katie in the public school system in her hometown, as well as starting a local support group for parents of children with disabilities. She lives with her husband, Nicholas (who wrote the previous essay), and three children in Alma, Michigan.

6. Through the Looking Glass

Phil Dougherty

It's the question no one has ever asked me: "What's it like, raising a child with autism, and how has it affected your life?"

I'm not talking about the early years—not the shock of the diagnosis, or wandering lost through a maze of medical, social, and educational services, or handling the grief that followed. I'm talking about years later—when we've adjusted to the new day.

My daughter Jenny was nearly four when we found out she had autism. It was August 6, 1997. Yeah, I remember the exact date. It was like something slammed a cleaver through our lives: from that date forward, our lives were defined by before we found out and after.

By August 1999, her diagnosis had been clarified to high-functioning autism. Although her doctors refused to make any long-term predictions about the chances of "full recovery," they agreed that Jenny had good potential so long as we worked with her continuously.

Now we're eight years post-diagnosis, and Jenny has been in various forms of therapy all along. Although she's improved markedly over time, it still requires a lot more effort for her to process incoming information than it does for a typically developing child, and to simply deal with the everyday trials and tribulations that we all have to deal with. She's starting 6th grade in September and turns 12 the same month. She's also edging into puberty, which is opening a whole new Pandora's Box of issues just as we finally resolve some of her childhood ones.

In school Jenny is able to handle the same academics as her peers. Her IQ tested right at normal in the spring of 2003. She's a whiz in some areas, such as math and spelling. She's in a regular class, but has an aide in the class to help keep her focused because she still can't do it herself. One of her biggest problems is impulse control. If the aide isn't there to help, Jenny might get up and wander or become fixated on something and begin loudly talking about it, no matter what's happening in class.

Jenny does not think in generalities. Her thoughts are specific and literal, and she says precisely what she's thinking. She's incredibly curious, and loves to grill me about everything imaginable. In one recent 15-minute period she asked: (1) "Is nitrogen flammable?" (2) "What's the temperature of a cold-blooded animal?" (3) "How deep is quicksand?" Simple answers didn't work: each answer required more detailed, follow up discussion. Most recently she has learned to understand the concept of jokes and, by God, she is even learning metaphors now.

Many people with autism have problems with obsessions, and so does Jenny. When she was three years old, she was obsessed with slugs. When she was eight, it was fire alarms. If we went into a building, she would have to scope out the building's interior first to identify where all the fire alarms were located and what they looked like. If we didn't take a look, she'd reward us with a ballistic tantrum. Sometimes she even wanted her picture taken by a fire alarm. We got used to the curious looks from bystanders. Currently her favorite is the recycling symbol on all recyclables. She looks for the symbol on everything she sees and points it out to whoever is near; several times a day, I'll hear her happily chirp, "reduce, reuse, recycle!"

Though many children with autism are socially withdrawn, Jenny has actually gotten more gregarious as she's gotten older. It's hard for me to see her approach some kids her age. After years of training and prompting, she's finally learned to look at people when she's having a conversation.

But she still doesn't understand the concept of "personal space," and has a tendency to get in a person's face and start a halting conversation, asking rudimentary questions; some of these kids aren't nice and either mouth off to her or ignore her. There's an odd bright side to this, though. Because of her limited understanding of social cues, she doesn't always realize she's just been snubbed. I can casually breeze in and distract her without her knowing what's happening.

She has many imaginary friends, mostly her stuffed bears. Her well-worn pink puffalump bear, "Snuggleshoe," is her favorite. She has some human friends too. Unfortunately, these friendships seldom translate into her being invited to meet her friends after school. I don't think this is intentional as much as her friends or their parents just don't think about it. Because in spite of the gains Jenny has made in the last eight years, she's still a different kind of girl.

Jenny knows she has autism. We've explained it to her in detail, and she's shown a surprising depth of understanding. Sometimes she's ashamed of it. Other times she admits to being scared and says she doesn't want to grow up. But often she seems happy and almost proud of who she is. She's always shown an incredible determination to learn and succeed. It's as if she realizes in spite of the obstacles she can still make a positive difference, not just in her life but in others, too.

She has a bright, fun streak, and a unique enthusiasm that makes us laugh. Her milestones make us particularly proud. We have dreams for the future, but they're different dreams, because every day—every single day—something happens to remind us of reality.

Society accepts us—but with an asterisk. We can never let our guard down. While many people we've had to deal with have been pretty decent about the problems Jenny sometimes creates, some—even (allegedly) well-educated adults—have been remarkably cold, not only to me, a grown man who expects it, but also to Jenny, a child who doesn't really understand why these people are acting the way they do.

As time has gone on I've become more polarized in my thinking and dealings with others when it comes to Jenny's autism. In spite of the progress, in spite of many people trying to understand, we still remain the odd family out. It's caused me to become more rigid when I deal with others. On the other hand, it makes it easier for me to stay focused on helping Jenny, and to be less concerned about how some of the decisions I have to make may impact others outside the family.

Another change I've noticed: absolutely no "disabled" and "retarded" jokes or stories that I still hear people tell in my everyday world strike me as funny. If I hear something like that starting, I'll get up and leave.

My family and I live in a parallel but alternative universe, both at ⸢ and neither. On particularly bad days I wonder if we live in a fantasy glass menagerie, ridiculously pretending we fit in when in reality we do not. But in spite of the daily disconnect we live with, it's one hell of a fascinating life. For that, I'm genuinely grateful. Jenny has taught me that even the smallest, most arcane detail—such as the light cover on a streetlight—is worth a look. Her questions and comments have forced me to think and to learn about much more in life than I otherwise would have. There really is a lot of cool stuff out there. Jenny has helped me see it.

I'm grateful, too, because of a change in my personal life that arose directly from Jenny's autism. Not long after her diagnosis, I joined a local group of families similarly affected. In Seattle in 1998, there was no one comprehensive "resource guide" available that could point parents to various area services that they could access to help their child. This group wanted to put such a resource guide together.

Though I'd been a journalism major when I was in college nearly 20 years earlier, I'd written virtually nothing since. Still, I volunteered to write the resource guide. I thought it would be an excellent way to help me learn what I needed to know. It took six months, but at the end I had completed a 73-page guide which was well received in the community. After it was published, I knew I was on to something and kept writing. I've had over 80 articles covering a range of topics published since, both locally and nationally. Writing has helped fill a void in my life, but it took Jenny's diagnosis for me to realize that.

Following routines is important for Jenny, and the bedtime routine is particularly important. If I deviate from it in the slightest, she yells at me until I get it right. She never told her mother or me that she loved us until she was eight. Thus the bedtime routine is a special pleasure for me: "Goodnight, Jenny." "Goodnight, Dad." "I love you." "I love you too."

Phil Dougherty lives in the Seattle area with his wife and their daughter Jenny. He works as a financial claims professional and is also a freelance writer. He has served on the board of directors of several nonprofit organizations that focus on autism, including the Autism Society of Washington.

Acknowledgement
This chapter is reprinted (in part) from *The Issaquah Press.*

7. My Will

Margaret Janger Flynn

The day we had the lesson on privacy, my son, Will, was three. I had gone into the bathroom and closed the door when he charged through without regard to the thought that I might want a few minutes to myself.

"Will, may I have some privacy, please?" I asked, trying to keep from sounding annoyed. So he left, closing the door. A few seconds later he shoved open the door again, this time with one hand held in a loose fist. He walked over and held out his fist as if to hand me something. Slowly, he uncurled his little fingers, gently depositing the imaginary something into my hand.

I was a bit puzzled... "Oh, thank you," I effused. "What is it?" "Privacy," he answered. Man, there's just something about that kid!

What I know now is that it was really a sign—a sign of what was to come...a sign that this child was different.

By the time Will was seven, we'd been working with our school's local screening committee for more than a year. Our goal was to find the appropriate way to work with our son who had problems that some saw as typical for a child his age, but others saw as more troubling. Indeed, it was Asperger's syndrome, and it was complicated by an additional diagnosis of Attention Deficit/Hyperactivity Disorder (ADHD). He would need psychological testing, social skills classes that included group therapy for parents, twice-monthly sessions with a psychiatrist, medication, and educational testing to determine academic impact.

More importantly, we would need to get to know him all over again. The boy that I thought I knew intimately was much more complex than I'd ever imagined. There was no assuming anything anymore, and the questions seemed endless: How did this happen? How will this affect him? Will he grow out of it? Will he grow up to be a happy and fulfilled adult? Does he see himself as being different? Should we tell him of the diagnosis? How do we best help him? Who are the experts? What about his older sister? What should we do, *first?*

Thankfully, what became very clear, initially, was that we were already on the right path. Our son was actually doing pretty well, because we had fortunately followed our instincts and had been strong advocates for him. But explaining all of this to his inner circle—when we had so much information to absorb ourselves—was difficult. While family members have been supportive, Will's behavior is even baffling to those closest to him. And it's a bit heartbreaking when he confides, "Mom, you're the only one who understands me."

Asperger's syndrome is a spectrum disorder which means that there are varying degrees of severity. Some of Will's issues are sensory: food, loud noises, some clothing, and certain odors can drive him to distraction and make him very unsettled. Interruptions to his activities will make him very angry. If toys don't operate as advertised, it will send him into a tirade. Furthermore, in his view, people should not deviate from the rules. If they do, he'll break all the rules to point out the deviation. To him, things and people should work properly. Even animals get admonished as evidenced one day by his booming declaration that he was "giving up [his] dream to be a fighter pilot," because he'd learned that orca whales were eating his highly regarded dolphins. In response, he'd become a whaler!

We encourage Will to tell us if something is bothering or frustrating him, because the executive function areas of his brain, which would normally react to previous experiences, do not communicate as they should. Instead, it takes him much longer to retain information in order to learn from his mistakes. This problem makes it exceedingly frustrating for a child whose whole being revolves around the logical.

It's amazing what physical work it is for Will to manage what many of us do without thinking: trying to control the urge to rage, trying to go with the flow, trying to understand why he takes these little pills, trying to cope with the classmate who won't follow directions, trying to ignore the noises or smells that get to him, trying to fit in, trying to recall names quickly so that he can return greetings to people in the hallway at school, trying to remember the appropriate ways to interact with kids and adults—don't forget eye contact—initiating a conversation or understanding the right time to join in, and leaving room in his head for his beloved facts that keep us all fascinated. It's exhausting for him. His brain cannot multitask like a person who is neurotypical.

Experience has shown that briefing Will ahead of time demystifies situations. Anticipating stimuli and talking about it ahead of time, while giving him the strategies to work around possible problems, helps him cope with his surroundings. It isn't always foolproof, though, and there still aren't many times when I feel comfortable dropping him off at activities, solo.

I can remember when, during his kindergarten and first grade years, I would take deep breaths as I strode into the school for my volunteer obligations. Often, I would be greeted with a story reported by one of his classmates about Will's being sent to the office because of disruptive behavior. "Hi, Mrs Will's Mom. He's having a tough day, today," little Stephen would say. And, forcing a smile, I'd reply, "Well, I guess we all have days like that, huh?"

We've learned that the numerous hours I've spent volunteering in the school have benefited Will's relationships with his peers. Seeing him periodically in his classroom, the cafeteria, or in the hallway has allowed me to coach him during the school day. I can help him engage in conversation. I can quietly feed him a classmate's name to use when saying "hi." I can see what he's been studying during the day, so we can talk about it at dinnertime.

I admit that there are days when, by 7:30 a.m., my bowl of patience, as we call it here in the land of the concrete, is nearly empty. Perhaps he couldn't find his favorite soccer shirt to wear. Maybe his waffle wasn't toasted quite right, so it didn't taste the same. There's a chance that school wasn't on his agenda for the day. It could be that his shoelaces won't lay flat. It's possible that he didn't hear me give the two-minute warning that it was time to catch the bus. And, by the way, can't the TV be turned on in the morning just once?

To some, it may sound like spoiled brat syndrome. To some, a tongue-lashing, a smack, or an old-fashioned spanking would solve this little problem. But for those of us who live with these children, it's the hugs when you can get them, the long talks after the meltdown subsides, and snuggles at night when the best secrets are revealed that remind us that we were entrusted with these children—for a reason. Patience, compassion, empathy, and being open minded about how the child sees the world are crucial ingredients to success. And, in a heated moment, when he asks in exasperation, "Why can't you cope with me?" I'm jolted back to his reality.

Will is now nine years old, and life is very different for us at this stage. Tantrums are fewer, and he doesn't break as many toys. His eye contact is better, and he's developed an outrageous sense of humor. He's a voracious reader, and can keep up a fact-filled conversation that includes meaningful questions and comments about military aircraft—both past and present—with his dad or any other willing participant. He has appropriate supports in place at school, and I still volunteer, often.

So… How did this happen? Somewhere in the gene pool. How will it affect him? For now, sensory overload and executive function will always be triggers. Will he grow out of it? We believe that he'll grow with it. Will he grow up to be a happy and fulfilled adult? He dreams of nothing less. Does he see himself as being different? Yes, but we encourage him to embrace his differences and we explain that they are not faults. Should we tell him of the diagnosis? It took a while, but we finally did. We explained that it means he'll need to work harder than others at certain things, but that it in no way affects how we feel about him. How do we best help him? We created a team of professionals who support him in ways that work for him and our family. Who are the experts? Start with Tony Attwood's books, and your family doctor. What about his older sister? She knows of his diagnosis and has been a wonderful influence through constant role playing and just treating him normally. What should we do *first?* Love, love, love… Because, man, there's just something about that kid!

Margaret Janger Flynn is a freelance writer in Burke, Virginia. She lives with her husband, Bill, and two children, Hayley, age 12, and, Will, age 9. Margi enjoys writing in her spare time and volunteering at her children's school. As a former teacher, Margi has written on various subjects including tips on birthday parties and seasonal craft ideas for children. She also participates as a guest panelist for Fairfax County Public School's educational series on *Recognizing and Teaching Students with Asperger's Syndrome.* According to Margi, parenting is either keeping her young, or causing her gray hairs.

8. Jenius

Nayma Glenn

In third grade, my son James's teacher gave him a hat with a "J" for James, but also for Jenius because of his many interests, questions, theories, and problem solving skills. That word stuck with me, genius with a "J"—that is Asperger's syndrome.

I used to pray for strength and understanding with my two boys, especially Jacob, my middle child. I would comfort myself with the thought that I was gifted with these amazing little souls because I had the strength to handle and guide them. I didn't know then how important that faith would be. I didn't know that these challenging spirits would lead me to discover something so vitally important about myself and my family that it would change our lives. The journey started the day Jacob tore his first grade classroom apart.

I remember walking into that room, looking at Jacob, and bursting into tears because I couldn't do it anymore. For a year prior I had homeschooled him. He had been removed from his kindergarten Montessori classroom for slightly milder versions of this episode. I successfully worked him through these problems that I thought were a response to the separation of his father and me. Jacob and his older brother entered school that fall. They wanted to know what public school was like, and I needed a break. So here was the little boy I had worked so hard to help, out of control, only much worse this time. I spent so much time praying about it not knowing that it actually *was* the answer to my prayers.

We returned to homeschooling while we waited for an opening at a school which specialized in behavioral issues. We had a difficult spring. By summer not even I could control Jacob, and he attempted to run away repeatedly. Only seven, he was the size of a ten-year-old and very strong. He suffered cruel treatment from children and even some parents, and became physically violent. I had to make the toughest decision of my life that summer…to admit Jacob for a 72-hour residential crisis stay. The center was cozy, clean, beautiful, professional, and so, so necessary. I cried all the way home, but I had the most peaceful three days I'd had in almost a year. Jacob would visit the residential center half a dozen times. He would also stay with his father the rest of that summer.

Jacob entered his new school in August. I cannot say how grateful I am for a place that could handle him *and* was proactively, kindly, and expertly working on his behavioral issues, as well as supporting my efforts to help him. We were very lucky. Too many children have to wait too long for services like these, or never get them at all.

Home and school support over several long months and hard work was the breakthrough for Jacob to start becoming self-managing. The school ruled out emotional disturbance, bipolar disorder, and other possible diagnoses that just didn't fit. We finally hit on Asperger's syndrome.

Then James, who *had* been doing very well, began to show signs of something wrong. James was in the third grade attending a wonderful alternative school, but had only tried full-time school briefly once before. By spring he started fighting at school, his only tool for dealing with teasing and exclusion. Watching James flap his hands like a bird when he was under stress at each of his basketball practices, I couldn't deny it any longer. James also had Asperger's.

In researching Asperger's and autism the odd behaviors of my children began to sift somewhere in my subconscious. Slowly the knowledge percolated to the surface that I was affected as well. When that piece fell into place, I could look back over my life experiences with an understanding I'd never had before. It was incredible, and for many months incredibly depressing. It's one thing to be eccentric and quirky. It is a world away to have a permanent neurological disorder.

It's better now. I've always loved being different even though I never really understood why I was so different. Why people often gave me funny looks after I spoke as if I had said something so bizarre or so profound it defied comment. Why as a child I would be so lonely most of the time I could only lay in my room and cry. Why I understood so much but often could not make myself understood. Why and why and why fell into place. I have no idea what "normal" looks or feels like. I will never know; it's not built into my wiring.

It is often hard for me not to doubt myself and my decisions for my children. Then I look back at the path my life has followed, the support, the information, the love… I may not know what normal looks like or *feels* like, but I know what right looks and more importantly feels like. That is what I hope to gift my children with: an ability to trust that amazing, intuitive, heartfelt part of themselves, to continue to be able to access and use it. Our intellect is a powerful tool, but it must be balanced by that part of us that *feels* what is right. That is Jenius.

It is an odd paradox of the child with Asperger's. Such a child has an intensely focused awareness of the world, otherworldly intuition many adults never learn to access and usually misunderstand, and often exceptional intelligence, all grounded by a great difficulty with social functioning, communication and personal awareness. Motor difficulties, extreme and unusual sensitivity to outside stimuli, and intense emotion are also present. They see and feel too much with minds that never shut off and none of our adult tools for coping.

So many amazing children are never recognized. The focus rivets entirely on their odd behavior, their bizarre rituals, how to *fix* them. People with autism are like frogs to the environment; if something is wrong in a system, they will be the first to show the signs of stress. Children with autism say with their bizarre physical movements, unreasonable behavior, blunt demands, and seemingly rude comments, tantrums, fear, and depression that there is something wrong. That knowledge needs to be honored.

So many children's trust in their own knowledge is lost to them as they are told over and over by adults how wrong they are. It hurts too much to be misunderstood; you become unmotivated, too tired to even try. These amazing little souls were gifted to me not only because I can guide them, or because I am strong enough to handle them. They were gifted to me to open the door to a world of understanding and potential I could have never found on my own.

I've learned it's alright to clap my hand rhythmically when I am stressed or to wear my sunglasses in the grocery store or to plug my ears, even in public. And I've learned that teaching my children to balance their time and their stress is more important than homework or chores done on time, that each of their needs is unique and that it is alright that their learning experience looks completely different from the mainstream model.

Both boys work daily learning to manage the challenges in their lives. Their growth inspires my own. I don't know where Jacob found the strength as such a young man to stand up and scream that something was very, very wrong, that he couldn't and *wouldn't* take it anymore. But I am grateful every day that he did. I'd like to think it was something I taught my children. I think I can at least take credit for hearing them, for being a safe place and an advocate in helping my children find a voice that is a little quieter but just as effective.

∾

Nayma Glenn lives with her three children in Eugene, Oregon. She loves having autism, reading books under a leafy tree in summer, floating in water, playing in shaving cream, eating chocolate, and of course, she loves her children. She offers the following advice to other parents: don't keep doing it alone. Help is a wonderful thing and it's out there waiting for you to ask for it. Ask lots of questions and find a quiet place in yourself to listen for answers.

9. School Days

Heidi J. Graff

Pencils, notebooks, loose-leaf paper… Crayons, markers, binders, and colored ink pens…back to school supplies. Bringing out our list means Labor Day…then the First Day of School. With that, all the anxiety, fear, worry, but especially hope comes to my heart as it does for so many other parents of children with special needs. Will my child be able to keep up with the work? Will he know where to go? Will he get teased? Who will be there to

help? My parental cocoon of protection will be opened. I want the world to see my child as I do: a wonderful, loving, unique boy with the tendency to need his private time. I want school to care how to help him learn best, to see his abilities. As trepidation and nervousness fill my soul and cooler breezes indicating fall is here touch his face: the beginning of a new school year has arrived.

This story actually began back on December 29, 1992 with the birth of our son, Jeffrey Benjamin (J.B.). J.B. was a little slower to blossom than other boys his age, and just a little different. Reassured by my pediatrician and the other playgroup moms, I believed he would catch up with his play. Yes, he lost the language he had been using, and he did line up his trains. Yes indeed he walked on his toes, flapped as if he would take flight, and often seemed lost, alone in thought. As an educator, I convinced myself that he was fine. I had worked with children on the autism spectrum in college and my little boy was not like those other children. However, by age two, I knew, with the help of many professionals, the undeniable truth: my child has autism.

The journey has been long and with many stumbling stones; however, through the hard work of our family and J.B.'s own continuous effort, he now functions scholastically on a relatively typical level. Yet, each year we are faced with a new teacher, new class, new rules, and new ways to implement his Individualized Education Plan (IEP) goals. For our son, J.B., newer is not better. In fact if nothing ever changed he would be happiest. When we fill his day with activities, trying to create new routines, his mantra is "I don't like new things." When we remind him that trying new things, whether a new food or store, is exciting, he remains steadfast in his unhappiness. During a recent summer excursion to the Delaware beaches, he reluctantly attempted, because there was nothing else, to eat a sandwich other than his usual peanut butter and fluff. While my reaction and that of my partner's was ecstatic, he firmly stated, "I don't like this, next time make it peanut butter, OK?" Instead of keeping up with the neighbors, at our home J.B. would be thrilled to keep it the same. It comes then as no surprise that the beginning of a new school year is a challenge, for us as parents, for J.B. as the student, and for the teachers and school.

Last year was one of our roughest. During our first parent–teacher conference, I was bombarded with stories of inappropriate behavior. I left feeling sad and disillusioned. I recall that the general education teacher said several times, "I do not think my classroom is the right place for your child." I was expecting to hear, "Let's talk about how we can make this work." This was only the third week of school.

The school and his special education teacher believed he was acting up because he was not able to follow the intermediate curriculum due to the emphasis on abstract concepts. The general education teacher believed his needs would best be met away from his typical peer group. I wanted the program of study modified to meet his needs. I discussed how positive second and third grade had been when he was fully included. I met with the special education teacher many times but most of my suggestions were not put into practice. My partner, who also works in the special education field, and I were in constant written and verbal communication with the school.

The last straw came in early October, the beginning of week four, when I was told by both the school guidance counselor and the teacher that "the other children in class are afraid of J.B." She continued, "You must understand, we need to think about all the children." The guidance counselor had apparently asked the class if anyone had a problem or issue with J.B. She relayed that several of the children had raised their hands. In my opinion, had she also asked if anyone had an issue or problem with *another* classmate, several of the children would have also raised their hands. After all, if in fourth grade you, as a student, haven't had an issue or problem with a classmate, where have you been? The teacher presented me with a list of what the other children had to say in connection to J.B. as evidence of their fears. I was very upset and felt that J.B. had been unfairly singled out. I began to wonder if this placement really was in our son's best interest. Certainly being with a general education teacher who didn't want him in her class and saw him as a scapegoat and a special education teacher who had lost instructional control was not a good choice.

The situation rapidly deteriorated. By the end of week four my son's behaviors got so out of control that he was placed in a self-contained, non-categorical class that supports children with a variety of disabilities including autism. At this crossroad there was a good deal of finger pointing, and accusations of not complying with the law and his IEP goals. I had lost faith in the school's judgment; I felt that no one was listening.

I needed a new set of eyes and ears inside the school—a more neutral person who was concerned only with J.B.'s best interests. I sought help from a woman who had known J.B. since he was initially diagnosed. She had a special education background and a good relationship with the school and was willing to act as an advocate on our son's behalf. After observing him at school, she let me know that J.B. seemed comfortable in his new class. Most encouraging was the optimism of his new special education teacher and her assistant. Eventually through the implementation of a structured positive reinforcement program, he was successfully placed back in the general education setting with a new teacher for science and social studies, lunch, and specials. Upon reminding school that math and reading were his better subjects, I was told of scheduling conflicts and personnel shortages. Upon reminding myself that all learning is progress, I was able to keep in mind that development can take place regardless of the setting.

With a great deal of effort from our advocate, everyone's feathers were smoothed and all involved finally fell into a comfortable exchange of mutual respect with J.B.'s best interest in mind. Confirmation of this placement came from J.B. himself when once again I eagerly began to hear in the morning, "Is it a school day?" Affirming stories began to be exchanged, like, "J.B. did great in science today," "He got 100% on a test," and "J.B. and his classmate worked together to build a magnet science experiment." His curriculum, especially in spelling, began to be modified to build on his other strong subjects. At that point, I realized that school had previously seen my role as that of an adversary: a difficult parent, not a knowledgeable professional. Until I got our relationship back on good footing as a parent, working as a team for J.B.'s best interest could not be accomplished. Escalating anger and upset on both sides did little to earn mutual respect. Now, I was able to make suggestions and be an integral part of his school education.

In a few short weeks, it will begin again. J.B. will be entering fifth grade. I believe I can reflect back on the last year to realize that attitudes, communication, and relationships can make or break a special education student's day to day existence. I realize I may never be one hundred percent satisfied with his placement, but a constructive, inventive, and caring teacher and assistant working cooperatively with parents can go a long way in achieving IEP goals. Having an advocate was so helpful in this regard that I will never wait to seek outside help again. I recognize that each year J.B. will begin again with hope and courage. Hope for a good year, for academic and social progress, and courage to work with the teachers in his school so they can look with encouragement toward his abilities.

Heidi J. Graff and her partner, Sarah, live in northern Virginia, about ten miles outside of Washington, D.C. They are the proud parents of two children: J.B., who is now 11, and Jessica, who is nine years old. Heidi has been in the education field for more than 15 years and has recently retired from a private practice working with children on the autism spectrum to complete her Ph.D. in special education at George Mason University. Since the diagnosis of her son, Heidi has been dedicated to the advocacy and teaching of children with special needs.

10. You Never Know

Nancy E. Ironside

I remember sitting and nursing our newborn to the sound of doors opening and closing. That was how George, our almost two-year-old, spent his days. I often tried to make the game purposeful by hiding in the closet myself and saying "peek-a-boo," but there was something about the doors swinging on their hinges that captivated him and I was unable to get him back. "He's the city's youngest doorman," people would often joke, and our friends and family thought he was just figuring out how the door works and would eventually be an engineer. I was consumed with worry about his behavior, and it was always the most troubling when I sat on the sofa nursing and was powerless to help. What would happen to my boy?

After weeks of harassing the pediatrician for help, more weeks of waiting for the doctor to see him, and more weeks waiting for her diagnosis, my husband and I sat in a small room with a very wise, but not particularly warm, psychologist who confirmed what we already feared about our silent boy. As I sat in that office, brokenhearted and angry, my husband asked the question that had haunted us for weeks. What would happen to our boy? What was the long-term prognosis for this condition? Dr X calmly answered that the two determining factors for success were parents and IQ. She told us that it was really too soon to tell what George's IQ was, but there were many therapies which were proven to help children on the autism spectrum make progress. Really what she meant was she didn't know and that it would be impossible to project his future while he was just two years old.

As we drove away with an armload of information and enough anger, self-pity, sadness, and confusion to fill our station wagon, we tried to move forward with Dr X's suggestions. We called each person that she recommended. Thanks to her, we enrolled George in a wonderful school and set him up with the best speech and behavioral therapists around. We felt fortunate that these people saw our son as we did—a bright, frustrated boy who had things to tell us and no way to communicate. With their help, our

prodding, and mostly his determination, George learned a few simple signs
and eventually words. He learned to tell us his wants and needs and even to
tell us his feelings. He learned to play with us and with his younger brother,
Charlie. He is learning how to cope with life's joys and disappointments
and is starting to allow new people into his intimate circle.

Some days have been easier than others. George loves his routine. We
are asked to read the same books, play the same games, and prepare the
same meals. He wants life to be predictable and, like all of us, he wants to
have control over his surroundings. We try to help him appreciate variety
and new things. Some days he is able to go with the flow. Sometimes he has
what we call "PDD days," when he is frustrated, cranky, and demanding.

Once when George was three and a half, he was bitterly disappointed
to find no blue M&Ms in his handful of candy. I tried to explain to my sob-
bing boy that you never know what color M&Ms come out of the bag.
Needless to say, he didn't listen to my philosophical explanation. He just
wanted one or two blue ones.

In George's busy schedule of school, therapy, and family life, he is often
met with the problem of his expectations differing from reality. He likes
things the way he likes them and is always curious if he will get the thing or
idea that he wants. Will we have our food served on blue plates at the restaurant? Will they have blue lollipops at the CVS today? Will the occupational
therapist bring the purple play-doh? "You get what you get," I tell him, "you
just never know."

Evidently, this is starting to have an impact. Last week, we drove to our
favorite diner for an early dinner and saw Katie, our favorite waitress,
through the window. Charlie pointed her out and I said that maybe Katie
would be our waitress tonight. "You never know," said George.

Along with George and Dr X, I have come to learn that you never do
know. Sure, we know some things. We know that every day with George
will be an adventure. We don't know what the adventure of that day will be.
We know that we will all work hard each day. We don't know if we will be
working towards learning and good interaction or if we'll be working to
make it to bedtime without going nuts. We know that we will go to bed
exhausted. We don't know if we will fall asleep crying tears of frustration
or overjoyed by a new development. We know we are doing the right
things to give George the help he needs. We don't know how far that will
take him. You never know.

Nancy E. Ironside received a bachelor's degree in secondary education from Westminster College in 1994, and a master's degree in education administration from Temple University in 2002. She taught for five years in the Philadelphia public school system. Since George was born in 1999, Nancy has been a full-time mom to him and his brother Charlie, born in 2001. She enjoys gardening, coming-of-age novels, festive holidays, and sleep, and hopes to return to teaching some day, in the special education arena. Nancy lives with her husband, Jim Beall, and her two boys in Oreland, Pennsylvania. Her family's pursuit of blue M&Ms continues.

11. Talk to Me, My Darling

Rosemary Johann-Liang

Christobee (my godson's nickname) is on the phone from New York. "Auntie," he says, "I come to your house? I want cookie…" He goes on with his cute two-year-old ramblings. Talking, asserting his wants and needs even over the phone to a person he has not seen in a while. Such is the wonderful exponential language growth of our little neurotypical youngsters. I get off the phone with a smile on my face but a crescendo in the longing in my heart. I long to have similar goofy nonsense conversation with my Jena, to see her beautiful rose lips form words that produce meaning and color.

My five-and-a-half-year-old daughter has autism and is not yet verbal. I say *not yet* with a forlorn emphasis because even while there is always the dull realization that she is falling farther and farther behind developmentally and may never speak, I hold onto hope. Hope that someday, not yet here,

Jena will talk to me. Many years ago, my older daughter Jumi asked me from the back of the car as I was in a mad rush to drive her to her group violin lesson, "Mommy, why did God place the tree of the knowledge of good and evil in the Garden of Eden?" "Auuh, let's see…," I said, and went on to do some explaining that in retrospect was probably pretty lame. Now, I am not asking for philosophical discussions or analytical debates like I used to have with my older daughter at that age. I just long for simple mother–daughter conversation, the everyday to and fro. I want to hear consonant and vowel sounds strung together into words, into sentences that produce meaning that express needs. I want to hear "I love you" and "I want to eat" and "Hug me" and "Isn't the flower pretty." I long to hear my Jena say "Mommy" and look up at me with expectant eyes.

Jena was my cuddle babe. Of my three children, she is the youngest and was the only child for whom I was able to get maternity leave from work. She was a gorgeous baby. Skin smooth as silk, perfect round forehead with just a trace of fuzz over her head and the cutest button nose. She and I were inseparable for three months. She was perched on my shoulder for most of her waking hours except when coming down to chest level to feed or cuddle. The sweet dependence of my cuddle babe left me with an incredible sense of satisfaction and an overpowering feeling of unconditional love.

Looking back now at the five years gone by since then, intertwined with the flooding images of my sweet, beautiful baby are my anxious feelings of dread: Why is she not yet sitting? Why is she not yet standing? Why is she not yet walking? Why is she not yet playing? Why is she not yet pointing? Why is she not yet running? Why is she not yet able to negotiate the playground? Why does she not yet imitate? Why does she not yet talk? There is that unrelenting and mounting drumbeat dread of the theme, *not yet.*

I guess on the positive note (since I am told that I am an insistent optimist although I beg to differ on many occasions), I should give a progress report of these historical "not yets." I mean Jena did eventually sit. She did eventually stand. She did eventually walk. She actually eventually learned to point (what a celebration day that was). She has now actually learned to play with a lot of work from play technicians and therapists. She did eventually learn to run. She has now actually learned to enjoy swinging and sliding in the playground (this has taken years). So, looking at things positively, I would say that Jena has truly come a long way. Now if we could only get beyond not yet imitating and not yet talking!

I don't think I had truly appreciated the importance of human beings imitating one another until Jena. It is intuitive for neurotypical children to imitate the world around them. This is a powerful source of learning and communicating. Jena (especially after the age of two) totally lost the ability to imitate. Actually that is not exactly it. She seemed to be totally devoid of the *need* to imitate. There was absolutely no interest in mimicking anything around her.

Jena retreated into her own world and spent most of her waking hours droning. She would sustain a low B-flat (I unfortunately have the gift of perfect pitch from many years of childhood music lessons) for hours, simultaneously flapping her right hand and keeping her left arm out in a *don't get near me* block position. We called this her "stim" position. She would assume this stance with the most intense and far away look in her face. This totally frustrated us and drove everyone insane. Her droning sound could penetrate even the thickest of walls and the house was filled with this constant super-irritating noise. Everyone around her tried hard to just ignore the noise as background white noise of loud low B-flat and...everyone always failed. To drive a long distance with Jena in the car "stimming" was just unbearable for the rest of the family. Recalling those hours in the car driving up highway I-95 from Maryland to visit my parents in New York, I still feel that total discord pain.

Applied behavioral therapy, discrete trials, play therapy, floortime... you name it, we've been there and done that...or as much as Jena will allow us to do. An around the clock home program coupled with specialized preschool and autism-class kindergarten has brought Jena to a place where she has gradually (painfully gradually, in my book) started to notice the world around her. Using her powerful motivator, which is food (especially fruit and chips), we have broken through many communication walls.

With the picture exchange card system, Jena began to ask for her wants and needs. She then began to comply with some nonverbal imitations. And then, about six months ago, she made the sound "Ahhh." It's not that she had not made this noise before, but this time she said "Ahhh" with a *purpose*. She did a verbal imitation to my prompting. She said "Ahhh" so that she could get the tantalizing spoonful of her favorite soy peach yogurt that was dangling in front of her mouth. I could not believe it! With my heart thumping, I quickly scooped up another mouthful of that yogurt and repeated "Jena, say Ahhh." Eyeing the spoon intently, she dropped her jaw and made the "Ahhh" noise again! "Sweetie...my sweet, sweet darling," I exclaimed and grabbed her in my arms. "You did it, yes, you did!" Jena squirmed in my arms, still eyeing the yogurt. I remember just holding her and thanking God for letting me hold onto my daughter and to the hope of *not yet*. No one else was home at that instance. I remember just quietly letting my tears come, letting the wet drops fall down my face and settle on my Jena's beautiful strands of hair. And that longing lump in my heart that had been congealing for so long liquefied a little that day.

Since the event of the purposeful "Ahhh," Jena has acquired "Eeee" as a request to eat. She is trying to verbally imitate many words. Sounds are not coming out the way they should for the most part, but she is trying! With a lot of prompting, she can now say "Mmm-ahh-mmm-eee" as well as "Ahheee Lahhhaav Eeeoo" and (this is key) look up at me expectantly. So, as I continue to long for that mundane conversation with my daughter, I hold onto the hope of "not yet." Someday, my darling will talk to me.

Rosemary Johann-Liang, M.D. is the mother of three very special children, ages 11, 10 and 5. The oldest is highly gifted and wrote an essay for this collection. The middle child was born premature and has cerebral palsy with autism (subject of the essay, *Why Am I So Resentful?*, written by his older sister). The youngest (subject of this essay) also has autism. Rosemary is an infectious diseases specialist physician who lives in Maryland and works full-time in the Anti-viral Division of the Center for Drug Evaluation and Research at the US Food and Drug Administration. She coordinates the home therapeutic programs for her younger two children when she is not at work or driving her oldest to various extracurricular activities.

12. Our Lives at the Edge of the Spectrum

Elizabeth Lipp

It would be simplistic to say that our family's journey with autism began on August 15, 2002, when my older son Nicolas was diagnosed with Pervasive Developmental Disorder–Not Otherwise Specified (PDD-NOS). The truth is, autism had been with me for much longer than that. But it took my son's diagnosis to understand that fact.

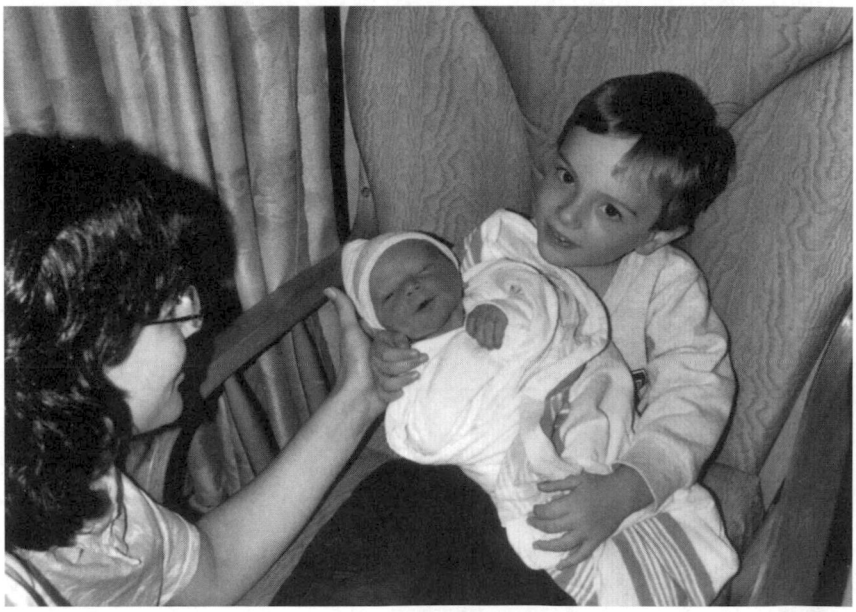

My husband, now a Ph.D. and a scientist by trade and training, had told me he had been speech delayed as a child—he didn't start speaking until after his third birthday. I, on the other hand, started speaking early—and often. My habit of using language far beyond that of my peers often landed me in trouble and remains a favorite topic of family lore.

"It's because I'm different!" I wailed to the school counselor shortly after a particularly difficult episode with my peers. I had often heard my mother and other adults say this about me from the time I started school and I was echoing their words. I didn't understand it, but I felt it must be true. "But how?" the counselor asked me repeatedly over the next two years. "How are you different?" I had no answer for her.

When the pediatric specialist who examined Nicolas on that fateful day quickly blamed my much-educated spouse for Nicolas's fate, I felt my first pangs of doubt. I knew the reasons for Nicolas's condition were a lot more complex than that, even if I didn't readily admit it to myself. "You said yourself that he isn't good at small talk, that he doesn't get jokes," the doctor told me. "That's right, but the same is true for me, too," I answered. He waved dismissively, "You're fine. I can see you have a fine sense of humor, you're very personable."

I reflected at the time, and many times afterward, that this doctor didn't know me at all. He had just met me and was drawing his conclusions based on a two-hour meeting with me and my son. I knew my own limitations. I have had 30-odd years to build my internal database with appropriate responses to thousands of situations, but I can still somehow manage to trip over the most simple and innocuous of social situations.

I threw myself headlong into researching autism and found more questions than answers. Was it lead exposure? Vaccinations? Was I exposed to some toxin during my pregnancy with Nic? Or was there really some genetic component to Nic's behaviors?

I started paying attention to my other family members. One of my sisters seems to have obsessive-compulsive tendencies; so does a nephew. A niece seems to be hyperlexic (and shows my tendency to mispronounce words she otherwise knows the meaning of). I realized that these traits were on my side of Nic's family tree.

On March 8, 2003, I attended an autism conference featuring Temple Grandin, an animal husbandry expert who has autism. I intended only to stay for her talk and then found myself caught up in the second session on Asperger's syndrome. That was when I finally made my own autism connection.

The speaker described the traits of Asperger's: hyperlexia, the little professor syndrome, the lack of peer relationships, just to name a few symptoms. I reflected on my own life and realized that this speaker could have been talking about me and my childhood and adolescence. When I reflected on my own immediate history—my father, long dead, an information technology specialist before the initials IT existed, and his mother, a woman with a gift for higher math, who married late—the pieces of the puzzle that is my son started to fall into place.

Well, sort of. The biggest problem I have is imposing my own aspie baggage on my son. The things that reduce me to tears often have no bearing on my happy-go-lucky little guy. For example, when a little boy of about eight years old called Nic a queer at the playground, I was furious and outraged and poised to reprimand. I had to remind myself that my son lives in this world and can't necessarily be sheltered from everything. What caused in me outrage, Nic simply shrugged off and went back to what he was doing. The boy, seeing his insult had no effect, followed Nic around for another minute or so, and then left him alone.

My son does not have classic autism. He is social, loves to play with other kids, and can make eye contact, although he needs to be pushed to do this (and so do I, even at my late age). His voice is full of expression, and he can take an accurate read of what someone else is thinking or feeling. I have seen him size up situations and amaze me tremendously with appropriate behavior. But social speech is a problem. He has difficulty formulating conversational speech, consequently, many of his responses are scripted from one of the over 300 stories he has memorized verbatim. One of his teachers told me how he recited a whole "Arthur" story, complete with different voices for different characters.

She was impressed. But I know that this is simply a part of who he is. His answers to questions are ready-made, in much the same way I used to rehearse answers to questions in the classroom in my head, repeating things mentally over and over, palms sweating, hoping I didn't trip over my own tongue. I wonder if Nic will do the same thing. And if he does, I wonder if he'll notice that he's doing it.

His obsession with road signs is another part of who he is. He knows enough about the meanings of road signs to take and pass his driver's test. He can even read the signs; he has been able to for over a year. We've used his obsession as part of an occupational therapy (OT) exercise, by encouraging him to cut out road signs—he can now use scissors pretty well. Our next big task is to encourage him to draw. At the age of four, he still doesn't have a firm preference for either his left hand or his right, which makes OT tricky for both his providers and his parents.

Nic gets speech therapy, occupational therapy, physical therapy, special education, and socialization, but perhaps his greatest education is in the world itself—at the playground, at the Barnes and Noble Thomas train table, at the library, and even playing with the five-year-old twins across the street. And my greatest education as a parent is to let him experience as much as possible. It's not as easy as it sounds. I want to shadow his every move. I hang on every interaction. I am poised, ready to jump in, only to have to remind myself not to hover, not to interfere (unless he is in some sort of danger), and to let him figure out for himself how the world—and other people—work.

I look at my beautiful boy and am amazed every day at his joy, his happiness, and his eagerness to explore his world. I tend to underestimate him more often than I overestimate him; I guess I'm afraid to watch him fail. At the same time, it is such a wonder, a marvel, a joy to watch him succeed. Every new phrase he learns, every developmental step he masters, is not something I take for granted.

When we are in the midst of (yet another) public meltdown, I head for the exit, looking neither left nor right, knowing full well the angry/judgmental/pitying gazes leveled our way. Fortunately, this doesn't happen often anymore. However, it does happen often enough for me to be grateful that it isn't a common occurrence. Interestingly, Nic never tantrums in school or while in the care of others. His tantrums are reserved strictly for mom and dad, which remains for us something of a mixed blessing.

As I sit here today, I am not sure what the future holds for my son. Most days, I feel confident that he will become a fully functioning member of society. But I often wonder, doubt, hope, and pray…

Elizabeth Lipp is a writer, editor, and adult with Asperger's syndrome. She lives in Montgomery County, Pennsylvania, with her husband and two sons. Her older son has a mild to moderate Autism Spectrum Disorder.

13. Pulling String

Irene Litherland

I am pulling the end of a wound ball of string. It is a very delicate string and tightly wound. In the beginning, only a very short end protruded from the middle. I had difficulty maintaining my grasp. Very small, careful movements were required to begin loosening the string from the ball. Forceful yanks were of no avail, producing only a remnant of broken string in my

hand. But slow, gradual pulls helped to bring more string out of the matted ball. By now, I have released a fair amount of string. Yet if I pull too hard, it breaks and I again have only a short end to grasp. Careful pulls are required, neither too slow nor too fast but steady and strong, without too much force. There is a lot of broken string along the way—reminders of lessons learned in how to pull and carefully wiggle the string loose. As the length of string outside of the ball increases, the requirements change. Relearning is a constant necessity.

My only child, Nishant, is a wonderful eight-year-old boy who was diagnosed with autism three long, string-pulling years ago. My husband and I have focused much of our time and energy on trying to increase his desire and ability to function in the world. It is extremely difficult. Too much demand and he retreats into his safe, solitary world without others. Too little coaxing and he remains in that world. Yet he is definitely not a string or even a ball of string. He is a full, complicated, unique human being. He has loves and fears just like others do, but his loves tend toward machines and electricity and his fears toward noises such as showers and unexpected machine sounds. He talks a great deal but is often repeating statements or questions about machines and power sources. His brain works in some different ways from the majority, ways that have recently been labeled as autism.

Little is really known about autism. There is an autism spectrum, a wide range of degrees and combinations of symptoms. I have met numerous children diagnosed with autism and have yet to find any whose combination of traits look exactly like those of my son. Likewise, I have not found any of the many treatment options alone to be a total solution for my son's major challenges. As a parent, I am tempted to try each and every treatment. Like treatment sampling, toys and games pile up as we parents hope that maybe this particular activity will loosen the entire ball of string and our child will suddenly find the world an easier place. Yet I am probably most helpful to my son when I stay focused on pulling gently on the string to increase his interactions with the world. I try to help him broaden the range of what he desires and attempts in the world without forcing leaps that are too big for him to negotiate and create hurt or fear. Patience and outside assistance are essential.

Nishant has come a very long way since being diagnosed three years ago. His play then consisted of lining up toys and using ribbons and string to hook them together. He did not look at people, verbalize his needs or desires, or interact appropriately with other children. He had a 16-second delay in responding to questions. He had learned not to respond since very few people would wait that long. He now responds in zero to five seconds but still has only limited social conversation. In the last year, he has done his first pointing, come to enjoy playing with a variety of toys, and shared spontaneously with us for the first time. Although he never had the strength or coordination to ride a tricycle, he recently began riding a bicycle with training wheels and proudly announced, "I'm a kid. I do kid stuff!" His self-image is improving as he is able to do more activities that other children do. However, the gap between his ability level and that of other children not only continues but threatens to widen.

I often feel that I am wearing blinders in order to stay focused on the present and prevent unproductive thoughts concerning the amount of string extracted or still wound. It has been a challenge to go from my former wide-angle view and involvement in the world to this narrow focus on my son and family. Yet the blinders are necessary as comparisons with other children or preoccupation with uninformed opinions of other people can distract me. I try to focus on how far my son has come, how he is feeling about himself, and how I can help him increase his comfort in the world. I need to reduce the natural tendency to compare his abilities with those of other children his age, with or without autism. Likewise, I need to not be thrown off course by comments of friends, family or service providers if they are questioning the path we are on or the progress being made in ways that are not helpful.

Wearing blinders does not prevent me from seeking supportive help or professional services from others. There is no way that my husband and I can provide adequately for our son without outside assistance. After years of working in service provider organizations, I am now a service consumer and spend untold hours arranging for services. This requires finding appropriate service providers, completing forms, making copies of evaluations and school reports, attending numerous appointments and meetings, and facilitating communication between a dozen or so professionals at any given time. Added to this are the occasional big struggles—such as going to mediation with the school district to get an appropriate placement. These take months of work, lots of anguish and money, deep emotional costs to my son, and delays in his development while the issue is moved through bureaucratic steps toward resolution. There is no end to the levels of challenge which autism brings to a family. We need assistance from outside our family and have to struggle on many levels to obtain it.

One of the greatest challenges in securing assistance is that providers range greatly in their experience and respect for the role and abilities of parents. We have had the luck to be able to work with many who have provided excellent assistance and guidance as well as respect and encouragement for our work as parents. But we have also worked with others who were patronizing, insulting, or discouraging and, although not intending to do so, demeaned our role as parents. Our greatest help has come from providers who have numerous years of experience, recognize the role and experience of parents, add it to their professional expertise, and provide thoughtful guidance accompanied by encouragement. Blinders keep me focused on those who are truly helpful.

More important than blinders has been a focus on my son's beauty as a person. I love him dearly as he is and that includes acceptance of his traits which have led to the label of autism, difficult as some of them are to live with at times. I wish that I could make life easier for him and reduce his anguish in our home and the world. He now wants to be in our world most of the time but social interactions are a challenge due to sensory processing differences. Not long ago, he made the alarming statement, "I am broken inside and I don't know how to fix it." He is aware that he faces challenges that are much harder than those faced by most children. They affect all aspects of his life, from academics to relationships. He needs assistance, understanding, and patience from many helpers.

How do I provide the right pull for him, neither too hard nor too soft? I first try to know who he is, what he himself needs, loves, hates, fears. His autism has produced many of those factors and they are now part of who he is. I struggle to accept him and provide him with tools to live happily in a world that doesn't understand these traits. So I don't expect him to perform well in an environment with loud noises or talk in a new setting. His interests are the links between his internal world and our external world. I meet him where he is and pull gently, adding an element or two to his focus to broaden his interests and include a bit more of our world also. His areas of beauty give me places to grasp the string if I use blinders to keep my focus on what is truly important—the whole beautiful person who is my son.

Irene Litherland lives with her son, Nishant, and husband, Dhruvkumar, in Oakland, California. She works part-time as Director of Finance at the World Institute on Disability. Irene has a master's degree in Public Administration and has worked in nonprofit finance and administration for 25 years. She worked for the sanctuary movement for Central American refugees for seven years and has visited refugee camps and resettlements in Central America on numerous occasions. The family has also visited Dhruvkumar's home country of India. Dhruvkumar works as a chemistry instructor in community colleges.

14. Still the Same Boy!

Mary Marmion

It is hard to tell when my life changed. Moments, glimpses of a time past when life seemed simpler flee through my memory. Then, the milestones. Pregnancy at 40, just as I was about to head off into a career in radio. Nathan and Pearl aged 13 and 10 and well able. The ultrasound at 16 weeks, "for reassurance," my doctor wrote on the letter. Two heartbeats

heading my way. I laughed hysterically. That sunny August morning when tiny Sam slipped into my life at barely 33 weeks. His twin Adam, laid back and breech, a harbinger of uphill days to come? We brought them home on our eighteenth wedding anniversary after the emotional rollercoaster of the special care unit.

If the birth of the twins was the change, I was too busy, tired, depressed, and exhausted to notice until Sam stopped leapfrogging his brother in development at 18 months. He was playing ball at Christmas, and by spring he was not calling his brother or responding to his name. He was slipping away from us.

Being an older mother carried some weight and my community nurse listened. Sam's hearing was checked. It seemed that he could hear but he was not responding. He was tuned in on another level. Then the nightmare of head jerks developing into full blown drops to the ground. Bloodied little lips and bruised forehead, a twilight gaze and his anxious twin observing. By summer we had a diagnosis of myoclonic epilepsy. Oh God—do babies get epilepsy!? Medication offered hope. I hung onto this hope, wracked by guilt when my anxiety and exhaustion reduced me to hysteria and depression, thus adding to my young family's burden that summer.

By autumn we also had an answer to Sam's obsessive paper tearing, string twirling, eating inanimate objects, and the elusive emotionless gaze beyond me. He had been slipping further away and his diagnosis was a turning point for all of us. The psychologist made two comments which sustained and remain. "Mothers are often aware at some level and therefore the diagnosis of autism isn't a stranger," and most important, "Sam is the same boy walking out of here as he was coming in."

The advice to seek occupational and speech therapy was a joke. These services didn't exist. In fact the Department of Education in Ireland did not formally recognize autism until 1998 when brave and pioneering parents challenged their children's right to education in the courts. The best I could do was throw myself into research.

Initially I knew nothing about autism. Well-meaning friends brought articles and copies of *Forrest Gump* and *Rainman*. The books available were dismal and spoke of institutional care and how parents needed a huge amount of support to cope with the challenge. Thankfully, I didn't have to rely on these as the internet opened up a world of information for me. I became my own consultant. I found myself educating doctors, teachers, family and friends, and other professionals about autism. "I am only a mother," I told them. I sought the elusive early intervention—whatever that was.

We started with play and making eye contact. Not wanting to let Sam slip away any further, I bombarded him with life. The sleep deprivation broke us several times. However it did not stop the endless efforts for Sam—sometimes it even fuelled them. Volunteering Sam as guinea pig for students of the Treatment and Education of Autistic and Related Communication Handicapped Children method (TEACCH) taught me that Sam was a visual learner. Functional objects encouraged rudimentary communication. This progressed to photographs. Picture schedules put structure on parts of Sam's day. This reduced his anxiety and began to give him some choice and control over his environment. Gradually he initiated communication using thumbnail line drawings which he carries in a small folder. The Hanen method helped us understand Sam's way of communicating.

Functional Analysis, ABA (Applied Behavior Analysis), diet, nutrition, genetics, sensory integration…I immersed myself in it all and soaked up every morsel that might help Sam. I arrived home from courses and workshops wild with enthusiasm for the next thing to try. Eventually I had to come to terms with the fact that I was human and could not handle it all together. So I set myself a rule of only trying one thing at a time and giving that thing one to three months' trial. I kept notes. That way I could be sure of any benefits. The most practical and sound advice I got was from other parents. It is the best network in the world. In recent times I have helped to develop a local parents' network with great satisfaction.

I regret that my focus on Sam has been at the expense of my other children and my marriage. I hope someday they will understand that I had to do this. Perhaps my efforts now will make life better for them all in the future because Sam will be a more able person. I regret that I missed my daughter's teen years. I was not the relaxed mother I wanted to be although I did try to make up by taking her away from time to time. I relied on her and maybe expected too much from her. My eldest son opted out somewhere along the line. It was hard to tell if it was because of the effects of autism that he didn't feel he belonged here. Not easy to bring your friends in when your mother is mad and your brother is running into the window and the walls and turning the lights on and off and worse. Often his twin laughs. It is all he knows and like so many siblings of children with autism he is wise beyond his years. "I wanted a normal brother," he told me, "but it could have been me." Sam will do anything for Adam. I never doubt their unique twin bond. I try to remind his brother and myself that it is the effects of the autism that I don't like; Sam is still the same boy.

Life is always changing. Thankfully, Sam has been seizure free for six years and off all medication. To my great joy he attends a special class in the same school as Adam. Interaction with his peers is vital for Sam. He loves people. His class offers an eclectic model of education including ABA and TEACCH programmes. At last his sensory needs are being addressed by occupational therapy. His daily routine includes skin brushing. This has greatly reduced his hyperactive behaviour and self harming. A listening programme is helping his language. He is now nine. While his academic progress is slow, he enjoys life skills and can set the table and wash and dress himself. His mischief has returned. His confidence has grown through involvement with Special Olympics Ireland where he is a natural swimmer and has his own friends. He tells me to "Go way Mammy" if he wants space in his room. He loves people who want to be with him. He is the best friend you could ever have because he takes you just as you are. He is the most intuitive person that I know. He comes with tenderness if I am upset. He loves to laugh and play. His smile lights up a day. It is contagious.

Some things must change. I challenge professionals to explore tools of assessment and follow up support for families. It was devastating to be told that Sam has a severe learning disability when he is obviously intelligent and clever. We just don't know the complex way he learns yet. And it is *us* who need to change.

Too often we have been left on a boat without oars on high seas with nowhere to turn. Too often we have not been paid the courtesy of being consulted regarding educational service provision for Sam. One size fits all doesn't work here. Regarding parents, professionals must always be aware that we are in some stage of grieving and our anger and frustration is usually not personal! Include us and play fair and honest. It is your job. It is our child!

I could never accept what I read in those early books on autism. My experience with Sam has taught me that the future is an open book and much is possible. I have to remind myself to trust my instinct and be brave for Sam. I rely on friends and a trusted counselor to help me through the dark days. For today, however, the wonder of a child of peace who lives in the moment and who looks into my eyes now with great passion and love is more than enough.

Mary Marmion was born in 1955 in Galway, Ireland. A Gemini flower child at heart, she left her job at the Bank of Ireland to pursue a career in journalism, community development, and holistic health. She worked for the Wicklow Times and has published regular articles on her personal experience with epilepsy, autism, and multiple births. She has lectured in the Marino Institute teacher training college on parents and autism. Currently she juggles home management with community broadcasting, reflexology, gardening, and cleaning the bathroom. Married to Ken O'Sullivan, they have adult children Nathan and Pearl and nine-year-old twins Adam and Sam. They live with autism in County Wicklow.

15. Stump the Cook

Lauren Goldman Marshall

When I used to cook for pleasure, I liked to listen to a culinary show on NPR called "The Splendid Table". It featured a segment called "Stump the Cook," in which the host would have to come up with a dish from preposterous ingredients proposed by callers. For example, what can you make with: duck egg yolks, spinach, pine nuts, baking soda, and yogurt starter?

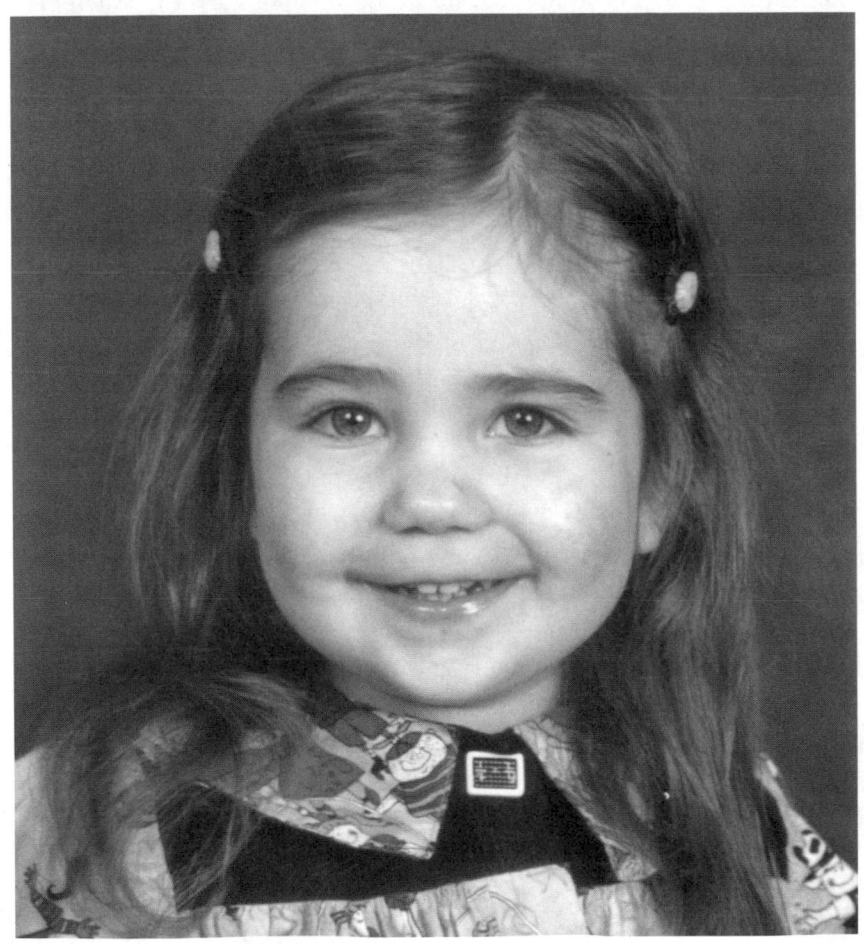

When parenting a child on a restricted diet, every day is like Stump the Cook. How do you make a birthday cake for a child who can't eat egg whites, flour, or sugar? How do you cook family meals for a husband who doesn't eat red meat and a daughter who can't eat grains, tofu, dairy, fish, or beans? Does gluten-free, casein-free, corn-free, soy-free, starch-free, and sugar-free also mean taste-free?

We started dietary intervention shortly after our daughter Hannah was diagnosed with an Autism Spectrum Disorder at the age of two. It is hypothesized that many children with autism have increased intestinal permeability, or "leaky gut." Gluten in wheat and casein in dairy are not properly broken down in the intestine and leak into the blood stream as morphine-like peptides, where they act as opiates on the brain.

For us, removing gluten and casein was only the beginning of the journey. Six weeks after we started the gluten-free, casein-free (GFCF) diet, Hannah ended up in the hospital for vomiting and diarrhea, which persisted over two weeks. We learned she had virtually no friendly bacteria in her intestines, was deficient in amylase (the enzyme that digests starch), and was allergic to rice, the mainstay of her GFCF diet!

A step-by-step process of food elimination began which continues to this day. We started the no-starch, no-sugar Specific Carbohydrate Diet (SCD), which meant eliminating all grains, as well as corn, soy, and potatoes. We have also incorporated some of the special foods of the Body Ecology Diet (BED) such as a delicious kefir made from young green coconuts. Both of these diets aim to *heal* the gut by eliminating foods that feed harmful bacteria and yeast.

The SCD diet marked the beginning of Hannah's turnaround, but that wasn't the end of our food exclusions. Soon, we were saying goodbye to egg whites (allergy), fish (mercury), and beans (too hard to digest). Honey and sweet fruits, such as bananas and grapes, mostly had to go because they feed bacteria and yeast, and because Hannah, like many children with autism, has a hard time processing the phenolic compounds found in these fruits. Now the list of what she can't eat is much longer than the list of what she *can* eat.

I constantly struggle with what it means to deprive our daughter of the pleasures of a bountiful table. What is summer without homemade blackberry jam? Easter without chocolate? Passover without matzoh?

I don't want Hannah to feel deprived, so I make sure she has a treat for special occasions. For her third birthday, I made an "ice cream cake" out of homemade frozen coconut yogurt and strawberry sherbet, decorated with strips of soft coconut. It was a work of art. Passover became her favorite holiday after she tasted my modified charoset, made from chopped apples, walnuts, blackcurrant juice, and cinnamon. For Easter, I filled plastic eggs with strawberries and hid them in the backyard. True, we missed out on the neighborhood chocolate scramble. But then we also avoided the tantrums that used to come like clockwork 20 minutes after chocolate touched her lips.

My creations aren't always successful. I set off the smoke alarms in my mother-in-law's house when my pumpkin pie crust, made from hazelnut flour and coconut oil, leaked onto the oven flour and began to burn. "Wouldn't some mandarin orange slices do just as well?" my mother-in-law asked, puzzling at my insistence that Hannah have Thanksgiving pie.

Hannah is well aware of what she is missing. Once, sitting at a restaurant, watching a plate of steaming naan (South Asian bread) pass by our table, she said "I want to go back to being two years old." "Why?" I asked. "So I can eat bread and toast again." Lately, she has begun to notice that her classmates' lunches are much more interesting than her own. One of her first peer interactions was to ask "Can I have your strawberry?" A popular game of hers is to go down to our basement pantry, where pasta, flours, apple juice, and other foods no longer in her diet are shelved away, and, pointing at various items, announce "That makes you sick. That makes you sick. That doesn't make you sick." She says philosophically: "When I grow up to be four years old, then I'll be able to eat wheat."

My husband didn't fall in love with me for my cooking, but he probably married me for it. When we were dating, he used to call me up from work to see what was on the menu. I enticed him over to my place with spanakopita, bouillabaisse, and lemongrass tofu, until pretty soon it just didn't make sense to pay two rents. Now he calls up to ask if it's chicken or beef day. If the latter, he stops at Taco del Mar on the way home. I eat what my daughter eats, so she won't feel left out. Instead, my husband gets left out. I might throw a pot of rice or pasta on the stove for him, but I just don't have the energy to cook two separate meals.

Eating out solves the problem of what to feed my husband, but it's hard to find restaurants that can accommodate our daughter's diet. Forget the starch-heavy kiddies menu. We order adult size meat and vegetable entrees for our three-year-old. I'm embarrassed by all the questions I have to ask the server, who usually fetches the chef, and, even then, we might not catch the cornstarch in the sauce or the gluten in the spice mixture. Despite these risks, we find our Saturday night dinners out are an essential way for our family to unwind. For my part, it gives me a much needed break from the kitchen.

Dietary intervention is truly a labor of love. Keeping up with demand for coconut kefir means sawing through the thick woody husks of 6–8 coconuts a week. It can take two hours to prepare Hannah's breakfast and lunch for school. It can take a day of cooking and a large ice chest to prep for a weekend vacation. At a recent hotel stay, there was not a single item in the huge breakfast buffet that Hannah could eat. It made me sad to watch the other children running around gaily helping themselves to cinnamon rolls and apple turnovers, while our daughter nibbled on warmed-over winter squash and watercress. But while Hannah's food becomes more different from that of other children, her behavior becomes more similar.

Twenty months ago, before we started dietary intervention, Hannah had a constant runny nose, was often home sick from daycare, and drooled so much she soaked the front of her shirt. She had explosive, runny poops that dripped out of her cotton diapers onto the liners, and rarely slept through the night. Back then, she refused most solid foods. She was too weak to walk from the house to the car. She insisted on being carried through doorways, and wouldn't touch her crayons or toys (but rather directed adults to manipulate them for her). Her only playground activity was making piles out of woodchips. She spoke a wide vocabulary but not to anyone in particular, didn't respond when I called her name, and didn't notice when I cried.

Today, at age three and a half, Hannah is a happy, busy preschooler, drawing pictures, building houses with blocks, making up stories, trying on dress-up clothes, and playing on the slide at the local playground. She rarely sniffles, doesn't drool, and didn't miss more than a day of preschool for illness last year. She sleeps through the night, is potty-trained and has one to three mostly formed stools a day. She rarely turns down a food for textural issues (unless it's peas) and indeed her most common response to a new food is "Can I eat that?" We take mile-long hikes. She notices my feelings and even shows compassion at times, for example, offering me some of her almond yogurt "because you spilled yours, Mommy." She seeks out me and my husband for play, and has begun joining her peers in silly antics. Through dietary intervention and other bio-medical treatments, she has come so far in less than two years that she is truly a different child.

How much of this transformation is due to diet is hard to say. Hannah attends an integrated preschool, where she receives ABA therapy. She also gets speech, occupational, and developmental movement therapy, and we do a form of relationship therapy called Relationship Development Intervention (RDI). Under the guidance of her doctor, we have started most of the treatments of the Defeat Autism Now (DAN) protocol, including vitamin and mineral supplementation, chelation, anti-fungal treatments, secretin, and intravenous immunoglobulin (IVIG) therapy. Each of these interventions has played an important role in her progress. At the very least, diet has made her healthier, happier, and better able to learn from her therapy. But I believe dietary intervention has also mitigated her behavioral symptoms. Many of her leaps forward have coincided with dietary changes, and when I try to slack off the diet she regresses.

Healing her gut has begun the process of healing her body and nourishing her brain. Dietary intervention has meant huge sacrifices—for Hannah who may never eat cotton candy at the fair, for my husband who misses the eggplant lasagne I used to make, and for me struggling to make creative meals out of limited ingredients. But then, without these restrictions, we might never have discovered spinach/duck yolk/pine nut yogurt pancakes, not to mention the delights of pumpkin seed pesto or crabapple kefir. Now nothing can stump this cook!

Lauren Goldman Marshall lives in Seattle with her husband Mike Schell and their daughter Hannah. Lauren is a produced and published playwright and award-winning travel writer. Prior to becoming a parent, Lauren was the artistic director of Seattle Public Theater. Mike is a composer and computer systems administrator. Lauren and Mike plan to adopt a baby girl from China in fall, 2005. Hannah looks forward to being a big sister, and asks, "What will the little sister eat?"

16. Taking the Bag Off

Shelley Milhous

Elliot climbed up and down every piece of furniture in the doctor's office as Lee and I waited for the developmental pediatrician to return. Knowing what would happen if we looked into each other's eyes, we protected Elliot and the furniture from harm, and simultaneously tried to make time go by faster and more slowly. We were trying to hold it together. I knew what the pediatrician was going to say. I had read all about it in *Time Magazine* and gave Elliot all the diagnostic tests myself. Still, I was clinging to the possibility that Elliot is merely the product of bad parenting and we are simply not up to the job. The footsteps. I don't want to know. The doorknob. I don't want to know. The words. "He has Pervasive Developmental Disorder (PDD). It's not so bad. Early intervention is the key."

She said more, but it was just a fog of words. She handed me articles, gave me websites and offered names. I wanted to vomit my own breath: first of all, when is it no longer "early"? He's only three. When am I going to run out of time? Clearly he is intelligent. He can recite an entire *Winnie the Pooh* video from beginning to end. He just never says "Hi Mommy." Surely we can teach him to talk to people. Surely he can be cured?

Panic, a race against time, fueled us for the next few months, until we were back at the hospital involved in a study linking wheat and dairy allergies to symptoms of autism. If I could prove it is an allergy, his symptoms would vanish and this nightmare would be ended. He would be cured. For the study they collected Elliot's urine to test for intestinal permeability. Lee and I were good sports, pretending to take it all with such maturity until it was time to take the plastic bag off of his penis. Just how much glue is necessary for a four-year-old's tender skin? He is screaming *this hurts, Mommy,* without words. Just his surprised, wild eyes meeting my surprised, helpless ones. The words, "Take the bag off!" finally came screaming out of him—but this was in the car as he was about to have an accident in his pants. Six months later.

More months went by in my search for the cure and we were back at the hospital investigating a white spot on Elliot's stomach. The geneticist that we saw suggested he have an MRI to rule out tuberous sclerosis, a sometimes fatal disease that often can be found on children with developmental delays. Fatality vs. MRI. What would any mom do? I was assured he would drink his sleeping potion and be sedated for the half-hour procedure. Even though a person needs three of these ash-leaf macules to meet the critical criteria of tuberous sclerosis, we decided to rule out fatality.

Although our appointment was at 9:45 a.m., it was close to 11:00 before a fasting Elliot got his promised juice—about one-eighth of a teaspoon of bright pink fluid. However, this was only a solution to "relax" him so they could put in an IV to sedate him. Guess what? The drink only seemed to make him a little drunk and cause him to slur his speech—which I found a little frightening since the whole nightmare began with Elliot's speech delay.

Nothing could relax this kid or me, and I end up helping one nurse pin him down while the other nurse misses her first attempt at finding a vein. Elliot is looking right at me and screaming, but he can't see me. It is a look that bores a hole through my heart, stops my breath and says, *You can't help me.* What is taking her so long? She is wasting time, saying calming things and complaining that he's not holding still. Another nurse barges in and gives needle nurse a piercing look that charges her with incompetence. I'm on the verge of screaming, *Your technique is completely horrendous* when, through some manner of grace, "Just how much longer is this supposed to take?" comes flying out of my mouth.

"Oh, about five more minutes," says needle nurse.

Five…more…minutes! Five more minutes of that look. Five more minutes of that scream. Five more minutes of veins popping out of his neck. Five more minutes of Elliot trying to rip the IV out. Five more minutes of watching the clock say 11:45. Five more minutes of holding my breath. I notice that my tears have made a puddle on the sheet next to his head. I try to remember why we're here. Silence. He's asleep. My little baby. My tortured little boy who recognized the roads to the hospital and thought we were on our way to Mimi and Poppop's house. And now his little hand is bruised and poked and wrapped so tightly in hospital tape to keep him from ripping his IV out. His face is wet with tears, his and mine. I hate you, needle nurse. I hate you, doctor who ordered this test. I hate you, children's hospital. I hate you, PDD. God, how could you maim my baby? He came out of me and he was perfect. Not only are they telling me he came with a neurological disorder, he now has the bruises and the tears to prove it.

They are wheeling him out, and I stand back to get out of their way. He is dead still and I am shaking. The nurses look like they've seen a ghost and I have a sick sense of satisfied retribution. Welcome to my world, baby. You just got a dose of my son full throttle, all stops pulled, no holds barred, tutti fortissimo. He took a bite right out of your confidence, chewed you up and spat you out. I saw the nurse write, "very hard to sedate." You got that right, sister.

They wheel him down to the room for the MRI. The technician starts to strap him in, looks at my wretched face and asks, "What's he in here for?" What's…he…in…here…for?! Doesn't anybody read charts? Nausea envelops my body. I realize that no one is actually in charge here, but I manage to patiently explain his symptoms to the technician like the good sport I am. The white patch, tuberous sclerosis, etc. She seems to understand me as if she'd asked me something as mundane as "Where is the peanut butter?"

She hands me gauze to wipe my tears because she has no tissue. I put in the required ear plugs. They leave. I sit and simultaneously watch Elliot's chest go up and down and his heart rate monitor show an even pattern. I read the Siemens label on the big machine about 500 times and stare at Elliot's dirty socks. An hour goes by just like this.

He wakes up two hours later uneventfully except that he throws up Juicy Juice all over my husband's shirt. Miraculously, he falls asleep in the car on the way home. I spend a fair amount of time fantasizing about a drive-up bar where we can just order a shooter or two, "grande red-eye," and be on our merry way.

Three weeks later, someone called from the geneticist's office to say that there is no evidence at this time to suggest Elliot has tuberous sclerosis.

"So he doesn't have it?" I eagerly, logically, and rightfully ask.

"There is no evidence at this time..." she repeats.

What is an appropriate response to this? What would any ravaged exhausted mother feel in this moment? Outrage. Betrayal. Righteous indignation. Pick one. I didn't feel any of them. I only had an overwhelming sense of calm. Resignation. I hung up the phone. And I hung up on the race. I finally saw myself as one of those stage-moms dragging her kid around from audition to audition with "Take the bag off, Mommy" ringing in my ears. I was attending to the experts whom I thought were in charge, unwittingly sacrificing my baby's humanity in order to bring relief to my own sense of helplessness. The truth is, he is perfect. He was perfect when he came out. And he is perfect with autism. It was time to embrace his gifts, embrace his challenges, and strive to make his the happiest, most satisfying life possible. For me, it was simply time to stop running, to allow myself to walk through the deepest sadness I have ever known, and to leave the bag behind.

This essay is taken from a book in progress entitled *The Mother of Intervention* by Shelley Milhous. The author lives in Doylestown, Pennsylvania, with her husband, Lee, and their two sons, Elliot and Christopher, ages five and two. Shelley and her husband are professional classical musicians and testify to Elliot's perfect pitch. Currently, Elliot enjoys reciprocal communication and articulates his ideas and feelings with increasing clarity. His therapy has consisted of a half-day preschool with speech and occupational therapies, and he is under the care of a psychologist. While Shelley attributes Elliot's progress mostly to the Floortime approach and his inclusive preschool program, it is Christopher who challenges Elliot's communication skills on a continual basis.

17. Truth:
The Parents' Spectrum

John Nelson

Immerse yourself in the culture of autism for longer than a coffee break and you will surely encounter the term *spectrum*. It is used repeatedly, perhaps to excess, in almost every article, book, and interview exploring the subject. In the five years since my son was diagnosed with autism, I have become aware of a different spectrum, the one that belongs to the parents: the spectrum of truth.

What is the truth about autism? Actually, there are manifold truths about the disorder, ranging from mildly impressive to severely important. Often they appear in conflict with each other, at once both contradictory and complementary. The following paragraphs explore three of these dichotomous truths of autism, ones I consider particularly vital: *hope, perspective,* and *expertise.*

The truth is, hope is the greatest victim of autism; the truth is, hope is the most critical element in fighting autism.

I once enrolled in a class on wilderness living and survival. On the first day, the instructor directed us to list, in order of importance, four elements essential to survival: oxygen, food, water, and the will to live. The order most of us chose was (1) oxygen; (2) will to live; (3) water; (4) food. Of course, we were all wrong. The instructor insisted that the will to live must come first. Without it, we would not even breathe. When it comes to battling your child's autism, hope is the expression of that will. It is the first and most necessary step.

Imagine, for a moment, how even more daunting your family's battle with autism would be without hope. Without hope, you would not hire therapists. Without hope, you would not enlist the help of friends and family. Without hope, you would not review Individualized Educational Plans (IEP). Without hope, you would not give your child birthday parties, attend Parents' Day, sign up for tee ball or sign up for anything. Without hope, you would not dare to dream. Without hope, autism wins and your child loses.

Perhaps right now it does not seem your child's life will ever improve. You may be beaten down. Your hope is like a lost dog that will not come back no matter how loud you shout or how long you cry. You are too strong to allow that. I know because you are reading this book and that means you are looking for answers.

However, if inspiration still eludes you, dwell on this; at no time in the history of humankind have more people been engaged in the struggle with autism than right now. There are legions of dedicated individuals working every day to improve therapies, adapt curriculums, track genes, develop medicines, organize fund drives, advocate legislature and raise awareness. And, they are all doing it on behalf of your child and others like him or her. *Hope.*

The truth is, autism is a curse that forges a tempest of challenges for your child, steals a mountain of resources from your family, and drains a torrent of emotional blood from your soul; the truth is, autism is a blessing that prevents you from ever taking your child's laugh, embrace, or verbalization for granted.

Reviewed separately, these two statements seem completely at odds with each other, but combined they help define a second truth on the parents' spectrum. If *hope* is the lever that lifts you out from under the sheets every morning, then *perspective* is the tack that keeps you from diving straight back under those sheets, the force that carries you through the peaks and valleys of the day.

What do I mean by this? Simple, count your blessings. Your child has autism and it is pervasive. Your child senses the world differently and that makes communication and education very complex. At least you have time to attack those challenges. Their life, although arduous, is not being cut short.

My little boy was speech delayed. Even today, he possesses a very limited use of language. However, that does not keep him from being impudently expressive. My wife and I have become accustomed to his conveyance of a myriad of emotions: sadness, happiness, pain, joy, boredom, excitement, stress, repose, defiance, love. He never even remotely seems to pity himself. Perhaps he does not have the ability. Perhaps he just accepts himself and his feelings, an ability we can all aspire to.

If my silver-lining outlook seems self-righteous, please remember, I know the dark side of autism as well. Hell sleeps outside my bedroom window. On some nights, the glass cracks and the flames seep in.

I remember one of the worst of those nights, my youngest daughter's first night home after being born. My little boy was not yet three. He became ill, developed diarrhea and a barking cough. Because of his tactile response to the bowel movements, he would vomit every time he had to go to the bathroom. On top of this, we had to attempt to keep steam in his face because the muscles in his throat were inflamed. He screamed for almost three hours straight in my arms, with only brief moments of silence during his withered gasps, until finally falling asleep, cradled against my chest on the couch, completely exhausted. My wife helped me when she could, but for the most part, we tried to isolate her and the baby so they would not get sick. At one point, the situation became so overwhelming I unleashed my own screams, shouting through the ceiling, through the moonlit clouds, "Why are you doing this to us?"

Sometimes people ask, "How does having a child with autism change you?" The answer lies in moments like that. How could anyone go through such an experience with their little boy and not change? Either you learn from the dreadfulness of such events or you let them drop you in an ever-tightening downward spiral. It took me months to understand what I had gleaned from this particular nightmare. Finally, I realized, the lesson was this; no matter how grueling my son's autism is on me, it is an exponentially greater challenge for him. *Perspective.*

The truth is, there are thousands of experts in the world that know more about autism than you do; truth is, there is no expert in the world that knows more about your child's autism than you do.

Although autism possesses many signature traits, it is still a distinctly individual disorder. My child's autism is not your child's autism. Eventually, we each become astute to our own child's unique way of seeing and reacting to the world. We become their personal expert.

I am not suggesting that parents are more learned about all aspects of autism than the multitude of professionals that have dedicated their lives to treating the disorder. In fact, quite the opposite is true. Because of the hard work of these professionals, a mountain of information is readily available for any parent striving to improve their child's life. The problem is you do not need the whole mountain, you only need the information pertinent to your son or daughter.

Think of yourself as a prospector. You might have to dig through tons of bedrock to find a vein of gold, but when you do, it makes all the sweat worthwhile. Concerning autism, gold is anything that improves your child's quality of life; it could be a better therapy, a better therapist, a new medicine, an improved IEP strategy, a new learning method or even an old one. My wife and I have read multi-hundred page books just to extract one meaningful passage.

Why is it important to become your child's expert? It is important because your resources are finite. Even if your finances are unlimited, your time and energy are not. You must allocate these resources discriminately, where they have the greatest effect. Do not be afraid of that pragmatic little voice inside you. It is there for a reason, and giving in to it, at least on occasion, can keep you from hiring the wrong person or spending months on an unproductive program. *Expertise.*

Hope. Perspective. Expertise. These three truths guide my wife and me in caring for our son. Lately, his increasingly physical reactions have challenged us. The stakes are high. If we cannot teach him to control his aggressive behaviors, his opportunities in the years to come might prove severely limited. The mere chance of that sickens us, but fear of the future will not help our little boy. Therefore, each day we strive to maintain hope, keep perspective, and increase our expertise.

Find your own place on the parents' spectrum. With a compass made of truths, either the ones I have highlighted or others that you discover on your own, you and your child can navigate through the unknown times ahead. Together, you can do it.

John Nelson is a 41-year-old, married father of four children, including his eight-year-old son who was diagnosed with autism at the age of three. John has a B.A. in Marketing and Business Administration from Eastern Washington University and currently works for Genuine Parts Company. He enjoys writing in his spare time, especially on topics as important as autism. He and his wife are active members of The Autism Society of Washington (ASW).

18. Listening to Macord

Eric Peter

You can measure my available writing time in minutes a week. It is down there with my reading time. Most of my time is devoted to my 13-year-old son, Macord, who has autism. I entered his life when he was five, and I adopted him on August 19, 1999, when he was eight years old.

As the adoptive father of a child with severe autism I admit that I've been guilty of pride. I can understand the disappointment that biological parents must feel when the autism bomb goes off, that they were dealt a bad hand, that nature served them up short. But I volunteered for this.

Yet even my pride is beginning to fade, giving way to exhaustion. Fatigue is the currency of daily living. Macord has amazing stamina. He can be up at 4:00 in the morning and not lie down to sleep until midnight. There was a period in his life when he would get up in the middle of the night and stay up for several hours. For many years I had trouble staying awake at work. Even today I can't sit through a meeting without nodding into sleep. I have developed stamina over the years, a gift from Macord.

As an adoptive father I have forsaken some rights. I cannot feel victimized. I cannot despair, although sometimes I do. I cannot give up. I cannot run away.

The responsibility of being Macord's father came at the right time in my life. I married Macord's mother, Joanne, when I was 43. I had never been married before. Prior to that I had lived for 20 years in a cabin with no running water in the Southeast Alaska rain forest. I had no one to worry about except myself. I read and dabbled in writing. I had all the time in the world to write but I lacked the discipline and focus. I worked at a variety of jobs: newspaper reporter, clerk, deck hand, but none for very long. I was satisfied with the poetic simplicity of one day fading into the next. Macord awakened in me the realization that I could actually be of use to someone. After years of false starts and no clear direction I was ready to be Joanne's husband. I was ready to be Macord's father.

If I had to place Macord on the new term of art, Autism Spectrum Disorders, I would have to place him on the lower functioning end, if only for the fact that so many other children with autism seem so much better off in communicative and cognitive ability. Joanne and I find it frustrating when we attend workshops and conferences on autism and find that they are talking about children far different from Macord.

At first I was enthralled by the mystery of autism. I kept searching for information that would add clarity to the mystery. I read books hoping that I would find one that cast a ray of light into the dark water of autism.

Macord is nonverbal, and I see this as being the central feature of his disability. The challenging behaviors he has shown over the years are the result of his inability to express himself. Clinical evaluations of Macord also describe him as mentally retarded. Joanne and I hate the "R" word, although we are often told it is necessary for Macord to receive the funding we need to keep him at home. Labels that describe a disability rob a person of individuality and usher in the challenge of describing just who Macord is.

Macord requires several medications, both to stabilize his behavior and to support his endocrine system. If he is in a cranky mood he spits out the meds. Our carpet is a stained testament to this fact. Every facet of his life requires attention. If he were a typical boy he would spend time with other boys running around the neighborhood. But his disability isolates him as it isolates Joanne and me. Very rarely do we have the opportunity to socialize, and when we do it is with family that accepts Macord. Isolation is a problem that many parents of special needs children face. Macord creates a solar system in which he is the center and he demands the constant tithing of work.

When Joanne and I are not working on Macord's physical care, we are working on ways to advocate for him. Every area of his life outside of the home, whether in school or in the community with his care providers, requires advocacy. We constantly write emails to Macord's teachers and providers. We frequently meet with school and support staff. We attend workshops. We continually try to improve the level of services Macord receives. We are continually educating ourselves about Macord's disability and how to cope with it.

The first time I saw Macord he was watching a video, an animated children's feature, with his face pressed up against the TV screen. He squealed with delight and flapped his hands in the air. This introduced me to Macord's principal obsession. Videos have always been an important part of his life, especially the classic Walt Disney features: *Pinocchio, 101 Dalmatians, Lady and the Tramp, Dumbo,* and *Jungle Book,* to name just a few.

When Macord was little he depended on someone else to play the videos for him. Soon he learned to do that by himself and he would watch them over and over from beginning to end. Then one of his care providers taught him to use the fast forward and reverse. That changed everything. Now Macord watches videos in brief segments, using fast forward and reverse to surgically watch and re-watch a scene. He will revisit the scene dozens of times before he moves on. Geppetto tells Figaro the cat, "Figaro, I forgot to open the window," again and again. Dumbo's first flight has taken place countless times. Perdy and Pongo have led their army of spotted puppies through the snowstorm hundreds of times.

As Macord has grown bigger, so have his challenging behaviors. At the root of this has been an intense and obsessive rage. Rage at having to do things that he does not want to do, rage at not having something that he wants. He hits and pinches painfully. He claws with his fingernails. He kicks, bites, and throws things. He yells and screams with furious wrath. His rages escalate until we cannot go near him. Over the years we tried a variety of medications: clonidine, Buspar, risperidol, amitriptyline, Ativan, Celexa, Abilify, all with varying degrees of success.

But Macord is more than challenging behavior. Locked within the mystery of his disability there is a boy. He can be kind and sweet. He displays remorse for causing pain. We hope that he can learn to take care of himself and to live within the community. Just as exhaustion is a currency of our lives, so is hope. Locked within the complexity of his behaviors are two boys: one who has autism and is severely limited by that, and a typical, rambunctious, opportunistic child. Separating the two is a challenge in itself.

The story of Pinocchio presents a potent metaphor. After all, it is the story of a puppet who longs to be a real boy. I wonder about the workings of Macord's mind, what he thinks about and what he longs for. I wonder if he realizes how his autism makes him different from other boys. Isolated within this little world, does he despair? Yet *Pinocchio* is also the story of Geppetto, a man who longs to be a real father. Macord has made me that father. With Macord I was transformed from a man who only had himself to worry about to one who is daily and intensely involved in the life of a child with a disability.

There are not many opportunities to sit down when caring for Macord, which is why it is such a relief once he is in bed or when he goes out with one of his care providers. Joanne and I do not have much time for ourselves and when we do we savor it. Things like going to a movie, going to church or being able to go to dinner with friends and family are precious commodities.

Joanne and I struggle with the question of whether we should place Macord in a special school or an assisted living setting. We have struggled with that question more and more recently as it is increasingly difficult to meet Macord's needs at home or in the community. It is a question that creates hope, guilt, and sorrow. Over the years we have vowed that we would never institutionalize Macord, that he would always live at home with us. Now I am not so certain that this is possible; not so much that we cannot handle his behavioral issues, but that we cannot provide him with the structured life that he requires or the tools and setting he needs to learn important life skills.

Life with Macord is a day-to-day process. His parenting and care create too many questions and uncertainties to have it any other way. How often have Joanne and I said, "How can we keep on doing this?" Hundreds? From the moment he wakes up in the morning until he finally falls asleep at night, each day is filled with challenge.

But then I think, I am 50 years old now. I can do this.

Eric Peter was born and raised in Juneau, Alaska, and continues to make Juneau his home. He works for the Alaska Department of Health and Social Services as an administrative assistant. Previously he has worked as a newspaper reporter, deckhand on commercial fishing boats, a laborer, and an office worker. He received a bachelor's degree in journalism from the University of Alaska Fairbanks. When he is not at work or parenting Macord, he enjoys reading and writing.

19. Parallel Worlds

Antonia Rowland

I never really encountered the world of special needs when I was growing up. It wasn't until our second son, Paul, was born with Down syndrome two years ago, that I ever encountered this parallel world. It's the same as everybody else's world: filled with love, laughter, good times and bad. But our days are also filled with countless therapies, appointments, and professionals.

We consider ourselves very fortunate to live in a community which is supportive, offering us a future that is bright and full of hope. When Paul was born, I knew that life wouldn't be easy, but I also felt a sense that the problems were manageable. We could handle them. Everything would be OK. Then, just when we thought we had everything under control along came another fastball. Our firstborn son, Sam, now four years old, was diagnosed this year with an Autism Spectrum Disorder (ASD). OK, I thought, I can handle this. I know Sam is bright, beautiful, and full of beans. We should just follow the same path as Paul's journey and we'll find out down the road that everything, difficult though it might be, will be OK… Right?

It's now five months since Sam's diagnosis; a diagnosis that didn't come out of the blue. We always knew Sam was different, but we never connected all the dots. Everything seemed to have an explanation: his absconding; horrific tantrums; screaming through every hair wash; never being able to sit; hardly sleeping; not eating; chronic diarrhea and on and on. We had explained each situation away and just accepted that he was a high-maintenance child.

It wasn't until his speech therapist suggested we consult a paediatrician that the penny dropped. One of life's little ironies was about to slap me in the face. A decade ago, I had graduated from university with a degree in psychology—I had even written my thesis on autism! And yet I had given birth to and lived with a child for four years and not even recognized he was on the autism spectrum. I tried desperately to remember everything I had learnt, but all that came flooding back were vague memories of the pub! Thankfully, I am reassured by my friends that being thirty-something and having young children is reason enough to not remember those days clearly. But following confirmation of Sam's diagnosis, and filled with a sense of fear that I knew nothing, my quest to clarify our now uncertain future began.

It began with every professional I knew through Paul. My laid-back carefree approach to life was on hold. A full-blown frenzy now ensued. It was only a tiny amount of common sense that prevented me from grabbing these professionals, and screaming, "Tell me everything you know." I restrained myself, and rather more calmly told them of Sam's diagnosis. There seemed to be a consensus amongst them that they should reply by asking me what I had decided about his education! "What? You tell me." I wanted to scream. "I don't know anything!"

Fortunately, we had Sam's educational future planned, being lucky enough to send him to private school. We had found the best. He was already attending his second year of nursery there. And the school, even with the knowledge of his diagnosis, remained enthusiastic about their dedication to him. The reality was, though, that even at the age of four, Sam had already slipped to the bottom of the class. He couldn't cope: participating was stressful for him. All the fun learning, fabulous facilities, and exciting opportunities to experience in a privileged world, and he just didn't get it.

I had begun to get it though, or so I thought. I spent many a supermarket trip shouting "Listen!" I had realized myself, that there was little point in saying anything else, unless I got his attention. It was a kind and wise professional who pointed out to me, though, that what I was actually doing was teaching him how not to listen. "Listen!" to him now means *I must run as fast as possible in the opposite direction to Mummy*. Not what I had planned!

I did get it when it came to realizing that not many people in the general public can see the parallel world of the autism spectrum. During my pregnancy with Paul, I was waiting at the supermarket checkout with Sam screaming around my ankles, swinging from the ends of the reins, when the old lady in front of me said "And you want more?" My humour has darkened enough now to see the funny side of that remark, but at the time it was less than helpful. More than two years on and I still get comments about his occasionally appalling behaviour. No one seems to look at us and think that my son requires special understanding. Instead, I get all sorts of comments that question my competence as a mother, leaving me feeling that it is a cold and unpleasant world out there.

I don't particularly care what people say anymore, but I am left with a feeling of sadness. Especially as I see the kindness and understanding that is offered to Paul. We have received occasional negative comments about Paul's Down syndrome, but most people are very positive and generous with their compliments for him. They see him, they judge him, and generally they accept him for what he is—a very cute two-year-old.

When their eyes shift to Sam though, they never see the special needs, and if I know them enough to share his diagnosis, I am met with complete astonishment. "He doesn't look autistic!" They question whether I shouldn't seek a second opinion. They tell me of all the little boys they know who have similar difficulties, but they're still "normal." With Paul we had a blood test, with Sam I've been left alone to argue that the diagnosis is the only thing we have that actually makes sense.

So where are we now, five months down the road? Well, I still vow to extract every pearl of wisdom from the continuing stream of professionals that I encounter, but now my focus is on how to best use the information that I have acquired. A lot of what is written about ASD isn't relevant to Sam. I need to find out what bits apply to him, and then just as I did with my information on Down syndrome, I want to turn the information into bite-size chunks that I can chew over and nourish my child's future with.

It's somehow not the same as my journey with Paul. There is a general understanding within society as to what Down syndrome is. Of course there is diversity within Down syndrome and society is evolving and boundaries changing, but we sure knew what we were dealing with. Life at our point on the autism spectrum is different. Life seems to revolve around a single issue, namely a complete lack of understanding. And it's not just the general public that doesn't get it...

After I recently attended a conference on autism, Whack! — it hit me: The child that I feed, dress, wash, and interact with every day was someone who I knew practically nothing about. I can't even describe to you how affected he is, other than to say he is verbal and not your stereotypical case of classic autism. *It's not just that Sam doesn't get the world; I don't understand his world either.* And if I don't see him clearly, how can his teachers? How can anyone?

I do see that sending Sam back to a school where he is bottom of the class is not the way forward, so I have taken him out of his private school. I await his future running between our local specialist school and our local primary school. I am afraid, because no amount of information can tell me what the future holds. Do I feel everything might turn out OK, like I feel with Paul? Well, not yet, but admittedly I do have hope. Hope in those professionals who do get it, who do understand and who generously dedicate their lives to helping families like mine. Living in a parallel world, I still have hopes and expectations for my children like everybody else. It's just that I need a pocketsize professional to carry around with me every day.

Antonia Rowland graduated with degrees in psychology and political science. She also obtained a certificate in counselling. Originally from the northeastern United States, she has settled in the UK with her husband, Simon, a security consultant. Currently, she is working as a full-time mum to her two special needs children: Sam, who is on the autism spectrum and Paul, who has Down syndrome. Due to the difficulties both of her children have with speech, she is now interested in training to become a speech therapist.

20. The Question

Shelley Stolaroff Segal

The question jolted me awake like Frankenstein's monster at 3:00 in the morning: What if my son, Josh, who developed severe autism, were to die? During normal hours, no maudlin thought like that was permitted to enter my psyche. Only during a fretful turn in the early morning would such an idea materialize.

What if my beautiful, brilliant little Jordan, Josh's much-adored and adoring twin sister were to die? Her death, equally unthinkable, would be just as tragic—but different. I tried, but couldn't control the compulsion to answer my own sick question. I am no stranger to dark thinking. After my son's initial diagnosis, when the protective shock wore off, I entertained a variety of morbid thoughts. Mainly, I was consumed with my own demise. One day I would panic at the idea of dying prematurely and abandoning a child who would always need me. The next day, usually a bad one, I would count how many years I had left on earth to endure the unyielding anguish of Josh's autism. But I got better, and so did he. I began to accept his condition, syndrome, disorder, disease, whatever you want to call it, and I loved and respected my courageous child even more.

Yet, the question tortured me. The fact is, if Josh were to suddenly vanish from our family's life, our life, as we know it, would disappear also. It stunned me to realize how married we were to Josh's condition. His diagnosis was the reason we fled Indiana to pursue help and services in another state. His diagnosis was the reason my husband quit a successful neurosurgery practice in order to research a cure for autism. It was the reason I stopped composing and creating music. It determined the meals we ate, the vacations we took, the restaurants we chose, and the absurdity level of a home revolving with therapists. It was responsible for our lack of privacy, sanity, wedded bliss, peace of mind, and energy. It determined where we lived, where we bought groceries, where the kids were schooled, how we socialized, how we politicized, and how we prayed.

My creative endeavors were carefully planned and executed around my son's inevitable regressions. My husband's dedication to his work included rushed and repeated trips to Washington, D.C. Indeed, all my speeding tickets were related either to D.C.-bound travel for an autism forum, rally, or press conference, or to one of Josh's medical emergencies. My consistent tardiness in making meetings, retrieving my daughter from school, attempting a lunch date, interrupting a lunch date, etc., were Josh-related. Jordan's innate sense of responsibility, otherworldliness, and character growth were Josh-related. My frequent depressions, as well as my euphoric states, were also Josh-related.

How can we ever extricate ourselves from the autism that defines and rules our lives? We can't. But it's OK. The beauty of Josh's spirit transcends our fate. Yes, his "problem" is painful. I hate the mystery of autism. At least a thousand times in the past several years I have fantasized about an autism-free existence, an existence where Josh says "I love you" freely and clearly. I've fretted that the agony of an unscripted future would crush my family. But our love for this incredible child is stronger than our fear of what's ahead. Our respect for his courage and sweetness, his humor and strength, far outweighs the ball and chain he bears daily. We grow wise with our son and daughter. Wise enough to put the question behind us.

Shelley Stolaroff Segal is a writer, composer, and performer living in Greensboro, North Carolina. After earning a degree in English literature in 1982 she moved to England where she completed postgraduate work at the University of London and received her theatrical training at The Drama Studio London. In 1989 she married Jeffrey Segal, a neurosurgeon and current autism researcher. Their fraternal twins, Josh and Jordan, were born in Indiana where Josh was diagnosed with autism in 1999. Her latest project was an original one-woman show performed in May 2004, entitled "Outing Your Autistic Child." All proceeds benefited her husband's research at the Wake Forest Autism Initiative.

21. Simply Perfect

Tanya Stanley

Christopher was born into this world simply perfect. He was a happy, seemingly normal baby. He reached all of his milestones on time, if not early. He cut his first tooth at four months, sat up by five months, and walked at eleven months. My husband and I never suspected anything to be wrong until Christopher was around 18 months old. He had approximately ten words by this time, but oddly, never repeated them.

Had he lost them? Did he ever really have those words in the first place? I could have sworn I heard him say, "tank tu." How cute for such a little guy to demonstrate manners so early! As time passed, I began questioning myself more. Soon thereafter it became clear that Christopher was speech delayed. The reason for his delay, however, did not reveal itself for another six months.

With a master's degree in clinical social work and training in the *Diagnostic and Statistical Manual of Mental Disorders, Fourth Edition* (DSM-IV), I began researching. Originally, I was looking at a diagnosis of selective mutism. Christopher just did not talk. He never said Mama or Dada. Then he started throwing severe tantrums, including head banging, which I attributed to him being in the "terrible twos" stage and having no verbal skills. Christopher grew more frustrated each day. I thought I was dealing with a smaller, albeit just as feisty, version of Helen Keller.

I had Christopher's hearing checked after it finally occurred to me that he would not turn around when I called his name. *Did he ever answer to his name?* I cannot recall. I thought about how excited he would get upon Daddy's return home from work. But that stopped, and I do not know exactly when.

I remember one late night in particular, looking through the DSM-IV, and thinking: *If Christopher has any diagnosis in this book, I can find it. Easy enough. I will start in the childhood diagnoses section.* I thumbed through the section and looked right past autism. *Sure, an autism diagnosis entails speech delay, but that couldn't be Christopher. He's too smart and affectionate to be autistic.* What embarrassing thoughts to admit to as a clinician.

I was naive. A few nights later, I would return to page 66 with its bold heading that read: "299.0 Autism." It finally sank in. The words under this heading fit my son. I read the criteria over and over, all the while leaving salty tears on that page. Within a month, Christopher was officially diagnosed. He was 25 months old.

I had to do something, and quick. I had read already about the brain's pruning processes. The clock was ticking. I was reading everything I could get my hands on, but I could not read fast enough. The more information I obtained, the more empowered I felt. Reading was like a drug. I would stay up practically all night, night after night. I learned that autism is not a hopeless diagnosis like it was once thought to be. With early intervention, some children actually "recover." Although no one can yet say a child has been cured of autism, realistic gains are attainable for all.

As for intervention, I have followed the premise, "If it can't hurt, it's worth a try." Unfortunately, present conventional medicine does not have many answers and consequently, I have felt compelled to seek alternative measures. Indeed, I will travel any road that offers some hint of promise, even if it makes me look desperate. I am desperate!

We have tried countless diets and supplements. Between the diets, my son's picky eating habits, and his sensory issues, he ate only six different foods at any given time for a year and a half. We saw neurologists, school psychologists, social workers, nutritionists, a geneticist, a holistic physician, and a neurodevelopmental pediatrician. Of course we had, and continue to have, many visits with Christopher's pediatrician who is exceptional. Speech therapy, occupational therapy, and Applied Behavior Analysis (ABA) are other interventions we subscribe to. It is ironic how routine six days of therapy a week can become. For our lives it is quite normal.

I am a firm believer that treatment needs to be tailored to the individual child. It is not uncommon to find that one method of treatment works well for one child with autism, but does little to nothing for the next child. Having said that, I believe there are two things that have helped my son the most. First, a casein-free diet. We noticed marked differences literally overnight. Christopher's eye contact improved, he was less frustrated, and he no longer banged his head. The second intervention that proved to be most beneficial was ABA therapy. Currently, I believe 75 to 80 percent of my son's receptive and expressive skills result from this type of direct instruction.

I decided to take on a teaching role with my son simply because I knew we could not afford ABA therapy long-term, and it seemed to have such a positive effect for him. I videotaped the therapies so I could learn from them, and Christopher's therapist consulted with me on how to teach him. I was already well versed in behavioral theory, but I had no applied skills for the autism population. Within a few months, I began working with my son, and a few months after that, I began data collection. Now, I develop targets and oversee his "book." Throughout much of this time I was also in the process of filing letters of appeal with our insurance company, which, at the time, did not reimburse ABA therapy. They do now. But in any case it can be, and is often, financially debilitating for families.

Still, I would go into debt ten times over because Christopher is a changed little boy. In two years, he went from having practically no verbal skills, to signing, to having a verbal vocabulary of approximately 400 words. He can sing songs (my favorites are "Old MacDonald" and "Itsy Bitsy Spider") and speak in four-to five-word sentences. Visual spatial skills and academics are his greatest strengths. Christopher, like so many other children with autism, is enamored with numbers and letters. Only four years old, he already can spell many words. That is not to say we are in the clear. We have a lot of therapy ahead of us. Christopher has little to no conversation skills. We are optimistic though, and believe he will obtain these skills in time.

As for me, I have changed too. Having a baby is a life-altering event. Discovering that that baby has autism is a life-altering event of the same magnitude, if not more. It is interesting to think of how a mere label can change lives so much, yet change them so little. Because, really, Christopher did not change in that single day he was diagnosed. It was we, as parents, who changed. Our perspectives changed. Our priorities changed. Labeling a child with autism is a sensitive topic, but one thing labeling provided me with was understanding, and from that understanding came a higher degree of patience. (Oh, how I need it!)

I have a strong appreciation for many things people often take for granted. In the beginning, we did not know if Christopher would be verbal. We had read that about one-third of individuals with autism never gain expressive language skills. I had no expectations. It was a wait and see process. When Christopher finally started talking, we knew we had crossed a major hurdle. Each new word was like a gift. Surely any gift is appreciated more when it is received unexpectedly. It still feels like we are receiving gifts. Most recently, Christopher and I shared our first conversation. We were in the car and it went like this:

Christopher: "Where going?"

Me: (excitedly stunned) "We are going to the store to get you a bed."

Christopher: "A bed?"

Me: "Yes, a bed. Do you want a new bed?"

Christopher: "Yes, please!"

Autism was a catalyst for change in our family. In many ways, I think we are a better family and better individuals as a result of it. We are still changing. We are still learning. Our journey through life is like everyone else's; it is just on a road that is less traveled. And there is one thing that has not changed: Christopher is still simply perfect.

Tanya Stanley was an individual and group therapist for chemically dependent and mentally ill populations before having her son, who she currently stays home to raise. She has been married for 11 years, and resides in Florida, where her husband is stationed as a pilot in the United States Navy. Christopher is their only child. Tanya enjoys snow skiing, reading, and spending time with family and friends.

22. On the Wings of Asperger's

Carol Anne Swett

On that crisp February day, white caps danced to the music of the screaming seagulls. Flashes of sunlight flickered like darts flung from the surface of the Chesapeake Bay. Rather than soaring with the gulls, my heart was heavy. "Mommy am I sick?" intruded the somber voice of my seven-year-old.

I knew instantly that my response would forever determine his reaction to life. I was about to chart the course of his future with no time to choose or polish my words. Would I set him free to sail on the wings of life? Would I forever chain him to a diagnosis he was yet too young to understand?

A seven-year journey that began when he was less than four weeks old had just ended in a doctor's office. The crank of a crib mobile launched our frenzied search. When the tinny sound engulfed the nursery, Will let out a scream which still echoes in my soul fourteen years later. He went taut and turned purple as the music drove him over some hidden cliff. I snatched him up and tried to shield his board-stiff body. What was this horror visited upon us?

He slept fitfully, napping only 45 minutes a day. I became weary in ways I couldn't explain. The world challenged him in ways that didn't make sense. He had fine and gross motor coordination deficits, motor planning difficulties, and was hypersensitive to sounds. Despite the challenges, he flourished.

He looked through industrial catalogs naming gauges and valves at 16 months. At office supply stores, he could name every type of computer printer on the market and list the pros and cons. Clocks and ceiling fans mesmerized him. No trip to the hardware store was complete without visiting those aisles. He quoted passages from "Rudolph the Red-Nosed Reindeer" by 16 months and potty trained at 18 months. Everyone agreed he was brilliant and would be the joy of his future teachers, but (tsk...tsk...) his mom was a neurotic basket case.

He was diagnosed with Attention Deficit/Hyperactivity Disorder (ADHD) at age three. Was our quest for answers over? Unsettling puzzle pieces left us uneasy with the diagnosis. He couldn't maintain eye contact. He asked to do "school work" yet couldn't focus for ten seconds. Tearfully, we struggled on, knowing the journey had only begun.

That Christmas season he occupied himself with Christmas lights: screwing in replacement bulbs, plugging in the cord, watching the string burn, unplugging the cord, and starting all over again. His Christmas list included a fax machine, a dot matrix printer, and a DCS machine (a Distributed Control Machine—used to control the operations of production machinery during the manufacturing process) like the one his engineer father programmed and installed in paper mills. Even though I made no conscious effort to teach him letters and sounds, he began to associate them.

When he was four, I told my husband that our son was brilliant but that testing would not plumb the depths of his ability. Despite kind comments from strangers, I knew that he would be a nightmare for many teachers. He would not be able to express what he learned in a way that satisfied the educational establishment.

His October birthday delayed entry to school for a year. We hoped it would give him time to be more "desk-ready." When finally, at age six, he began to play make believe with peers, he could only sustain the play if it involved outer space travel. The Weather Channel was a source of endless fascination. When he was tested, I mentioned to the educational psychologist that I believed his Intelligence Quotient (IQ) scores would be in the 120 range for verbal and the 80 range for performance. As he nodded I felt patronized and thought I saw the words "neurotic mom" flash across his bemused mind. He seemed less cavalier when he reported that both scores were within five points of my predictions.

"He will have an LD [Learning Disability]," came the explanation. "Until he spends some time in a school setting, we won't know how it will manifest itself or what compensatory skills he will develop." The psychologist went on to explain that he felt there was no test instrument that could adequately quantify Will's IQ. "He is far brighter than these results indicate. We don't have a test that can adequately assess what he can do."

By the middle of first grade, we realized that traditional school would never work. We worked on spelling 45 minutes a day, six days a week. We used rocks, sand, Lego, and shaving cream to form words. They escaped him at test time. Math flash cards and timed drills put him into a frenzied state. "Mom, I am smart. I work so hard but I never get an S+ or a happy face." He cried on the way to and from school.

I sobbed out our frustrations to the pediatrician. I told her we were going to homeschool. I needed help to figure out why my child struggled despite being so bright. "You are right," she said soothingly. "Will is unusual. Other seven-year-olds talk about Power Rangers. He wants to run the centrifuge in the lab." Within days we had a referral and an answer.

With the answer came the question that would define our lives. "Mommy, am I sick?" The answer would either liberate or imprison. We had an answer to the why: Asperger's syndrome. The hows to be answered lay like depth charges in that far off ocean called "The Future."

I stroked the blond mop framing the puzzled little face. "No, honey. You are not sick. The doctor helped us understand the way you think and organize information. We've learned some things that will help us as we teach you. You won't find school as frustrating. You aren't sick. You are brilliant. You are fearfully and wonderfully made."

We restructured life and learning in baby steps. We never lost hope that William would soar as freely as those gulls over the bay that February day. In the seven years since, we have coped with the hows of life and found they weren't so scary after all.

His fear of heights gave way to the desire to hike up a mountain. The mountain prepared him to tackle a ski lift. The child who descended flights of stairs on his bottom became the young man riding a ski lift without the bar over his lap. He still refuses escalators but will, I suppose, conquer those in time. He worked for two years learning to jump rope. His determination kept him at it until he could skip 25 turns without missing. It was one of his proudest moments. He loves to ski, skate, and swim.

I watch amazed as he approaches new situations. He is the first to make eye contact, extend his hand, and greet new friends. His poised confidence puts them at ease. While he struggles with social nuances, he has friends of both sexes and all ages. He has participated in talent shows, youth choirs, puppet teams, and mission trips.

Will won a scholarship for piano instruction, plays at community events, and is composing orchestral scores. In defiance of the prediction that he would never learn to spell, he writes with cleverness and wit. He has built several computers and has completed many computer repairs. Math is still a struggle, but he has maintained a B average working at grade level. He loves science and history and thinks he'd like to go to Oxford.

He forges ahead on a path uniquely his own in search of other horizons to conquer. He recently spoke publicly about his diagnosis for the first time. I asked if it was awkward or sad. With characteristic grace he replied, "You know, I don't think about AS too much. It doesn't define who I am. It just means I have to work harder at some things than some people. Everyone has challenges. I don't mind talking about AS as long as I am an encouragement and not just an example."

I realized as he spoke that he makes his dad and me look like much better parents than we are. I close my eyes and see the bay. The seagulls call to me from that lonely day long ago and far away. I open my eyes and watch him with humble awe. I am the one who soars.

❧

Carol Anne Swett holds a B.S. in Family/Child Development and has taught in special education settings. She has homeschooled William and his younger brother Isaac for the last seven years. While her son Isaac hates "school" he has filled a notebook with his first draft of a 250-page book.

As a conference organizer and speaker, Carol Anne finds fulfillment encouraging other moms. Subsequent to William's diagnosis, her husband, Jeffrey, was formally diagnosed with AS. Will is completing his eighth grade school year in their hometown in South Carolina and trying to decide what to pursue in college. He believes he will write a stunning end to this story. His brother, Isaac, loves karate and is working toward his black belt. Isaac is very busy being seven; he never stops moving and hopes to conquer the world one day.

23. Learning to Embrace the "A" Word

Elaine Tarutis

When I learned in November that my three-year-old son Ethan had a diagnosis on the autism spectrum, I was delighted. An odd reaction, perhaps, but I hoped that a diagnosis meant answers. Since the spring, my husband and I had struggled to find a solution for Ethan's increasingly frustrating

behavior. His unpredictable tantrums were throwing our family into chaos. We never knew what would set him off or how aggressively he would react.

Things were worse when we went out. He might be fine, or he might scream and kick and push another child for no apparent reason. I had to watch his every move. I learned to limit my outings with Ethan and frequently turned down play dates. He would never play with the other kids anyway—he'd find a quiet place away from the other children and look at a book or play with a toy train. It became less stressful to stay home with Ethan, to keep him in a familiar environment surrounded by his favorite train books and train videos. But I felt more and more isolated.

Ethan's behavior wasn't just affecting me. My six-year-old son, Jonathan, grew more resentful of Ethan daily. Every time Ethan ignored Jonathan's invitations to play, crumpled up his drawings or screamed during an "Arthur" episode, Jonathan complained that his little brother was "dumb" and "bad." Our family was in turmoil and the responsibility of fixing it fell to me.

But solving the problem meant that I had to understand what the problem was. And I didn't. Ethan attended an integrated preschool where he received speech and physical therapy, so I started there. I spoke with his teacher and his therapists. They increased the services he received in school and suggested strategies for me to try at home, but nothing helped.

Meanwhile our home-life kept deteriorating. We all tip-toed around the house, never knowing what would set Ethan off into an uncontrollable tantrum. At three years old, he was the uncrowned king of our family. When a good friend trained in special education suggested that Ethan might have a Pervasive Developmental Disorder (PDD), it seemed worth exploring. I hoped that a diagnosis would provide me with a clear path to solving Ethan's behavior problems and help my family return to normal.

In August I arranged for a developmental pediatrician to evaluate Ethan. The earliest appointment was in November. During the next three months I took notes about Ethan's behavior and read up on PDD and the autism spectrum. I grew convinced that PDD explained Ethan's unpredictable tantrums, why he wasn't interested in other children, and why, at nearly four years old, he had never given anyone a hug or kiss.

So when the doctor told me in November that Ethan's symptoms and behavior were consistent with Pervasive Developmental Disorder–Not Otherwise Specified (PDD-NOS), I barely managed to suppress my smile. Finally, we had an answer: PDD-NOS, an Autism Spectrum Disorder. We had identified the problem and could work towards a solution. I left that appointment relieved and happy. But my smile soon faded.

After immersing myself in information about PDD, I realized two important things. The first was that PDD is a lifelong disability—it doesn't go away. Yes, Ethan was on the "high-functioning" end of the autism spectrum (he talked and could already read) and he could likely learn compensatory strategies to help him function in everyday life, but there is no cure, no way of solving the problem.

That meant Ethan's issues were not short-term. He would be dealing with PDD for the rest of his life. Which meant that *I* would be dealing with PDD for a long time too. This was not a problem that I could fix. I was in a marathon, not a sprint.

The second thing I learned was the power of the word "autism." When Ethan was initially diagnosed, I wondered what to tell people—that Ethan had PDD, an Autism Spectrum Disorder, or simply autism? I knew that autism rates had increased dramatically over the past several years, so I assumed people would be familiar with autism as a spectrum of disorders, as more than classic autism—a silent, unresponsive child unconnected to the world. My husband disagreed. He felt the term "autism" carried a stigma, since many children with autism also have mental retardation. He advised telling people Ethan had PDD and not even mentioning the "A" word.

About a week later, a conversation with my chiropractor, who knew me and my family well, convinced me of the power of the "A" word. As usual, he asked me about my boys, whom he had met many times. "Jonathan's doing great in kindergarten," I said, "and Ethan will be starting more speech and occupational therapy at his preschool." "Oh. What prompted that?" he asked. "Well, he was recently diagnosed with PDD, which is on the autism spectrum. His pediatrician recommended more intensive intervention," I explained.

I'll never forget the next moment. First, there was silence. Heavy silence. I couldn't see his face, but I knew when he replied that the only word he had heard me say was "autism." "What's the…um…what's the prognosis…for that kind of thing?" he asked hesitantly. My mind raced as I considered the implications of his question. *The prognosis?* He made it sound like a terminal disease! And this guy *knew* Ethan! He'd met him and talked to him many times. What will people who don't know Ethan think when they hear he has autism? What assumptions will they make about his abilities and his future?

I tried to respond nonchalantly. "Well…pretty good, actually. He just needs help interacting with other kids," I said. "He's doing well cognitively," I felt compelled to add. I left the office dumbstruck. I had underestimated the power of the "A" word. Just because autism rates were skyrocketing across the world didn't mean everyone understood the latest view of autism as a spectrum disorder.

So where did that leave Ethan? And me? Should I become Autism Ambassador and try to educate everyone I know? Should I use the term PDD and not mention the "A" word? Should I read books on autism in secret? What about the book I bought for Jonathan, titled *My Brother with Autism*? Should I return it and look for a book called *My Brother with PDD*?

I had hoped that a diagnosis would lead to answers, but I realized sadly that the diagnosis itself was problematic. I didn't want to ban the "A" word from my family's vocabulary because that would imply that autism, and therefore Ethan, was something to be ashamed of. That would send the wrong message to Jonathan about his little brother. But how could I prevent people from hearing the "A" word and letting their inaccurate ideas about autism define how they saw Ethan?

It's April now, about four months since Ethan's diagnosis. My bookcases are crammed with books and articles I've read about autism spectrum disorders. I've been to workshops. I recently joined a support group for mothers with children on the autism spectrum.

I've grown more comfortable with the "A" word. Yes, it has power. And yes, some people have outdated notions of autism. But how will people expand their views of autism unless someone explains it? So I've cautiously accepted the role of "Autism Ambassador" and I'm learning to embrace the "A" word. It's the healthiest way forward for me and my family. There may be times when I say Ethan has "PDD" rather than "autism," but I recognize now that the "A" word is as powerful as I let it be. I will not let it control me. And I won't let it define anyone's view of who Ethan is. Interestingly, April is Autism Awareness Month so it seems fitting to embrace the "A" word and realize that no diagnosis can limit Ethan's potential.

Just the other night, in fact, Ethan proved this to be true. He and I were sitting in his room reading his favorite train book. As I reached to turn the page, Ethan turned his big brown eyes to me and kissed my cheek. The next moment he was focused back on the book, saying "Read, Mommy, read." I swallowed hard, fought back my tears, and quickly finished reading the book. But my thoughts were elsewhere. My little boy had just kissed me for the first time. Unprompted, I was overwhelmed with love for him and with hope for his future. For this Mother's Day, I'm asking for an autism awareness bracelet, which I plan to wear proudly.

Elaine Tarutis earned her bachelor's and master's degrees in English from Boston College. She also pursued doctoral work at the University of New Hampshire and graduate studies in education at Boston College. She has taught literature and writing at high school and college levels. She currently teaches at Boston College and is working on a memoir chronicling her experience as a mother of a child with autism.

Elaine lives with her husband and sons in Norfolk, Massachusetts. She is active on the Parent Advisory Committee at the public school that both of her children attend. Elaine also supports the national Alliance for Autism Research and participates in their annual "Walk FAR for NAAR" to raise money for autism research.

24. On Eating Biscuits: Life with Autism

Eileen Teyssou

Looking into the eyes of a beautiful child is a humbling experience at any time. To see reflected the beauty of innocence and truth, trust and love in the eyes of your own child inspires feelings that are comforting and reassuring but which are, for the most part, unarticulated and undefined. My experience as a parent of a child with autism has allowed, and sometimes forced, me to examine these emotions and to examine life in its essence.

Conan was born on April 10, 1998, a snowy morning, four weeks after the death of my father. While his birth was a moving occasion, it was made bittersweet by the fact that I had assured my father that this child would be another boy child and would be named Conan, a Gaelic name, signifying intelligence and wisdom. His birth day had the further significance of seeing the signing of the Good Friday Agreement, bringing an era of relative peace in Northern Ireland.

Conan's early months showed him to be a calm child, content with his own company, who slept without difficulty, unlike his older brother, and who achieved his gross motor milestones with ease. I often feel, in hindsight, that one of the gifts of autism is that it allows you time to know and understand your child and gradually come to the realisation that there is *un certain je ne sais quoi* (a certain something) about the child that marks him out as different from others.

Without doubt many parents and families grieve for the child that could have been. I have, however, always felt that autism is a fundamental part of who Conan is and is as much a part of him as his huge green wells for eyes and his blond hair. His brothers, from time to time, question whether I wish Conan did not have autism. I invariably answer no. I cannot separate my son from his autism and cannot deny him part of who he is. Where does autism start and where would it end? I wouldn't like to lose any part of him. I would, however, wish for more patience. His younger brother, Fionn, comments that Conan is weird. That's fine; he can be weird but I don't see that weird has to be a negative trait, it can be very positive. Don't many of us strive to be different, to be individuals after all?

When Conan's diagnosis of autism came in May 2000, it was a positive event. It validated my intuition about Conan and I felt that understanding autism would allow me to commune more fully with him. I felt that it also validated who he was and gave weight to what otherwise were simply idiosyncrasies: laughing at the wallpaper or standing in the shade of trees laughing at the leaves moving in the breeze or not being able to eat a circular biscuit without it being broken or, oddly, without having a second one to hold while eating the first one. Things always come full circle: now my third son refuses to eat biscuits if they are at all broken!

Although I try to maintain a positive outlook there have been some very difficult times. Shortly after his third birthday, Conan went through a period of several months where he literally screamed and screamed and threw himself on floors kicking like a beast from morning to night. I have no notion to this day what precipitated this distress or what ended it.

This period was extremely stressful for all of the family. My son Yann, then aged five, said to me one evening that he thought Conan was going to run out of breath from screaming and die. The mental strain of having to

ease those fears and ensure that this violence would not have a detrimental
effect on my other boys was compounded by the questions their father and
I had to ask of ourselves and each other. Are we able to emotionally and
physically cope with this strain? How do we deal with this? What are our
core values that will allow us to get through this period? Sometimes there
were answers, other times the situation looked ominous.

The day I broke down and cried in Conan's preschool after he had
screamed getting up, screamed getting dressed, screamed getting into the
car, screamed on getting out of it, screamed being carried fighting into
school, I think I learned one of life's most valuable lessons: that to admit
your vulnerability and let people help is ultimately a sign of strength. It
does not mean that the problems disappear but somehow makes them a little less demanding.

While the summer of 2001 was an incredibly trying time, things have
never reached that breaking point since. I have learned that Conan's behaviour is cyclical and that each year from April to late August and September
he is at his most anxious, and have put measures in place to cope with this
period, from awareness of what is happening to medication when
necessary. I have benefited from the professional help accorded by his
multi-disciplinary support team and we often avail ourselves of respite care.

Conan is now seven and is in his second year of primary school. I have,
over the years, learned many things from Conan and from the world of
people with disabilities. The foremost of these is the innate dignity of all
human beings. I have seen, time and time again, that Conan has his unique
contribution to make; whether this is the smile on someone's face when he
robs a chip from their tray in McDonalds and breaks our social rules or
whether it's the gift of wonder that we have lost that you see when he pulls
down your socks to check if they have left any lines on your legs. I have
seen the unconditional love of a child who cannot verbalize or rationalize
what he feels. I have seen the essence of life through his eyes when the
socially constructed world that we live in is bared down to one without any
trace of hypocrisy or agenda of malice or gain, but one rich in the me and
you and laughter and tears and the vulnerability and dignity in dependence. I have learned that we all have our capabilities and that there is truth
to the cliché that no man is an island.

The second major lesson that has been brought home to me is that of
the complementarity of things. Whilst Conan will always, to a greater or
lesser degree, be dependent on others, there are always others who have a
vocation to be caregivers of one form or another. I have encountered many

people who have touched Conan's life, and thus mine, by their gift of giving time, care, expertise, and understanding.

I have seen that for some of us many, many words are wasted in talking too much, in not saying what we mean or meaning what we say, in withholding what we actually mean when a touch or hand held can say infinitely more. I have seen that to listen means more than simply listening to words.

I have seen that each person has a gift that marks him out from others. My first child is a born talker, an outgoing, lively, and caring child who will always have someone to talk to. My third child has the glint of devilment in his eye and music in his bones. But my second child, *the one with the disability*, can swing higher on his swing than any other child in the neighbourhood, can do the handstands that his brothers cannot, and can, despite many impediments, get people to love him for who he is.

Eileen Teyssou, aged 37, lives in Sligo, an Atlantic coastal town of 20,000 people in the northwest of Ireland. Mother to three boys, she works full-time as an administrative manager and is currently undertaking a Master of Arts degree by research in the area of higher education development part-time. Reading modern literature and catching up with friends fill in whatever spare time she finds.

25. Katie's Question

Lauren Yaffe

If I think Katie will enjoy a particular book, I never suggest she read it. I leave it lying around. Not until it has gathered an air of familiarity will she pick it up. One book I left lying around was *Asperger Syndrome, the Universe and Everything*. In it, ten-year-old Kenneth Hall describes his life: the "jammie days" when he lounges around the house, books he likes, his singular devotion to grated Red Leicester cheese, his problems controlling his temper and being around other people, the behavior modification program his mother uses with him, and how he came to be homeschooled and to pass England's math achievements six years early. A simple book, really, but it was like a window into my daughter. Katie, like Kenneth Hall, has been diagnosed with Asperger's syndrome, which in the most simplistic of terms means having characteristics of autism, with a great deal of cognitive and verbal ability coupled with challenges in social skills and various sensory issues.

When Katie found the book, she devoured it. She particularly liked the notion of "jammie days," an activity to which we already subscribed. A few days after reading the book, Katie, then age seven, asked, "Do I have Asperger's syndrome?"

I paused. For me, the jury was still out on that question. As with most kids with special needs, my child's constellation of idiosyncrasies fall sloppily inside and outside of all the boxes of possible diagnoses. I started to say, "You have some features of…," then stopped, caught up in the ambiguities I was constantly mulling over in my mind. No, I thought. She needs an answer. I said, "Yes, you have Asperger's syndrome."

"I'm so relieved," Katie said.

"Relieved?" I asked, unsure if I was.

"Yes. I always knew I thought differently than other people. I like that I'm special. Like Kenneth Hall is special too."

For the next few months, while I expected Katie to struggle with this new information, she felt she had gained a new understanding of herself.

Some expressed disapproval that I would tell Katie this about herself at such a young age. And I had my own concerns.

I worried she would tell the world she had Asperger's. And she did. She revealed this personal matter indiscriminately, without consideration for how others might regard her (or her parents)—or for the potency of her words. Asperger's. Autism. Both terms set my scalp ringing when I was first told they might have a bearing on my family. It is only through a rigorous reeducation that I have begun to dismantle the negative wallop those words packed for me. How was Katie to understand that, while she had no more choice in having Asperger's than a diabetic does about having diabetes, the world did not yet comprehend this? She would be judged, excluded, dismissed, pitied.

I worried that she would use Asperger's syndrome as an excuse to back out of situations that overwhelmed her. And she did. She told the gym teacher that Asperger's was the reason she couldn't participate in gym. This got her sent to the principal's office for insolence. In truth, it was a valid excuse, but because of her Asperger's she could not articulate that the noise and fast pace of the gym class quite literally overloaded her nervous system, basically causing her to short-circuit—in this case, by prancing back and forth along the sidelines and whistling frantically to block out the external chaos.

While I worried about how her new-found identity would affect her self-esteem, Katie was helping me come to terms, continually pointing out the wonderful gifts and qualities that go along with having Asperger's. It *is* good to think and feel differently than others and not be overly concerned about others' opinions, to be bright and curious, unaccepting of established modes of thought and behavior. My concerns aside, Asperger's gave Katie a name for what she perceived, but could not express, about how she differed from her peers.

While society spends much time addressing the negatives of labelling (that is, seeing a person only for one aspect of him/herself), nonlabelling, denying or not acknowledging an aspect of a person, is equally dangerous. If I shunned the word "Asperger's" Katie might conclude, *If no one wants to say what I am, I must be bad.* An infinitely more sinister problem to overcome than labelling is shame—internal labelling (of the negative kind). Despite the ambiguities of Katie's diagnosis, assuming (for the time being) that it is correct, frees us—me and her both—from the confusing sea of possibilities one can become mired in when something is not right, when something, in fact, is very wrong, but we don't know what it is. Diagnosis gives us a way out of the confusion, an approach to try.

A year and a half after Katie asked her question, she has only a rudimentary understanding of what Asperger's means. For that matter, so do I. It may be that, in time, this name will not fit her, or not well enough. But doesn't every child—every person, for that matter—grapple with such questions? Identity is a fluid, organically developing thing. Titles like artist, mother, friend, activist are lenses through which to view ourselves, locate ourselves in the world. We also, sometimes unconsciously, define ourselves in other ways: sensitive, middle child, night owl, asthmatic, victim. Even labels with negative connotations can serve positive purposes: to understand, to initiate change (hopefully for the better), self-acceptance. Achieving any of these ends, especially the last, self-acceptance, is impossible without first recognizing a facet of ourselves and putting a name to it.

Lauren Yaffe, parent of two, is a writer, avid gardener, and vermiculturist, which means worms eat her garbage. Her essays and short stories have been published in magazines and literary journals such as *Frigate, Mediphors, Cottonwood, Alaska Quarterly Review, Sassy, Calliope,* and *Word.* She is currently writing a novel based in Brazil, an animation screenplay about worms, and a series of essays about parenting her very special kids—a daughter (now 10), diagnosed with ADHD and Asperger's syndrome, and a son (6) with ADHD and Central Auditory Processing Dysfunction (CAPD). She lives with her husband, kids, and several thousand worms in Brooklyn, NY. You can read her blog at www.especiallymom. blogspot.com.

Part 2: The Grandparents' Connection

A parent's job never ends. The grandparents who have contributed to this book illustrate the lifelong value of the supportive extended family. Grandparents can have as hard a time accepting autism as parents do, or even harder since they have less contact with their grandchild, and their acceptance can take longer. Grandparents worry about their grandchild and also have to watch their child struggle. They face the double grief of their grandchild's diagnosis and their own child's pain.

This second level of grief often renders the grandparents powerless to offer the support that their son or daughter longs for. Grandparents may despair that they could not protect their child from this fate; they may worry that they have passed on a defective gene and that it could appear again in another grandchild. They may also feel overwhelmed and guilty that they cannot help more. Undoubtedly most were looking forward to a warm, indulging role with their grandchildren, without the responsibilities of being a primary authority figure. Being involved with the new generation can be a source of special pride and satisfaction, but when confronted by autism, the role of the grandparent may not be what they expected.

Grandparents may lose their dreamed-for grandchild who was to be their legacy to future generations just as the parents often lose their dream-child. Getting to know their actual grandchild can be more difficult because they are often removed from the child's everyday life and because they may face the dual challenge of supporting their adult child in a time of tremendous need.

With the experience and wisdom gained from raising their own children, grandparents may have much to offer in sharing coping strategies and in discerning which issues are linked to the disability and which ones are the normal challenges of childrearing. They may also have the time needed to help with many of the demands of caring for a grandchild with special needs. The grandparents who have contributed to this book are true role models.

26. Barefooted Band-Aid Boy

Patricia E. Gardocki

My four-year-old grandson stared at the end of the broom handle he was twirling. Without realizing it I entered the descending orbital path. My head and his handle collided. Normally my grandson showed no emotion for such everyday crashes, but this night was different. "Dad. Mom-mom has boo-boo. I go get band-aid." The barefooted boy bounded up the basement stairs. Moments later he returned with a tissue and patted my forehead. "Thanks, Brandon," I said when he surprised me with a kiss, "It's much better now."

What was better? Brandon's ability to express himself and my new understanding about autism. A couple of years ago things were different.

"Ouch! Don't pinch me," my daughter-in-law yelled at the toddler toted on her hip. "No-ooo," he wailed, then slapped her face. "Don't hit me either." After a repeat performance I jumped from the dining room chair. "That's it," I said grabbing Brandon out of her arms and bolting up the stairs. "If you can't treat your mommy any better than that, you can't have her."

"Ma, Ma...." (sob, sob) "No. No" (high-pitched screams). I kicked the bedroom door shut, plopped on the rocker, and tightened my grip on the *screaming demon*. He straightened his arms, pushing me away, and stiffened his body trying to break loose. When that didn't work, he punched me. I held his hand. "No-ooo. No-ooo. Ma, Ma...," his sobs and screams continued.

I tried to calm him down by cuddling, rocking, and rubbing his back. I even sang a soothing melody. But he continued to squirm, kick, and push me away. When I finally let go, he threw himself down and pounded the floor. "You can't keep acting like this," I explained trying to convince him this plan of his wasn't working. "If you want to go back downstairs, stop hitting and screaming."

"No-oooo. No, no, no!" Then he gagged and tried to vomit. *If you do, I'll just clean it up,* I thought to myself. *You're not getting off that easy.* Then he changed tactics and peed his pants instead. We sat together in the same room, but worlds apart.

Why was Brandon so "hateful," so prone to temper tantrums? How could my son let this behavior continue? Why couldn't a mom with a degree in early childhood education control her own child? How would anybody teach him? Why did he push me away when I tried to console him? How do I reach him? Those questions stayed with me long after I freed Brandon from the bedroom. He ran to his mom and I returned to my home five hours away.

This episode began to change my perspective on how to deal with Brandon and autism. I have learned many lessons since that day. Here are some of the most important lessons I've learned. Lesson one: Traditional disciplinary measures often don't work with children who have autism. Lesson two: Learn to adjust.

At first they called it "sensory issues." Now we know it's autism. The pediatric neurologist warned Brandon's parents they would have to exercise forgiveness to each other, to Brandon, and to people who don't understand autism. I asked them to forgive me, and they did. Now we work together to help each other.

I started reading books about autism and connected with information sources, like the Autism Society of America. Two other helpful organizations have been Parents of Autistic Children (POAC) and Pennsylvania Training and Technical Assistance Network (PATTAN). I've attended seminars on Applied Behavior Analysis, reading instruction, and autism in the family. Through all of this I feel better equipped to understand autism, the way it affects a child's ability to learn, and the pressure it puts on families.

"Put your shoes on *now*," Brandon's mom yelled grabbing her coat. "We've got to go." He sat on the floor kicking the dreaded brown objects. "I can't get him to wear those," she explained and ran upstairs to retrieve a pair of worn out sneakers. "Here. See if you can get him to put these on." So I knelt beside the barefooted boy and tried to coax him to slip on the sneakers. He kicked the one. "No," he yelled and threw the other one across the room. His mom came inside from scraping ice off the car, "He wants his water shoes."

"Well then," I responded, "guess he wears water shoes to preschool today." "But what will people think?" his mom asked. "They're for summer." "Who cares? He won't be out in snow and he can't go barefoot." She leaned over and eased his foot into the multi-colored slipper. Brandon stood up then stared at his feet and smiled. He was ready to face his day at school.

Lesson three: We all have more to learn. Brandon didn't know the difference between a tissue and a band-aid, but he knew he wanted to do something. His vocabulary is increasing as well as his ability to communicate his strong desires. I don't live close enough to be as much help as I'd like but I'm trying to learn and to love as much as I can. He's trying and so am I.

"Thanks, Brandon, for the tissue," I said wiping away my tears. "Your kiss made it better."

Patricia E. Gardocki is a teacher and former nurse. Her five-year-old grandson, Brandon, is one of four siblings, three of whom have autism. He has an older sister and two brothers, ages 7 (PDD) and 13 (Asperger's). Brandon receives Applied Behavior Analysis through the Dr Gertrude A. Barber Center in Erie (www.drbarbercenter.org). His parents are also training there. Brandon's dad pioneered a program establishing autism services for other local families. Patricia Gardocki is familiar with limitations. She has dystonia (a neurological movement disorder) and writes a column for the National Spasmodic Torticollis Association as well as other inspirational articles.

27. Lap Time

Dan Gottlieb

"In darkness, the pupil dilates searching for light. In adversity, the heart dilates looking for God."

Victor Hugo

I'm not a theologian or a biblical scholar. I don't know what God is, but the church around the corner from me says that "God is love." That makes sense to me. The heart dilates and it's about love. We suffer because we love; we work because we love; we are here because we love. From the moment babies open their eyes, they love.

I'm pretty new to this business of autism. I'm pretty new to this business of grandparenting also. I don't want to write much here about my wonderful grandson Sam who was diagnosed with autism at the age of three. I want to write about my daughter Debbie and about *lap time*.

When Debbie was four years old, I broke my neck and became a quadriplegic. I was home on a weekend pass from the rehabilitation hospital, and she was sitting on my lap, when she said to me, "Daddy, I'm glad you weren't hurt worse in the accident."

It was a confusing statement and I asked her, "Why?" At the time, I didn't care whether I was hurt worse or not. I wished for death. She answered me, "I am glad you weren't hurt worse because now I have a Daddy." She helped me to realize two important things: (1) that I was loved, and (2) that I had a responsibility for the rest of my life.

About ten years later, her mother left us and Debbie and I went out for breakfast to talk about it. She told me how depressed she was and how hopeless she felt. My inclination was to make her feel better by saying the kind of stupid things that parents always say like, "Mom and I won't always be enemies." Stupid parent talk I call it. We do that.

Instead I said nothing and I cried with her. I knew then that my job as a parent was to listen and to care. But more than just listen, I felt protective of her because she had a father with a disability. I felt even more protective when her mother left and I became her only parent. I cared fiercely for her suffering.

That's why I worried after Sam was born. I would call every day and ask her how Sam was. She would say the same thing every day, "Sam is perfect." I worried about that. Nobody is perfect and I was afraid she would be hurt some day. Nevertheless I kind of ignored it because I was enamored watching my child be a mother. I was in awe of this.

That's why I struggled when I first noticed there was something wrong with Sam. He didn't seem to be hearing. I didn't know if he wasn't hearing or wasn't listening. Should I be at that point the father she depended on; the father with psychological training? Or should I be at that point the father who was supportive and had faith in her maternal instincts? My struggle with these issues goes on every time we are together. If I open my mouth, am I being controlling? If I keep my mouth shut, am I denying her some advice that might be helpful?

One thing became clear to me when Sam was about six months old. Speaking of *lap time*, Debbie put him on my lap. They were visiting at my house, and she went downstairs with her husband to pack up and get ready to leave. Sam squirmed and fell off my lap and onto the floor. It was a thick rug and he didn't get hurt physically, but he was shook up and he bellowed. Debbie came running up the stairs. It was the first time. We all remember the first time they fall in the bath tub. She was completely upset and agitated and I pretended to be calm. Of course everybody was OK.

The next day I called her, and I said, "Debbie, I know the answer, but I have to ask it anyway. Would you ever let Sam sit on my lap again?" I knew who was in charge. I was her assistant now, and that was my job.

For lots of reasons, it took me about six months to adopt Sam as mine. I don't know why. It also took Sam about six months to adopt me as his Pop. It's easy to understand how I took to him. He's my grandson. He's the child of my daughter. He's beautiful.

Why did he take to me? I live three hours away. I was not there for bonding. He didn't understand *grandfather* at the young age of six to nine months. Yet all he wants to do now is run up to me and sit on my lap. That's all he wants to do. Maybe it is a gene. Why? Well maybe he's intrigued with the wheelchair. You know—an autism thing, but I see it differently. I believe at a certain level he knows we are kindred spirits. He knows about my vulnerability, about my weakness. He knows I can't do what others do.

In time Sam will understand my differentness, my alienation. In time, he will understand his own. Part of my job is to teach him how to tolerate his alienation, how to navigate the waters of his own differentness. Part of my job is to also help him never ever to forget what he knows right now. He knows more about giving and receiving love than most adults on this planet.

The road ahead looks like it might be a bit bumpy. I couldn't wish for better parents for him; they both understand adversity and are not afraid of it. As Sam gets older, I will tell him how I've learned to cope with people staring at me or treating me differently. We can talk about fear, injustice, God, and the tiny little gifts that sometimes live inside of adversity.

I no longer worry when Debbie says that Sam is perfect (yes, she still does). Finally, I understand what she means. His body is not perfect, nor is his brain. She meant his soul. Sam has a perfect soul.

Dan Gottlieb, Ph.D. is the host of "Voices in the Family," on WHYY radio, Philadelphia's public radio station. He is also a psychologist and family therapist in private practice. Dr. Gottlieb is a nationally recognized lecturer in the field of mental health, and a regular columnist for *The Philadelphia Inquirer*. He is the author of two books, *Voices in the Family: Healing in the Heart of the Family* (Penguin, 1993) and *Voices of Conflict; Voices of Healing: A Collection of Articles by a Much-Loved Philadelphia Inquirer Columnist* (iUniverse, 2001). His new book in press at Sterling Publishers, due to be released in 2006, is *Letters to Sam*. You can read his columns and listen to his radio shows at his website, www.drdangottlieb.com.

Acknowledgement

This essay was based upon a presentation made as part of the Parent Panel at the 2002 conference of the Interdisciplinary Council on Developmental and Learning Disorders (ICDL).

28. An Unexpected Gift of Love

Oscar and Sally Olson

Our 17-year-old twin grandsons were diagnosed with autism at about two-and-a-half years of age. Although this is an increasingly growing event in today's world, we could not help but wonder why this happened to our family. As grandparents, our first concern was the heartache and seemingly overwhelming problems this would bring to our son and his wife.

Through the years we have watched and helped as much as possible as various treatment approaches were tried. The Option Institute "one on one" sessions, with a host of volunteers working in special rooms with each boy, was implemented in their home. We marveled at the efforts of music therapy, gymnastic training, and the ability of their father (our son) to create a world of activities for them—hiking, swimming, camping, canoeing, bicycling, Boy Scouts, Special Olympics. All of this, while their mother took them to training programs at Eastern Mennonite College in Harrisonburg, Virginia, and Shenandoah University in Winchester, Virginia, prepared regular reports to the local school on all the homeschooling work being done, established a small private school for teenagers with special needs, and arranged for the local high school to provide several hours a day of special education.

What started as a catastrophic "sentence" has flowered into a gift of love and admiration in what can be done when parents, friends, and family unite to accept and learn from life's challenges. Our grandsons, Kevin and Carl, can now go to restaurants, movies, church, and sit in a family gathering as well as most teenagers.

Autism teaches those who are involved in it many lessons. We observed much about ourselves as we learned to relate to these boys. One of the main skills is communication. Most of us talk more than we listen, relying on the spoken word alone. With Kevin and Carl we were challenged by having to find alternative ways of expressing feelings—smiles, looks, touching, laughing, a wide variety of role modeling. Their response is so rewarding when it is on their terms.

Another lesson in this area of interpersonal communication is an awesome new dimension of give and take. Our grandsons see more, hear more, and feel more than one would ever suspect simply by observing their external behavior. Our son had placed one-way windows on the doors to the rooms where we worked with the boys. Outsiders in the hall could look in without the inside participants being aware of the observation. At first we felt like we were always out in the hall looking in—for all the recognition and feedback the boys could give us. They hardly seemed aware of us. We gradually learned that for them it was like that one-way glass was turned around. We were being observed closely and clearly by them without even realizing it. They saw us in their unique way of seeing others. It was rather surprising when we caught on.

We have also learned more about our fears. We considered ourselves appropriately safety conscious when we raised our four children. With Kevin and Carl those normal protective instincts were elevated to a higher level. When they were younger they loved to climb the towering trees in their yard. They scrambled up trees that rose higher than their house and perched themselves 30 or 40 feet above the ground. When we mentioned our concern to their parents they persuaded us those fears were groundless. They knew their sons' strengths and coordination.

We used to walk the boys down to a creek in the thick woods behind their mountain home. Their mom and dad finally put a stop to that when we reported that the boys could run faster than we could and sometimes did not heed our shouts to come back. One of our worst fears was nearly realized on the night of their uncle's wedding rehearsal dinner. Shortly before everyone was ready to sit down to eat, a phone call came that Carl, 11 years old, had darted out into the road in front of their house, was hit by a car, and was being rushed to a hospital. Thankfully he had only been badly bruised and shaken up.

We can only marvel that so many dangers have been escaped by our obviously super-vulnerable grandsons. We can only respect the vigilance and skill of the parents for allowing their sons to experience every risky venture a youngster needs to grow up strong without undue and restricting alarm.

Another lesson is to appreciate the problems these children experience in a world where people stare at them, many times disapprovingly. Many children with autism are handsome and have no visible disability so others are challenged in how they react to their differences in behavior. We adults have much to learn in the field of acceptance and adaptability to those who are different than what we think of as "normal."

Until directly involved with autism, most of us think of the movie *Rainman* as the way it is. Of course, there are many savants, but most children with autism are not so exquisitely advanced in these kinds of skills. However, if we observe them carefully, there is more there than most of us see. Kevin has always done well with puzzles. Carl has memorized phrases from TV shows and songs which he can use as conversation with uncanny appropriateness. For example, when being sedated for some type of medical exam, as he lay on the table, he commented, "Have a good night sleep on us. Mattress Discounters", and when hearing a minister quote a Bible passage about only the righteous would enter the kingdom of heaven, he quipped, "No more Mr Nice Guy!"

We belong to a very special fellowship—relatives of family members who have autism. There are bumper stickers, periodicals, and all sorts of rallies and conferences. It creates a bond that is very rewarding as we grow in mutual attempts to understand and cope with these very loveable members of our population who are to be admired, loved, and accepted by those of us who are enriched by knowing them.

∾

Oscar W. Olson, Kevin and Carl's grandfather, is a retired mental health chaplain, a minister in the United Church of Christ. He did his master's thesis on Carl Jung. Sally W. Olson, their grandmother, was a high school English teacher turned telephone company service representative. They live in Woodbridge, Virginia. All together they have three children and five beautiful grandchildren. They also lost a daughter who was killed in Rome, Italy while studying classics during her junior year of college. At ages 81 and 79, Oscar and Sally Olson live 60 miles from their very special twin grandsons with whom they continue a familiar and rewarding relationship.

29. A Grandmother's Story

Elizabeth Nedler

On January 7, 2000, my daughter gave birth to her first child and my grandson. She named him Daniel. The pregnancy was uncomplicated and my daughter received good prenatal care. When Daniel was eight months old he had heart surgery to repair a ventral septal defect (VSD). After surgery he remained incubated for approximately four weeks. Over a month later and back at home he gradually started to regain his strength. His health was very weak. He finally started to crawl around 18 months and finally at 20 months he was walking. I blamed the delays on the drugs and the incubation period during the hospital stay.

It was around this time that I started to notice Daniel flapping his fingers when he got excited. He also enjoyed spinning himself around while looking out of the corner of his eye. He would drag his head on the carpet and every now and then he walked on his toes. Daniel rarely made eye contact with any one of us. Time and again I would see him licking the television or sometimes the walls. My daughter and I had few conversations regarding Daniel's unusual behavior; after all we had more important things to talk about, for example, his remarkable memory and the enormous interest he showed in numbers and letters at such a young age.

It became clear to everyone in my family that Daniel was different and it was especially noticeable when he was in the same room with another child of similar age. One day, my mother mailed me a newspaper clipping about a story of a boy who had autism. At the end of the story was a checklist of symptoms that are consistent with a diagnosis of autism. I quickly compared them to Daniel and placed a mental checkmark next to the ones that sounded familiar. At the end of the quiz I realized that I had checked off more than half of the list. I was overwhelmed with the results. This was when reality truly set in: the reality of my grandson having autism. Depression and sadness quickly followed.

Without delay, my daughter scheduled an appointment for a developmental evaluation. This evaluation included several doctors who each monitored Daniel's behavior and intelligence by using simple games, puzzles, and other structured activities. He was supposed to follow the evaluator's lead. During much of the evaluation Daniel ignored people in the room and hardly ever imitated their actions.

The evaluation lasted several hours and we were then led to a small office with the evaluators for a discussion of the results. Each professional spoke about their part of the evaluation and explained why/what they were testing for. The speeches were short and to the point. Every doctor on the team agreed that Daniel was somewhere on the autism spectrum. My daughter and I sat in silence; we asked one or two questions, picked up Daniel and drove directly home. The rest of the day I felt dazed and miserable and my daughter did too. Despite the fact that we had suspected autism long before the actual diagnosis it was still very hard to accept. Daniel was 2 years, 3 months and 11 days old.

Immediately, my daughter and I started to read every library book and newspaper article we could get our hands on. In a strange way I felt like this was our private mission. I needed to be part of this for two important reasons: (1) to provide my daughter with as much support as necessary (she was a newlywed at the time and not doing well with the news about her son), and (2) to strengthen my own relationship with my grandson.

I knew very little about autism. I spent hours and hours on the internet searching for websites and reading everything I could. I would rush home with a stack of library books and scan the pages, skipping chapters from beginning to end because I didn't have time to read the story; I was desperately searching for the chapter that described the "magical cure" and I was determined to find it! This "magical cure" would pull Daniel out of his strange world and give back my precious little grandson so we could continue living as if nothing ever happened.

After many months of research, diets, vitamins, and time to heal from the initial shock, my daughter and I finally found the closest thing we could to that "magical cure." We didn't find it in a book or in a recipe. As a matter of fact, it was here all along yet at the time it was the furthest solution from my mind: it is called early intervention. I would not actually claim that early intervention will cure autism; however, it is essential that every child be enrolled in a special program.

Daniel started a Child Find Program when he was two years and nine months old. The first semester I didn't see much of an improvement. He was constantly screaming and knew only a little bit of hand signing as a form of communication. The following summer my daughter enrolled him in a different program and this was when he showed a remarkable improvement. Daniel attends school four days a week. He enjoys his new teachers and especially likes riding the bus every morning to and from school. He has five of the most wonderful and amazing teachers and therapists who work very hard with him every day.

In this last year Daniel has progressed in all areas of development including potty training! Although he hasn't mastered potty training yet, I'm pleased with what he has learned so far. He doesn't scream as often anymore and is talking more than ever; even if much of the time his words are echoing ours. Not so long ago my "grandma name" was a loud, high pitched scream. It has been replaced by the more common name of "Nana," which is certainly more calming to my ears. Daniel can follow simple instructions and has learned that if he wants something he must ask for help. There have been days when I have heard him say, "Help Nana" at least 40 to 50 times, which is just fine with me.

Daniel is now four years old. He is a handsome little boy. He smiles, laughs, loves his family, and shows us affection. He is extremely smart and obsessed with computers. He will zoom directly to his favorite websites and insist that he navigate the mouse the entire time. He lives with his mother, stepfather, and younger sister. They are exceptionally proud of him. My husband and I live only a few miles away. Two days of the week Daniel comes over to our house to spend the night. Not only does this give us time with him but also it allows my daughter to spend time with her family and for herself.

During my daughter's second pregnancy I was worried and scared for Daniel. I thought with a new baby in the family, little by little my daughter would forget how important it was for her to continue learning about autism. I was absolutely wrong. Daniel's sister is the greatest person that has come into his life. Her name is Kaiah and she is two and a half years old. She loves her brother and he has learned a lot because of her. They laugh, play, chase each other, share toys, and like most siblings they often fight with one another. Daniel is learning how to wait his turn and have patience and, most important, how to have fun and be a kid. This behavior comes naturally and easily for Kaiah, but for Daniel this is a daily struggle. My daughter once said to me, "Together they are each other's best teachers," and I completely agree with her.

Not everything is wonderful; Daniel has numerous days when he is very difficult and would rather drift into his own world. I'm certain his sister is curious, confused, and wonders why he does things differently than her. Occasionally, I see her observing Daniel. As she matures she will understand why he could not do the simple things she did and the reason why we accepted his screams as a replacement for communication instead of treating it as bad behavior. In return, I believe she will grow up to become a more caring, thoughtful, and considerate adult who understands the challenges of living with a disability.

Autism is a frightening word. Until a genuine medical cure is available it is here to stay. The past two and a half years have been very stressful and complicated. However, it has not destroyed my family. I am blessed with two grandchildren who love me and whom I love dearly. One with a head full of curls who likes to play with dolls and puppies. Another who'd rather climb trees and has autism. It does not make my job harder, just more important!

Elizabeth Nedler is a grandmother with a four-year-old grandson with autism. She has lived in Albuquerque, New Mexico, for the past 18 years. She has never written a book on autism, however, she does have a special interest in starting one.

30. Come with me, Grandma

Frances S. Rosenfield

My grandson Daniel is bright, loveable, and irresistible. He charms everyone he meets with his smile and big brown eyes. My grandson Daniel is a blessing. My grandson Daniel has autism.

As a grandparent when I was told that this precious child, once so vibrant and so much a part of my world, was now residing in his own world, I was crushed. I felt so helpless. As a grandparent I felt the pain for my child as well as for my grandchild. I watch with admiration the life my son and daughter-in-law build around Daniel and for Daniel. The interventions, the therapies, the diets, hour after hour, day after day of love, patience, teaching. The beauty of their interactions, the depth of their commitment. I am so proud of Jeff and Norma.

We are a family, a warm, loving, close family. We are all there for Daniel, thrilling in his every victory, understanding the difficult times. And Daniel knows. One lovely day when we were all together and Daniel was resting on Grandma's bed he called each of us into the room, one by one, telling us to "sitted" on the bed. When we were all together he went from one to the other naming us, and then with an ear-to-ear grin, he said "my family."

I have dealt with my feelings of sadness and helplessness by seeking information and getting involved. I have joined autism groups, helping to raise awareness as well as funds. I have read a great deal about autism, and I am now working on getting a grandparents' group together to offer our support wherever needed.

I have learned so much from Daniel. I have learned patience and have readjusted my sense of values. I don't sweat the little things as I once did. A long-time advocate for social justice, working to bring some joy into the lives of abused and disabled children, I often become impatient and discouraged. Now I say to myself, how does this setback compare to Daniel and what he works at to achieve? His delight in the antics of a cartoon character, splashing in a pool, painting with PaPa, hugging Brianna and Loren, his big sisters, roughing it with Uncle Bill, laughing with Auntie Shari, gives me new appreciation for the simple things in life that too often I have taken for granted. My wish is that the grandparents of all children with autism will discover the joy and beauty in their own Daniels.

My family and I try to do as much as we can to influence the future for children with autism. There is so much to be done. We write to our legislators defending our children's rights to the services they need. We have to build for their tomorrows. Daniel is only six but there are so many years ahead. We have to lean on our state and federal governments to make sure that these precious souls are not the children left behind.

What I do, I do from a full heart. Daniel has my love and devotion. He and his parents have my promise to keep working towards a better tomorrow for him. My pride in all my family for the roles they have chosen to assume in Daniel's life is immense. We thank God for this gift of love, this beauty that is Daniel. I will love him for all of my life and beyond.

Fran Rosenfield is 77 years old and has been married to the man she still loves dearly for 56 years. She is the vice president of their temple, and has been working with the Alliance for the Care of Abused Children for 13 years, as well as other organizations that believe in the Hebrew words, *tikkun olam*, which means the responsibility to repair the world. Last Christmas she was responsible for collecting 900 gifts for underprivileged children. She delights in her roles as a wife, mother, grandmother, activist, and woman.

Part 3: The Sibling Experience

Brothers and sisters have life's longest relationship. They share experiences and memories of warm, compassionate, loving feelings mixed with the inevitable rivalry and jealousy that exists among siblings. They share the special kind of laughter that you can enjoy with a brother or sister. There is the love and loyalty that is easy to talk about. On the other hand, the darker, more difficult side of emotional life is also there simultaneously. Over-emphasizing sibling rivalry tends to accentuate the negative, while ignoring it denies an integral part of the reality that bonds siblings.

It's a story as old as humankind. Cain killed his brother, Abel. It's a story about the wish to get rid of a sibling. There is a certain amount of shame in admitting competitive and angry feelings. After all, don't we all love and respect our brothers and sisters unconditionally? Everyone who grew up with siblings can access these deep mixed feelings. Most, if not all, parents aspire to have a perfect family with warm unqualified love between brothers and sisters. For the children who have a sibling on the autism spectrum, they unavoidably wonder about and miss the brother or sister they might have had. Life is not fair when your parents are overwhelmed and bereaved by the unrelenting demands of caring for a sibling's special needs while usually expecting the needs of the typically developing sibling to be minimal.

Frequently the feelings and attitudes of siblings mirror those of parents. We can certainly see this in the contributions of the brothers and sisters who have contributed their heartfelt feelings and words to this collection.

31. An Unexpected Blessing

Kimberly M. Bittner

My little sister is my hero—she always has been. Kristy is eight years younger than me, but I have always looked up to her. She carries a myriad of diagnoses: Obsessive Compulsive Disorder, Attention Deficit Disorder, mild cerebral palsy, severe verbal apraxia, Anxiety Disorder, and most recently, Pervasive Developmental Disorder.

I can remember back to when she was born and how I anxiously waited for her to come home with my parents. I remember thinking how lucky I was to finally have a baby sister to grow up with. We would do lots of things together…you know, the "girly things" I couldn't do with my brother—the endless conversations, the sharing of secrets, the shopping, and the close bond that only sisters can share.

When Kristy came home, we were the typical happy family with a new addition to love. She grew up and we all marveled at her developmental milestones. I remember being in the pediatrician's office and my mother worrying that although Kristy was meeting those milestones, they were later than for my brother and me. I can still hear the doctor saying "Don't worry, she'll catch up." We went back home and waited for her to "catch up." At age five, my parents took Kristy to Children's Hospital of Philadelphia for a neurological workup. Kristy was going to take a test, we were told. The receptionist called my parents and Kristy in, and my brother and I were left to wait. Finally, after what seemed like hours, my parents and Kristy emerged. What could have happened in there to make my parents look so upset? Why were they crying? I would find out that the neurologist told my parents that Kristy was "severely retarded" and "she would not ever be able to do anything on her own" and it was best for us "to put her in an institution and forget about her." Biting words from someone who only knew Kristy for a couple of hours. (And, by the way, as Kristy got older we saw just how wrong this doctor was and how much Kristy has accomplished over the years!) Luckily, my family was stronger than this doctor's words, and we began the search for appropriate help for Kristy. And with that, Kristy became the center of our family—bringing with it all sorts of emotions.

Growing up with a sibling who has special needs is not always an easy road—that is certainly true for our family. Being the oldest, I became like a second mommy to Kristy. A big responsibility for anybody, but I loved it. When Kristy went off to school for the first time, there I was with my mom reading her copybook to see how she did in school that day. When Kristy had her private speech therapy, there I hid at the top of the stairs listening to the exercises so I could do them with her later. When Kristy had an Individualized Education Plan (IEP) meeting at school, I went with her to help plan for Kristy's new goals for the upcoming year. When Kristy received yet another diagnosis, I was there to ask questions and support her however I could.

I didn't always grasp it so much then, but as I grew up I realized I gave up a lot to play such a large part in Kristy's upbringing. I was always the quiet one everywhere I went. I had school friends, but they didn't come over my house to play. Outside of school, Kristy was my friend. Besides, I thought the other kids at school would not understand Kristy or accept her complex needs like I could. I did not realize until I got older how lonely I was growing up. How guilty I felt that I was jealous of all the attention Kristy got—from my parents, family, therapists...everyone. Besides my immediate family, I did not have anyone else to talk to who would understand and validate all the emotions I was keeping inside.

I did not know anyone else with a family member who was "special." I remember thinking how horrible I was for feeling jealousy for things that my sister *needed* and I only *wanted*. I was afraid to talk about it with my parents; afraid they would think I was a rotten sister for feeling all these feelings—some good...and some not so good. Finally, I needed to get some of these emotions out, so I tried to write them down. I watched in amazement, as the following seemed to flow out of my pen...

> Lost.
> Lost in a sea of emotions.
> How this came to be cannot exactly be determined—yet, it wasn't in an instant.
> It happened over years of shattered hopes, misplaced feelings and altered dreams.
> This came to be through no fault of my own, but by a higher and much stronger power.
> A power that brought a blessing.
> A blessing that would cause empathy, care, resentment, hatred and an overwhelming sense of unconditional love.
> This blessing has been a most positive influence on my life.
> It has veered me toward the right path in life—both personally and professionally.
> It has enabled me to see through another's eyes, hear through another's ears, talk through another's mouth, and walk in another's shoes.
> This blessing has thrown me into a sea of emotions where I get lost easily—until the blessing itself pulls me onto stable land where I can once again find my path in life.
> This blessing is my hero...
> This blessing is a very "special" person...
> This blessing is my sister.

That was in 1991. Now, many years later, I look back on this poem and I can relive every feeling that I had growing up. Kristy will always be the center of our family. She continues to live at home with our parents, and works in a sheltered workshop setting. Kristy is proud of her work—and should be, as she is considered one of the hardest-working employees in her section. She has overcome many obstacles that have been thrown into her life path and has grown from them. I could not be prouder of Kristy and all that she has accomplished over the years.

Today, I work in a nonprofit school teaching preschoolers with autism and their families how to communicate with pictures. Growing up in the family I did allows me to see the children from both a personal and professional perspective. I experienced first-hand what some of these families are going through. I am thankful now for everything I had to go through and grow from.

Kristy has truly been, and continues to be, a huge blessing in my life. I would not be who I am today without her and all the things we experienced together. I now understand it is okay and typical to feel all those things I was experiencing. And I realize how important it is for all siblings to know it's okay for them too. In spite of it all, I feel grateful and blessed to have Kristy in my life. In many ways, she has always been, and will always be, my hero.

Kimberly M. Bittner has been working with children with autism and developmental delays since age 13—beginning as a camp counselor for an agency in Philadelphia. While continuing her career at this agency, she earned a degree and teaching certificate in special education from Holy Family University. After teaching both integrated and specialized preschool classes, she helped develop a pilot program addressing the needs of preschool-aged children with autism. Through experiences teaching this class, she witnessed first-hand how children diagnosed within the autism spectrum could communicate through exchanging pictures. She pursued training in this specialized area and began working as a communication therapist at Bancroft NeuroHealth, a specialized nonprofit school for students with developmental disabilities and behavioral challenges. She lives with her partner and two dogs in Audubon, New Jersey.

32. Growing Up with Bradley

Stephanie Coyle

I knew from the time that Brad was born that I was a big sister. I just didn't get to know him as a brother since he didn't live at home. We lived in Bemidji, Minnesota. Bradley was diagnosed with autism when he was 18 months old and went to live in foster homes so he could get the schooling he needed. First he lived in Wayzata, Minnesota, and then he moved to Duluth.

I always wanted my brother at home with us. When I was in third grade, I wrote a letter to Santa as part of a letter writing competition sponsored by our local newspaper. In my letter I wrote, "All I want for Christmas is for my brother to come home and live with us." I got my wish a few months later. He was home. I always say now, "Be careful what you wish for!" All of a sudden, I had to share my mom and then learn how to cope with his "differences." My life with autism...

I never meant to be "one of those kids." The ones that teased, the ones that tortured, harassed, and picked on peers with disabilities. I wasn't brought up that way. I accepted Brad for who he was...different. At least I tried. My actions spoke louder than my words.

I wanted to defend him when kids teased him. I got into fist fights on a number of occasions. Sometimes, I just looked the other way. I changed the subject when kids talked about him; I walked away and pretended I didn't care what happened. "Guess what dumb thing Brad did today?" "You should have heard what Brad said to the teacher!" I got really sick of it. If I listened to it, I had to make up an excuse for his actions. If I didn't listen, I felt guilty.

I couldn't wrap my teenage brain around having a "different" brother. I saw other kids and their siblings playing in the park together, playing games together, and even fighting! It was amazing to me that siblings could do that! It wasn't something I was used to, but I dreamed about it every day. What would it be like to watch a movie, or play a board game with my brother and have him understand it?

Sure we got into arguments, but Brad never understood what we were fighting about. He just knew that I wasn't happy and that bothered him. One big argument around our house was him being nosy! Get this...I had a phone in my room and when I was talking on it, he'd sit outside my bedroom door and listen. I knew he was doing this because soon I'd hear my mom yelling at me to come downstairs. Brad had repeated verbatim everything I'd said to my friend over the phone. Of course this was one sided but my mom got the drift of what was being talked about. Picture a teenage girl talking to a boy on the phone or a girl friend on the phone about a boy! Brad got me into some trouble. Okay, it was my word choice that got me into trouble...but I wouldn't have been in trouble if he hadn't been snooping!

I got all the "negative" attention growing up. I was in trouble a lot. But when Mom was lecturing me, it was attention all on me. One-on-one with me and Mom. This was something I craved a lot growing up. So the trouble

I got into was a blessing. I knew that she'd yell at me, so I knew she had to talk to me and only me.

Another big issue I faced was embarrassment. I'd spend the night at friends' houses and go to their houses on weekends a lot. It was so exciting to me to be able to do this and get out of my house. I liked to see other families that I thought were "normal." I'd see brothers picking on sisters, moms and dads hugging, and laughter. But then there were times when my friends would ask if we could come to my house and I'd come up with excuses why not. "My mom is sick." "We have company." "We are remodeling our house so there isn't room." Then I got very creative. "A tree fell on our roof." Anything I could think of so that my friends wouldn't have to see my brother. I wouldn't have to explain him.

Some of my best friends didn't even know I had a brother! He was my secret. Keeping him a secret was hard so when the kids found out that he was my brother all of a sudden, "I was adopted!" Knowing that my brother didn't fit in, I thought if people knew that he was related to me in any way, I would be an outcast too. Taking this chance was not an option for me.

I just wanted to be like everyone else. Having Brad for a brother wasn't like everyone else. I thought my family stuck out like a sore thumb. In restaurants, Brad would throw temper tantrums. In the mall, a teen's second home, Brad would cry and yell and scream. I would imagine crawling under a clothes rack and just living there for the rest of my life!

I struggled in school partly because I was dealing with so much at home. I had the wrong crowd of friends because fitting in with the "in" crowd wasn't going well. Keeping Brad my secret or just dealing with the daily struggles that our family was going through was too much for me. I couldn't do homework, I had to help with Brad. By the time my class was graduating, I was sitting at home raising my first child which Bradley named Nathaniel. I didn't know what I was going to do. I wanted to move out and get away from what seemed to be holding me back...Bradley.

I don't blame Bradley or his autism, but I just couldn't deal with everything at once. It was so bad compared to other girls my age that I didn't see a way out. I was still dealing with Bradley's issues. He was still in need of care all the time and Mom was at work. I didn't want to be his primary caregiver and it seemed I was.

One day, I remember sitting in the stadium and watching Bradley walk the aisle for his high school graduation. I cried hard because I was so proud of him. There goes a guy that was said would never make it past kindergarten and he's going to get his diploma! Wait a minute! I'm older; I was supposed to graduate before him! I then decided to go back to school and make something of myself. I got my General Equivalency Diploma (GED).

Eventually, I went to college and was really proud of myself for taking this step. I wound up getting married and dropping out of school again though. I worked some, but my new home life was bad. I moved home again. I now had two kids. Bradley helped me through this. He was so supportive every time I moved out and then moved back home. I did this a lot.

Living at home with Bradley, my kids, and my mom was hard. I had a curfew again. I had chores and felt I was being treated like a child. But I had responsibilities. I had to be my kids' chauffeur not to mention Brad's too. I had housework from five people and I couldn't keep up with anything. I was extremely depressed. Bradley helped me out so much. He watched my kids for me when I needed him to and he cheered me up by being himself. We still fought a lot living together as adults, but we got through it.

Growing up with Bradley was a challenge. It made life hard and interesting all at the same time. I've always been a firm advocate of supporting the siblings of children with disabilities in dealing with the issues that they face. At times, I think, these issues are overlooked by parents, teachers, and others. I don't believe that they are overlooked on purpose, but we siblings seem to have our share of hardships related to our brothers or sisters that have autism or some other disability. Embarrassment, humiliation, pride, courage, humor, and love are all things we go through together every day. Learning about disability has been a lifetime research project for my family.

In retrospect, Bradley has also been an inspiration to me. When he couldn't get something, he worked till he got it. When he was told he couldn't do something, he tried anyway and often did it. He thrived in life and is still achieving goals every day. He is a role model to people around him. One day he told me, "In school, I didn't care if kids teased me, they just didn't know me." How could I have not seen that? His autism actually helped him to develop a strong character. Today, Brad and I are very close and we spend a lot of time together. He's a terrific uncle to my boys and he's a great friend to me. If Brad can overcome his obstacles, which he does every day, there's hope for me!

Stephanie Coyle lives in Bemidji, Minnesota, with her husband Todd and her two sons. Nathaniel is nine, Nicholas is six. Todd and Stephanie were married in October of 2004. Todd has been an over the road truck driver for the past 10 years. Nathaniel is in third grade this year and Nicholas is in kindergarten. In addition to being siblings, Bradley and Stephanie are best friends and he continues to be an inspiration to her and everyone who gets to know him.

33. Living Life

Katherine Flaschen

You know how they say life's not fair? Well, mine definitely isn't. It's always the same: DJ first, me second. As long as he's happy, my mom's happy, as long as my mom's happy, my dad's happy, but what about me? Where do I fit in? My parents, ever cautious and scared of dealing it too tough to their poor little boy, reproach him so that even the most sensitive person in the world would not get upset. At most, he gets time out for 60 seconds (of course, he has to count), whereas I get sent to my room with at least one privilege taken away and a hurting heart.

Although I may be embellishing the truth a little, this is how it *feels* to me to have a brother with autism, and I'm sure we all know that sometimes the intensity of our emotions can carry us away. In fact, sometimes we're so vulnerable that even the slightest imposition can send us through the roof.

And I'm at the most vulnerable time in a person's life—adolescence. Hello?! Doesn't anybody care? I'm becoming a woman here!

DJ goes on a hitting rampage, or as we like to call it, "bonking on the head," and you can't even tell him that you're mad at him or that cute, irresistible face will scrunch up. He'll cry, "You're not mad!" and go into a tantrum, hitting himself on the head and wearing my mom down until she feels guilty for being upset with him in the first place. I mean, come on! He's two years my junior and he has my whole family wrapped around his pinkie finger. Everybody loves DJ, blah, blah, blah—sometimes I go to bed with those three words repeating themselves over and over again in my head.

And yes, I've succumbed to his charm, too. In fact, I think I take more pleasure and pride in his accomplishments than anyone else. I watch in complete adoration every little thing he does. How can I resist that rosy little face peeking around my door in the morning after knocking vigorously, not waiting for a "Come in!" or even an I-don't-want-to-get-up groan. He clambers onto my bed with his enveloping, feathery "white blankie." (Comfort is very important to the males in our family—anyone allergic to down, beware the Flaschen household!) "Good morning, Katie," or perhaps a recent big-boy development, "Kate," pipes a sweet voice. Even that small tweak to his ever-charming innocence makes me cringe a little. I can't even think of what it will be like when his adorable, squeaky child voice becomes a man's.

Everyone's drawn to DJ, and I think one of the main reasons is because of his purity and his constant joy. He's the epitome of human happiness—what we all wish we still felt like after getting up on a Monday morning, or totally blowing an audition, or failing a test, or even just having a really bad day. You look at him; feel warmed by his toothy grin, his welcoming body language, his wish to just cuddle and make all your worries melt away, and that character, that outlook on life is infectious.

If you look around you, people are so caught up in what they need to do, what needs to be fixed, what's not working right. But the wonderful thing about DJ is that he takes pleasure in every soft pillow, every delicious dinner... It's all a dream come true for him. He doesn't know about destitution, hunger, or even war. You look at him and you think, "This kid's got it made, I wish I could be just like him." But the irony is you don't, not in a million years you don't. Imagine a cloud fogging your brain day in and day out, and the only way to let the sun's rays penetrate the darkness is to fight it with all your might. You try to reach in and pull out a piece of information, to respond in any way you can, but every part of you, every fiber in your being, is working against you.

Of late, I've witnessed a change in DJ's behavior. Recently, we took DJ off some medicine that was very helpful to him, in order to let his liver recover. This has made it extremely hard for him to stay with us in the "real world." Before, when he was in his head, he'd kind of just flap his arms and giggle to himself as he recited lines from movies over and over again, playing each detailed scene repeatedly in his overwhelmed brain. But recently, his constant happiness has broken a little bit. He's been covering his eyes and exclaiming, "No questions! My head's busy!" He knows that when he feels this way he has to fight even harder to stay with us. And now he wants to be with us.

Yet he's also lucky because no one has expectations for him. As a person who sets perfectionist goals for herself and feels that everyone around her is bearing down on her all the time, to me DJ seems like he's got it made. We're constantly working with him, pushing him to achieve, and striving for, for…something. What are we striving for? We don't know. We don't know what DJ will ultimately accomplish and so we keep pushing, but he's the one who determines the pace. His future depends on what's in him, and although the rest of us can do all we can to help him along, he's the one who will ultimately decide his own future.

And so we all come to realize that DJ's just like the rest of us, for we determine who we are, what we become. And this scary realization hits home with us every day, yet it does not with DJ. He takes pleasure in every single day, in the joys of life. What humans were put on this world to experience; not to become the smartest person in the world, or the richest, or even the kindest. Life's about living it, and that's exactly what my 12-year old, learning-disabled little brother plans on doing.

Katherine Flaschen is 16 years old and lives in Brookline, Massachusetts, with her parents David and Deborah and her 14-year-old brother DJ. Currently, she is a sophomore at Brookline High School. She loves spending time with her friends and enjoys playing sports, especially soccer and track. She also feels it is important to share her thoughts and feelings, and cherishes her writing because it allows her to do just that. As the sister of a brother on the autism spectrum, Katherine has made presentations at national and local forums on the subject of living life as a special sibling. Her first article recently appeared in the premier issue of TAP Magazine (The Autism Perspective). Katherine's next goal is to become a licensed driver.

Acknowledgement

This essay was based upon a presentation made as part of the Parent Panel at the 2002 conference of the Interdisciplinary Council on Developmental and Learning Disorders (ICDL).

34. Their Sound Has Gone Out

Susan Ironside

My sister Nancy was the most serene pregnant woman I have ever met. She and her husband, Jim, were excited about becoming parents, but their excitement had an air of serenity about it. They bought a crib and set up the nursery and waited patiently. I recall the day that I went to the hospital to meet my nephew, George, for the first time. Nancy and Jim were calm about their new identity as parents. They were filled with joy, too. But their joy was whispered, not shouted.

My sister Nancy is a serene mother, much more so than I am. She approaches temper tantrums and strong-willed behaviors with a quiet voice and a mild manner. When we started noticing that George was different, our family suspected that the quiet serenity of my sister was somehow granting my nephew permission to run amuck. Now, when I think of those earlier suspicions, I feel embarrassed that my family would be so short-sighted. We are educated people. We are compassionate people. We had misdiagnosed the source of the problem.

George was not a serene baby. He was fussy. It was difficult to keep him comfortable. When our family would gather for events, he seemed to be miserable. Nancy would spend most of the time that we were all together comforting George, rocking him or walking him outside in his stroller. I remember when George came with Nancy to join us for our annual family beach vacation. Our family spent the day lying out on blankets while my children and the other cousins raced around in the sand, playing the usual beach games. Nancy couldn't join us that day. George didn't like the sand. He didn't like the sounds of the waves crashing or the screams of the playful children. I recall watching Nancy's back as she left the beach with George, in pursuit of a park with some familiar grass and playground equipment. She didn't say anything that day. Neither did I. I just watched her leave with a quiet determination to soothe her son.

In the few years that have passed since that day on the beach, much is different and much is the same. We no longer go to the beach with Nancy, Jim, and George. But we do other things. We meet for lunch sometimes at a park. My children like George. He is an easy companion. He watches them and lets them lead. He speaks infrequently when he is with other people. Even when he does speak, he is difficult to understand so we rely mainly on Nancy for translation. As a family, we have learned about Picture Exchange Communication System (PECS), sign language, and early intervention. We have come to anticipate unexpected cancellations or changes in family plans.

We have adapted to my nephew's presence and, in some ways, my sister's absence. Nancy remains calm and serene. She does not speak much about George's deficits. She tells us stories of his successes, with potty training and writing his name. Nancy says "PDD-NOS" and explains what that means (Pervasive Developmental Disorder–Not Otherwise Specified). Her husband, Jim, says "autism" sometimes, but Nancy would prefer that he not use the "A" word. She is a mother, she explains, and she does not like what that word means.

Sometimes I miss Nancy. Being George's mother has taken her deeper into herself and further away from me and the rest of our family. Her quiet serenity, which is a soothing balm for George, can sometimes feel to me like a separation and barrier. Thinking about it in those terms, though, seems selfish. Nancy's peaceful nature balances the chaos of George's autism. Rather than causing her son's autism, Nancy's calm presence creates a salutary environment to nurture such a unique child.

"Although they have no words or language, and their voices are not heard, their sound has gone out into all lands, and their message to the ends of the earth." King David wrote these words in praise of creation, but these words remind me of my sister and her son, George. Nancy's serenity is like a blanket that she held, folded in her lap when she was pregnant. She unfolded her blanket of serenity at George's birth and covered him with it when he began to cry. She enfolded him within it whenever the stimuli of the world started to distract and frighten him. George, too, has a blanket of serenity. In many ways his autism is a blanket that he lives under. Nancy and George dwell together underneath their blankets, which have twisted together: the blanket of Nancy's peaceful spirit along with the blanket of George's pervasive developmental delay. The hope is that, at some point, George's blanket will begin to unravel. I am convinced that when that happens, Nancy will be able to gather her own blanket around George in such a way that he will be strengthened and supported as he creates a new blanket of his own making and for his own shelter. But for now they sit together. They sit there, wordlessly most times, comforting and loving each other.

And yet it would be inaccurate to say that the blanket muffles their sound. "Their sound has gone out into all lands, and their message to the ends of the earth." George's smile sounds like the breaking of the waves on the sand; Nancy's peace sounds like the whisper of the wind. The sound of their mutual love is often wordless but echoes of the truth of their mutual language, which indeed travels to the ends of the earth.

Susan Ironside is a nurse who has extensive experience working with adults with developmental disabilities. For many years she was a nurse-investigator for Adult Protective Services and in that capacity, assisted families in creating long-term care plans for adults with autism. She is also a mother of two children and the sister of Nancy Ironside who is raising Susan's nephew, George, with compassion and wisdom.

35. Why Am I So Resentful?

Lydia Liang

My brother has cerebral palsy from being born too early and as it turned out, he has autism too. Sometimes I think that the reason I am so resentful toward my brother is that I started feeling like that so long ago. Since I didn't understand what his problem was when I was little, I thought he was just being rude and misbehaving. These feelings have stayed with me and I still think this way a lot, sort of subconsciously.

Whatever my brother does, whether he rocks back and forth, freaks out about touching his toes, or simply stares off into space, it aggravates and frustrates me so badly that I just want to tear the house down. It's just not normal and that's just not what normal people do!

If he hadn't had autism, and if he only had cerebral palsy, that would've been much easier. At least then he would still be able to think and imagine and we could talk, even though he couldn't walk and run around with me. If he didn't have autism, he would be able to think up his own sentences and play games and not have obsessions and weird behavioral issues. He would be much easier to get along with overall. Although I'm slightly better at controlling my anger now, I still have frequent outbursts of frustration which I simply can't seem to help. And I blame my brother's autism.

What is autism, anyway? There are many theories about autism, and some people are completely clueless. But to me, autism is simply a problem that my brother has. It really annoys me because there's nothing my brother or I can do about it. My brother's autism prevents me from really liking him as a friend or from actually appreciating him. Whenever he's doing something that's really bad and you tell him that, he'll act up because he wants to be told that he's a good boy. But if you tell him he's a good boy when he's behaving badly, he'll think it's OK to keep doing what he's doing. So I often feel sort of stuck because I really do want to avoid a major breakdown for either my brother or for me.

I try to find positive things about my brother and really, there are some. Like sometimes he says something that he's heard somebody else say at a really unusual time and it's really funny. It's great when he can make me laugh. He can also sing really well, and has a great memory. And even though he's very persistent and that can be annoying, it does help him out sometimes. I tell myself these things and I try to be grateful instead of resentful that I have this unique brother. Even though he is a pain, there are still good things about him. Through it all, he's my brother and I love him.

Lydia Jumi Liang is 11 years old and will be entering seventh grade middle school at a center for the highly gifted in Maryland. She plays violin with a classic youth orchestra and performs various folk dances with a Korean dance company. Her forte is the three-drum dance where she gets to pound away. She loves birds and takes care of a bird-feeding area in her backyard. Lydia is the oldest of three. Her younger siblings both have autism. She escapes by reading fantasy and science fiction books, her absolute favorite pastime.

36. My Brother…Ahhhhhhh!

Zoë Naseef

Data

My brother Tariq has autism and mental retardation. He is 25 years old and 14 years older than me. He lives in a special home with three other people with different disabilities. I visit him once in a while but he scares me.

My mom once told me that I shouldn't be afraid of Tariq because he is like a big two-year-old. I guess she is right but I am still afraid of him.

Tariq used to live at home but that was before I was born. When I was little he came to visit but I don't really remember that. What I remember is visiting him and going out to eat. He used to steal my pizza but now he is on a pizza strike. In other words, he used to love pizza, but suddenly he won't eat it. He still steals chips and ice cream though. It is embarrassing to tell people that I am afraid of my own big brother. Sometimes I wish I could have a normal big brother; you know, the kind who teases you and annoys you, but then Tariq just wouldn't be himself.

Feelings, life, or both

What do you think are the feelings you have about the people you love with autism? Are they really true feelings or are they just life hiding in itself? Like if feelings are a part of life and some people don't consider them that way then they might be hiding their feelings. Hiding feelings and not expressing them is hiding life inside itself instead of letting life express itself. Expression is good for the soul.

Bad things come with good things

Good things seem to always come with bad things. For example, you can't just jump up in the air and fly; eventually you have to land. You get what you want (you feel free from gravity for a moment, like free from reality—what really matters), but you also get something you don't want (but then all reality returns as your feet hit the ground). And to add to that, if a person with and a person without autism jumped at the same time you wouldn't be able to tell when they were in the air which one had autism, but when they landed you would know right away. Some people think that getting a relative or friend with autism is a bad thing. But it also can come as a good thing. Like sometimes I get an ice cream and a half because after I eat half, my brother steals it so then I get a whole new ice cream. I have to suffer him stealing the first one, but I get something good for it. Or maybe you get other good things. Like Tariq's autism gave my dad good ideas for book topics.

Dad hogging

My brother always hogs my dad when we visit him. I wrote something short about that when I was ten, here it is:

DAD HOGGER
Dad hogger definition: a sibling who constantly hogs a dad.
Sentence: My brother is an all around dad hogger.
D-A-D H-O-G-G-E-R.
Whenever we go canoeing: dad hogger.
When we go hiking: dad hogger.
Every time he is around and I try to go near my dad: dad hogger.
As you can see, my brother is a dad hogger from head to toe.
He can't help it.

Tariq

I haven't talked too much about my brother's personality. Tariq can't speak regular English but he still makes a lot of noise. He bangs on windows and plays with his tongue and makes loud, strange sounds. And somehow he manages to tell us things, like when we are in the car, he makes sure everyone is wearing their seatbelt. If you don't put it on yourself, he will reach over and put it on for you.

Here is a poem I also wrote about Tariq when I was 10:

> Everyone is Special in a Different Way
> I am Special my brother is Special Ed
> When I go to school he jumps on a bed
> One day when we went out for lunch my pizza is what he took
> I forgave him though because I know he is not a crook
> Sometimes he makes it go ballistic
> But that makes life realistic
> My sister is special, I am special too
> My brother is Special Ed
> That's enough for me and maybe even you

Zoë Naseef is 11 years old and in the fifth grade. She lives in the Philadelphia area with her parents, her sister Kara, and some pets. The pets include three cats named Cuddles, Peaches-n-Cream, and Tiger Lily, Zoë's two turtles, Sparki and Lightning, and Kara's goldfish, Zippidy. Zoë enjoys ballet and jazz dancing, acting, playing the violin and saxophone, and sports—especially basketball. She is excellent in math and science, and hates writing.

Part 4: Diagnosed on the Spectrum

Every parent and family member, every teacher, therapist, and doctor wishes for the kind of outcome that is reflected in this group of essays by people who are living with the diagnosis of Asperger's syndrome. Although nobody can predict the destiny of individual children, it is natural to hope and often pray for a virtual recovery from the early devastating symptoms. For the overwhelming majority of children and adults, this will not be the reality, and this makes the contributions of these writers vitally important to the autism community. Hearing from people who live with the signs and symptoms of the autism spectrum (including two of their spouses) provides all readers with essential information that is available from no other source.

What is it like to live with sensory issues? Or to experience the world and think in a distinctly different way as the reader can discern in these essays? People who live on the spectrum spend a lifetime struggling to understand the rules and conventions of society. It seems overdue for that society to learn to understand the culture of people who were born and remain different.

This group of essays demonstrates the similarities and differences of people diagnosed on the spectrum with all humanity. These men and women have the same heartaches and the same needs and desires as people who are not diagnosed. They say so clearly, "Love and accept me as I am." They appreciate those who treat them as whole people despite and maybe because of their differences. We are grateful and proud to present these outstanding and extraordinary contributions. They help the rest of us understand that autism is not just something that a person has, but is a way of being.

37. No! You Don't Understand!

Beth Adler

The loneliest thing in the world is having nobody understand you. I'd tried for years to explain about myself to the piano professor I studied with. I'd tell him about something that frustrated me and he'd respond with either a suggestion or sympathy. But useful suggestions require deep understanding, and sympathy is a dead end. Obviously I hadn't been explaining myself very well.

So I started wondering how many others don't have a clue what I'm going through. What if I could tell some of the people I've encountered over the years why I act as I do? What do I want them to understand about me?

I'd like to start out by telling my neighbors that I'm really not crazy. I know how it must have looked when I started screaming my lungs out just outside my house, but you really didn't have to call the cops. It was just a fly. An ordinary insect. The feel and sound of it buzzing in my ear so suddenly felt like an atomic bomb exploding. What's that you say? That's impossible? How can a fly buzzing in your ear feel like a bomb?

Please understand that I'm not like you. I feel things differently. My senses are so hyper-aware, that the most ordinary sound or touch or movement causes a reaction of epidemic proportions. I don't want to be this way. I'd quite prefer to be released from the agony this causes. But I can't control what I feel. And if you could get to know me, I think you'd find I'm quite sane.

Do you remember me, sir? You were standing behind me in line at the dollar store as I was about to pay the cashier. I had to cover my ears from the unbearable sound of your whistling. I reached over my head with my left arm, covering my right ear with my left hand and my left ear with my upper left arm, leaving my right hand free to get my wallet out.

I heard what you said. You fumbled with your own wallet, shook your head from side to side and said, "Ah well, it takes all kinds." *All kinds?* Is that what I am? A *kind?* I felt sick to my stomach. You said it loudly enough for me to hear you but looked at the cashier to pretend you weren't referring to me.

Why did covering my ears make you so uncomfortable? I can't brush off hurtful acts like most people. They burrow into my gut and lie there twisting and writhing like a snake being poked with a stick. Your remark will live in my memory forever—taunting, burning, seething.

Hi! Please come in. I really need this second phone line for my computer since I'm online all day. Yes, I'd like it put in my office, right there by the computer.

Smack. Chomp. Pop. Oh god, no. He's chewing gum. Loudly. This is triple agony for me because of the noise, the stench, and the sight of his mouth constantly opening and closing. Uh, could you please stop chewing gum?

Why have you stiffened like that? You're staring at me. Did I grow a third eye or something? I'm being unreasonable? You've suddenly acquired such hatred in your eyes. But it's such a simple request! Well I'll just hold my nose and look away from you as you work since you won't stop chomping and popping. What? I'm insulting you? *I'm* insulting *you?* How would it harm you to stop chewing for a few minutes? Why did you turn into King Kong just because I feel things differently than you do?

Wow! This is so neat! I'm a tutor and grader in the math department at Arizona State University. I'm proud of what I do and I love to watch people's faces when I tell them I tutor calculus.

Aaaaarrrrrgggggghhhhh!!!!! That was excruciating! I don't care that it's 'only' an eraser. It's like being shot in the head. Those long, skinny erasers in colorful plastic cases with notches on the sides are very popular among students. But they don't click them only when they need more eraser, *they play with them!* They click them up and down constantly. What? I can't work here any more? Just because I screamed and knocked over a chair when someone clicked an eraser?

At least I can still be a grader. Grading algebra homework is perfect for me because I can take the papers home where I'm alone. But now it's the beginning of a new semester and I have to contact three different instructors. I really did try but it's so difficult. It's like there's this fog in my head that turns to glue every time I think about how to contact someone. Oh please no. I've lost this job too?

Hi Karen. Remember me? I'm the one you kicked out of your therapy group for behaving inappropriately. Things were fine at first. I really liked you. But when my sensitivity to sounds increased and I jumped in shock at noise outside the room or when someone drummed their fingers on the arm of their chair, do you remember what you said? You said, "Well can't you just put up with it so we can continue the session?"

Uh, no Karen I could not. Could you put up with half a dozen firecrackers going off in your ear without reacting? Once you even had everyone in the room cover my ears with their hands to see what "came up" for me. I guess I was supposed to dredge up some forgotten childhood memory of a grade school teacher abusing me in a noisy classroom while he tapped his fingers. But of course I didn't. No surprise there since my sensitivities are caused by my internal wiring, not a repressed memory.

Mom. Dad. You've been gone a long time now. I know how much you loved me, but what I remember most about my childhood was you two yelling at me all the time. "Why do you keep whining like that?" "Why haven't you set the table yet?" "Why were you so rude to Aunt Essie?"

I didn't know I was autistic until I was 45, long after both of you passed away. Your angry faces scared me, and the sound of your yelling was so painful I had to whine to drown you out. It was also difficult for me to suddenly pull myself out of my solitary activities. I was far too engrossed in my self-contained world to step into the real world at a moment's notice. And I never meant to be rude to relatives and friends; blurting out the first thing I thought of was the only way I could communicate. I didn't understand the rules of social behavior that seemed to come so easily to most children. Did you have to call me 'miserable child' and 'rotten kid'? I'm sorry I wasn't everything you wanted me to be, but your anger and your words hurt so deeply, the pain never went away.

Okay. Now that I've gotten some of the things I wanted to tell *specific* people off my chest, the question still remains what do I want people *in general* to understand about me?

My first thought was to tell you that just because I don't talk to you doesn't mean I don't want to. People mistakenly think I'm anti-social and want to be left alone (sometimes I do). But being ignored because I can't initiate a conversation only increases my isolation. Or maybe what I need people to understand is how angry I am that life has dealt me such pain, poverty, and, most of all, loneliness. My struggle to cope with daily living, difficult enough with support, can be insurmountable without it.

Frankly though, neither of these conclusions get to the core of what I want people to know about me. I've thought and thought until my brain felt like it had been beaten to a pulp, but I still can't explain who or what I am given my current stage of evolution. Perhaps, for now, the best conclusion is that there is no conclusion. My persona, like autism itself, is best understood through an ongoing process of empathy, patience and time.

Beth Adler lives on 9½ acres in the Arizona desert. She has a bachelor's degree in piano performance and has been teaching piano for 20 years. She performs regularly in student recitals and with a local music group. Beth has always loved horses, and in the fall of 2003 won a free trip to the Arabian National Championship Horse Show. She had an article she wrote about the trip published in the February/March 2004 issue of *Arabian Horse Magazine*. She is a member of the Internet Writing Workshop. Beth's website is www.bethadler.com.

38. It Never Rains…

Simon Brodie

"Poor social skills?" I ask.

"Definitely," my wife Sarah responds.

"Unnatural fascination with specific hobbies/activity?"

"Of course."

"Easily offends others with no understanding of what they have said?"

"Do you have to ask?" she says.

"Gets upset when their routine is disturbed?"

Sarah just laughs at this point. "Guess that's a 'Yes' then," I said.

We were sitting on the couch reading through the list of clinical symptoms of Asperger's syndrome. We had known for a while that one of our daughters was not quite "right." She had her eldest sister's Sensory Integration Dysfunction (but not her dyspraxia, nor hypermotive joints). However, there was something else. As caring parents, we read every article we could find on her symptoms and did extensive research over the internet. After weeks of investigation, we arrived at "Asperger's," which fit her symptoms "like a glove." Today, however, we were not discussing her, we were discussing me!

Well that explains everything. It explains why I have always been somewhat out of phase with those around me. It explains why I couldn't cry when my dad died last year, or when my dog died two months earlier. It explains why, to this day, I don't feel (to my shame) any loss for either of them. It explains why I feel alone in a room full of people. It explains why, when there is a lot happening around me, I feel the whole world is imploding into my head. It explains why, despite loving my family more than life, when I get home from work all I want to do is dive onto my computer or into my gaming books to the exclusion of everything. It explains why I never made friends at school and still find it hard to make really good friends. In fact, my handful of friends are all war-gamers. I suppose that should concern me, but it doesn't!

I remember the problems I had fitting in at school; socializing and making friends just didn't interest me. No, that's not quite true. Like the Aesop's fable, I probably convinced myself that I didn't want to make friends after realizing that I just didn't have the ability for it. I remember being bullied in primary school, no doubt because, being different, I was an easy target. This set the pattern for my social activities throughout high school. I knew that there was something not quite "right" with me but, with no obvious mental or physical "defects," I believed I just wasn't any good at socializing—which was right, I guess. I remember wanting to have a girl-friend, like all the boys at school, although I convinced myself otherwise.

Not surprisingly, there were certain school subjects I was excellent at and ones I was embarrassingly poor at. Maths, physics, and chemistry were my favourites; they all had simple rules which (apart from quantum mechanics) never change. If the subject can be summarized as $A+B=C$ then I was good at it. Art, music, and English however, were a different story. I still don't understand art; I know what I like and that is that. Music, well let's not even discuss the disasters that were my music lessons. English was different. I understood grammar and punctuation as they were ordered; everything had a meaning and a set of rules. However, the interpretive ele-ment of English was always beyond me. Who knows what Lady Macbeth was thinking with her "Out, out, damn spot," or what *The Catcher in the Rye* was all about and quite frankly, who cares!

I left school with a good set of qualifications (despite spending all of my spare time war-gaming instead of studying) and joined the armed forces as an engineer. Now that was something I could do. Engineering was all physics and mathematics, so I wasn't going to have a problem there. Well, I was partially correct. Whilst the engineering bit was easy (I graduated in the top class and with the best possible qualifications), there was the social element, which I definitely wasn't prepared for. Being someone with poor social skills in an environment with hundreds of testosterone-fueled indi-viduals, having parties, drinking in the pub, etc., all trying to find their own social status, was not pleasant.

I thought that I had left the "social outcast" tag when I left school, but unfortunately real life doesn't work like that. To make my life even more challenging, I went for a commission early on in my career and I have been an officer for many years now. Think of it, someone with poor social skills as a military leader. Don't get me wrong, I haven't "wormed" my way to the top, I have worked tremendously hard for everything I have (significantly harder, I have always felt, than my contemporaries) and I have definitely earned everything I have achieved. I led some of the first troops into the

Balkans for the conflict in Kosovo, I have commanded troops on numerous exercises, I have been responsible for millions of pounds of equipment, and I have managed projects worth over £100 million, all the while without realizing I was "disabled."

It was whilst I was undergoing my engineering training that my life took its first positive step. My best friend became my girlfriend, and then later my wife and we now have a house full of lovely daughters, which is where we began this story. My wife, without knowing anything about Asperger's syndrome, has "saved" my life. She taught me how to act in social situations without my offending everyone in earshot. She taught me that, whilst I might not have any concept of fashion, it is important to create the right impression in the right situation. It has taken me three years to learn to dress my daughters without being accused of crimes against fashion.

I still don't like social events but at least I know how to behave. This is where an "Aspie" might have an edge. A benefit of being a member of my extended "special family" is that you remember all sorts of useless information. You can turn a subconscious social activity (which we "Aspies" are poor at) into a mechanical, regimented process (which we are good at). To this end, one of the most useful pieces of useless information for an "Aspie" to learn is human psychology. If you know how "neurotypical" people act (personal space, body language, etc.), you can identify what people are "saying" by reading (in an objective manner) what those around you pick up intuitively. This also lets you project the appropriate body language by adopting the specific body language you want, rather than what you may be comfortable with which is probably sending completely the wrong message.

However, whilst the Asperger's syndrome tag may explain me, it certainly doesn't define me—I refuse to let it! After all, only a few weeks ago I was a regular guy who had problems with my social skills, now I'm an "Aspie." Same person, same weaknesses, just that now I have a label for my problems. It doesn't change them, it doesn't offer any solutions, but it does mean that I am now aware of the thousands of people out there who are "just like me" even though they probably feel that there is no one "just like them." Now that I have found this plethora of "brothers" and "sisters," I intend to do what I can to help them. To educate their parents/guardians, their families, their schools, etc., so that they can reach their full potential, and not be written off as useless by their parents, their family, society or (worst of all) by themselves.

I shudder to think where I would be now if Sarah had not seen the potential in me and spent the time she has turning me into someone who can live a relatively "normal" life. This article is dedicated to her and to all of the unappreciated parents, guardians, and partners of every "Aspie" out there. We do appreciate everything you have done, and continue to do, for us. On behalf of those of us who cannot express their thanks and appreciation to those who help them through life…Thank You!

Simon Brodie was born in Edinburgh, in June 1969. He is married to the enchanting Sarah and has three adorable daughters, Caitlin, Eilidh, and Maia. He is an engineering officer in the Royal Air Force, currently based in southern England. This is his first ever serious article to make print, hopefully not his last. Having recently found out he has Asperger's, he would gladly give it up for Lent, were he not Jewish. He is a typical Gemini and, as such, does not believe in the Zodiac.

39. ...It Pours

Sarah Brodie

After her assessment last August, our eldest daughter was diagnosed with Sensory Integration Dysfunction. The occupational therapist told us that this was part of a wider group of ailments known as Autism Spectrum Disorders. Up to that point, I was not aware of any direct contact with autism in my home life. Being a nurse, I had encountered autism at work, but certainly not in my personal life, or so I thought.

Around this time, it also became apparent that our middle daughter had some problems. As most parents would do, we got her referred for specialist assessment. We saw her pediatrician who, after examining her, said that she obviously had "significant social and communication difficulties." We were asked what we thought was "wrong" with her and we said that we felt it was something in the autism spectrum. The pediatrician agreed, but would not make any specific diagnosis without further investigation. So now, another of my daughters was tagged with the label of autism.

On coming home, I was upset that the doctor had not found something wrong with my daughter. My husband, however, took the view that we already knew that there was something wrong, now we were starting to find out what it was. He had absolutely no idea why I might be upset at the pediatrician's assessment. On looking up "Autism" on the internet, we found huge amounts of information to wade through. Eventually we identified a set of symptoms or behavioral responses that exactly matched our daughter, "Asperger's syndrome." Relief, you may think, that at last we had a term to use for her problems, which is true. The "but" element is that these symptoms also described my husband perfectly!

My husband and I met whilst at school together and quickly became friends. He was always seen as being a bit odd, a bit of a loner. He would make inappropriate remarks and seemed completely unaware of having done so. He seemed lonely and was certainly not the most approachable of people. It was obvious that he was clever but he seemed very self-involved. However, we did have a similar interest, that of role-playing games. Outside of schoolwork, this was his main topic of conversation, and still is, nearly 20 years later!

Due to my nursing training occuring in Scotland and Simon's training being in England, we could only meet up every couple of months or so as our respective work schedules allowed. This meant that we communicated mostly by letters which, looking back on it, was probably a good thing. By writing, it made it easier for Simon to communicate and I still have the most amazing collection of letters!

Socially, it was incredibly difficult at times. I recall regularly apologizing to offended friends and relatives after each of his visits home. I was asked all the usual questions by family and friends: "Why him? Why not someone nearer home who would treat you better, and not embarrass you in public?" Throughout the whole of our courtship, he managed to offend all of my friends and was even banned from the house by my dad. This was all the more remarkable because he was completely oblivious to it. He just did not understand that not everyone understood things on his level, or shared his sense of humor. Away from everyone he seemed to relax and he was (and still is) a very caring and understanding partner with a good sense of humor.

For the record, I had other offers but I loved Simon and I finally realized what the problem was (or so I thought). I blamed his parents. I assumed, in my arrogance, that they had not taught him any social skills and were obviously not well-equipped socially themselves. These assumptions, although based on inaccurate ideas, led me to realize that he had to be taught how to interact socially. This presented me with the unenviable task of teaching him the rules of a game that he wasn't even aware he was supposed to be playing. However, this had to be done without either offending him or belittling him.

I found over the years (we were now over three years into our relationship) that the best method of communicating with him was without any ambiguity at all. Therefore, as the situations arose, I would explain how they might have been dealt with better with varying degrees of success. We eventually got married and lived together and it was then that a whole new facet of Simon's behavior was revealed to me: I had no idea how rigid his routines were and I am sure these were reinforced by military training. At first it was totally bizarre how trivial the things were that could throw his day totally out of sync. It took me a long time to realize what the triggers were that set the reactions off.

We have now known each other for nearly 20 years, been together as a couple for 15 years, and married for 10 of them. We have had four miscarriages and now have three amazing daughters. We have been through a lot in those years: family bereavements, Simon being posted to the Falklands for six months immediately after our second daughter was born, and his disappearing off to take part in various wars and military exercises. This is not helped by Simon's posting "cycle" which means that we have moved house seven times in ten years adding a good bit of pressure to both our lives and our children's. We have come to unwritten understandings regarding his need for routines and all the other compromises that people need to make in order to live together. I would not wish to live with anyone else.

Now, nearly 15 years later, I find that the majority of the difficulties in our relationship were largely attributable to Simon having Asperger's syndrome. Now I wonder why it was never picked up when he was younger. To realize that my partner doesn't just not understand my emotional reactions, but can't, is difficult, to put it mildly. What is hardest for me to deal with is the comprehension of all of the difficulties in everyday living that he has had to overcome in order to get to where he is today. The thought of him feeling isolated and overwhelmed in social situations causes me pain and sadness, both for him and for our daughter who will have all this to come. However, Simon is an amazing father. His role in our children's lives is immeasurable; they adore him and they get all the warmth, nurturing, and loving they could wish for.

My husband has not let his condition slow him down. He has excellent qualifications, Higher National Certificates and a BEng Honours degree amongst them, and he has also been considered for an MSc placement. He is an officer in the UK armed forces and, although he may not be aware of it, he has made many friends along the way. From my own point of view, he is my husband, the man with whom I will spend the rest of my life. He does have Asperger's syndrome but that is not his sum total and it does not define him; he is more than the total of his parts. Simon is an individual. In his case a very special one, as we all are. Our daughter is only four but she will have all the help and support that her father did not. She is a very special little girl who will greatly benefit from her dad's "inside" knowledge.

Sarah Brodie (née Wallace) was born in Edinburgh, in June 1969. She is married to Simon, who wrote the previous essay and who was recently diagnosed with Asperger's syndrome. They have three adorable daughters, Caitlin (who has dyspraxia, hypermotile joints, Sensory Integration Dysfunction, and possibly Asperger's), Eilidh (who is diagnosed with Sensory Integration Dysfunction and Asperger's), and Maia (who has nothing identified, but is a whirlwind of trouble and chaos). Sarah is a registered general nurse and currently lives with her family in southern England.

40. Melt(d)ing Down

Rauidhri Finn

A meltdown is when you get cross and can't remember things and break things and scream and a freak-out is when you just get confused and scared and can't talk.

One day I was painting and I was 15 and I put water for the brushes in a glass bucket thing and my father saw and got cross with me and tried to stop me while I was painting and I had the biggest meltdown ever and I picked up the bucket and threw it and it hit him on the head and he fell down and then there is a hole in my memory and then I was sitting on top of him and I was holding a piece of glass in my hand and I was going to cut his throat then my mother and uncle walked in and I ran away. And then another big hole in my memory and next day I was in my head again. And so I knew that maybe I could kill people and that I had to be very careful not to get cross and I made a promise to myself never to hit anyone again and I have kept that promise except only twice and then not hard so that's OK and there was a boy who was Asperger's like me in England who killed his brother when he had a meltdown so I am lucky. But I wasn't really so sorry cos he wasn't a nice person and my mother didn't think so either cos one day and my brother said it to me and showed me the bullet in the door when she took out a gun to shoot him and missed and so she is not a good shot.

Once when I was studying for an exam at night and my mother and father started fighting about the gin and I took it away from them and threw it away and they hit me and he ran away and then I left home and didn't have a home anymore. But I passed the exam and had to go and find him very late at night and couldn't study. I was still young and 17 and then had to look after myself and find how to go to university and get qualifications and get money and everything and lots of nice people helped.

When I was in hospital for the first time and the psychiatrist said was the best thing for me I was 20 years old and was at a friend's house and he had taken me there to have lunch and we were going to eat steak and I like eating steak and then he asked his girlfriend and I got really upset now cos she was coming and wasn't jealous or anything but I was upset cos he didn't properly say to stay for lunch but then I knew they were cooking steak for me to eat and that was what I wanted but cos I didn't hear him say to stay for lunch I ran away and got a hole in my memory again and couldn't talk anymore and nobody could understand that he had to say it and that only then could I stay and so I had to go to hospital and they gave me lots of Complan which is baby food and I wasn't a baby cos they said I didn't eat properly and sometimes I stop eating cos I don't get hungry much. So it was quite a big freak-out and just a bit of meltdown. And then they gave me tablets cos I thought it would be a good idea to stand in front of a bus.

When I told them my father ran over me with his car they said that I had to go to the neuroward of the big mental hospital [1963] and I did and what they did was terrible and they wanted to x-ray my brain and they didn't have proper machines and put a needle in my back and took out fluid and then air into me and it went in my brain and my head was going to burst and it was very bad and they x-rayed and then they tried to do EEGs and the machine went mad and they said to me that the needle they used was dirty. That's not nice. And they said I'm a bit neurological and now they say I'm autistic or Asperger's. And then I became unconscious and I woke up the next day and they said my brain was funny.

And last year or one more before they did an MRI scan and it was not so bad but the EEGs were funny cos there was too much delta and they taught me how to stop it cos I used to fall asleep but now I don't. And I know how to make alpha brain waves and also once learnt to change how my heart works by making the sounds of a drum in my head and it was like playing the drum. I take lots of medicines for my epilepsy and autism and everything and don't get cross now.

I had a big meltdown that is a good word to say what I was like when my wife wanted to bring her friend home and I said no she must go to her house and my wife said no and then I had to run away and I jumped through a big window but it was closed and lots of glass broken and I learnt how people in films jump through windows it is OK if it is quick and there was only a little blood and I went to hospital and they sewed me up and I told the nurse and she said oh.

I got the best marks at the university and then got a teachers' diploma and then got scholarships to study at London University for an MA and then a Ph.D. at another university and became a professor. And I was supposed to go to a garden party with the Queen but didn't. But now I think it was a big mistake even though it was a very good Ph.D. cos I would have been much happier if I was a painter and not a writer. Now I paint on the computer and when I am on the computer it is good cos I don't need words excepting like now and then my mind is not here in the same way and it is much better. But best would have been a zookeeper.

So if I get upset I run away and stop talking but have been working on this and am better now that I am older but it was difficult for my wife and children and I am very lucky to have a special family.

I have two different voices an inside voice and a Ph.D. voice and this is the inside voice and the Ph.D. voice is very different.

The Ph.D. voice says things like:

I am a retired professional and have developed an intellectualized external voice, but I also have an "inner voice" which I used in the brief autobiographical account above. The "inner" and "outer" voices are very different.

A severely impaired personal memory (an under-researched AS characteristic) has led me to create an autobiography composed of dispersed fragments and unresolved, misunderstood events. The formulation of goals and direction were determined entirely by chance and the advice and intrusion of friends.

Decisions, which have had a radical impact on my life, were made without an understanding of how I functioned, leading to much suffering and unhappiness. A simple comment like, "You are autistic which impacts on your ability to…" would have been unbelievably beneficial in enabling an awareness and understanding of otherwise inexplicable behaviours, which indeed made me feel I was a madman.

For the adult with AS, modification of external behaviours enables social participation and adaptation to some extent but does little to alleviate the internal pain. Diagnosis should be seen as a way of identifying those in need of assistance so as to minimize the negative effects of the syndrome. The diagnosis in itself alleviates suffering and in fact can also cause transformation. Subsequent to a diagnosis, new awareness can lead to adaptive behaviours and to a reinterpretation thus a re-conceptualization of self by self and others. In this way, the diagnosis can be critical to the process of healing—discovery / re-invention.

Rauidhri Finn is a 62-year-old adult from South Africa, recently diagnosed with Asperger's syndrome. Before retiring, he was a professor and taught at a university for 33 years. He asserts that Asperger's syndrome/autism has devastated his life and impacted negatively on family and friends. He is certain that the survival of his marriage owes much to his wife's extraordinary and invaluable love, intelligence, and support.

41. Relativity

Aurelia van Hulsteyn (Finn's spouse)

In order to begin this essay I had to get rid of a toothpick, a grubby old bandage, a large bible, and wipe the "mouse" covered with sticky stuff. (The computer belongs to my husband, who wrote the previous essay.) My former erudite approach has been entirely dismembered. This is not an unfamiliar experience.

I have known my partner for 44 years. We met in the drawing room of the Fine Arts Department, where he was singled out for his flamboyant charcoal oak leaf drawing. The rest of us were immediately intimidated and I changed to Psychology as a major. Forty-three years later, armed with the insight of my grown up children, a diagnosis was made.

"Hasn't Dad got Asperger's?" "Yes," it appears so, and what a relief. Most of the inexplicable behaviors we, as his family, could not rationalize, can now be contextualized and a lot of negative assumptions and interpretations released. Of course not everything falls under the Asperger's diagnosis; personalities differ and are rooted in primal family of origin backgrounds. One cannot relegate all responsibility to a diagnosis.

As personalities he and I could not be more different. I work as a clinical psychologist and am interested in the nuances of relating. For my husband nuances do not exist. I am over-empathic with fragile boundaries, whilst his boundaries are impermeable especially when doing a task, and empathy is often a good guess based on rationalizing. Misinterpretations are continuous, and used to cause hurt to both of us and the family. Even now when looking back, we might have been living on different planets, based on our inner experience over a wide range of areas and issues. What has changed now is that the "sting" and hurts have diminished through understanding the syndrome. Where once there would have been a week-long upset and breakdown in communication, we can now sort things out in an hour or two. I also attempt to live more "in the moment," which simplifies.

Still, daily misinterpretations happen, and I find I bottle up in an attempt to interpret according to the new (for me) Asperger's paradigm, and then blow a gasket. His pragmatic response is killing for me—and strange in view of the fact of his dealing with lecturing in abstract cognitive realities for over 30 years. I sometimes simply cannot believe that he has missed the point again, and focused on some trivial detail. I find deep breathing and one of my tranquilizers usually does the trick. I used to rationalize for hours until I discovered that this was a total waste of energy. What I do now is listen, and try to stand in his shoes. If it goes well he will sometimes swap shoes with me.

There is a growing trust that reality can become consensual, when one has translated it into the framework of "the other." One of the things that triggered me was his continual underlying anger, which would burst out inappropriately (it seemed), anywhere. Now when the signs are there I can recognize and find a source sometimes, and he is learning to self-talk and contain. This makes an enormous difference to my anxiety level and allows more sharing of ordinary things whereas before we lived emotionally isolated, doing our own thing, and walking on eggs.

Having a non-dogma orientated spiritual base, in which there is understanding of something greater than personality, ego, and relationships, has contained us at core-level. His spiritual knowledge and my experiential orientation to energy in my work and philosophy give us a deep inner resource for coping. This infuses growth—often painful—with hope.

It seems possible now to not only reinterpret the past in light of new knowledge and compassion, but to also change the definition of ourselves and our relationship. When this happens to one member of a partnership it must affect the other—in our case with a sense of positive open-endedness.

Aurelia van Hulsteyn, aged 62, is the mother of four, and grandmother of three. She is a clinical psychologist and Reiki Master, practicing energetic medicine, and chakric meditation (based on Dwaj Kuhl) in their hometown in South Africa. Aurelia is an animal lover, reader of heavy psychological thrillers, lover of red wine and Leonard Cohen. She is also blessed by many friendships, and a loving family.

42. Essay on Autism

Heidi Kunisch

What is Asperger's syndrome? The first time I asked that question was about three years ago, sitting in a child psychologist's office. I was trying to figure out whether my son Joey even needed to be seen by a child psychologist. He was struggling at daycare, and I was struggling with the people running the daycare. My son is not a bad kid. I was sure there were good reasons for his behavior. But trying to gain the understanding and cooperation of the teachers was becoming a full-time job.

We had gone through four daycares in less than two years, and the same scenario always occurred. At first I'd be treated like an overprotective mother, then as a mother who spoils her child. Next I'd be given advice on how to discipline my child. Finally, the big hit: "It's not working out." The last daycare center—the one that ended our "Age of Daycares"—referred us to speech therapy.

So began the evaluation process, and Joey started seeing a speech therapist. I thought it was simple: I had not recognized my son's speech needs and now things would get better. But a year passed, and there was little change in his behavior. The daycare supervisor later told me that they had hoped "other" things would come out as a result of his evaluation. I questioned this and she answered with a casual "You know, psychological issues are sometimes associated with signs of neglect and abuse." I was stunned—how had I missed their attitude toward us? What problem was my son having that would make them think something like this?

I pulled my son out of daycare—which pleased Joey—but we were back at square one. I watched other children interact with their mothers and each other and noticed how everything seemed to fall into place with them. I came to think that I just wasn't doing something that all these other mothers already knew how to do. Feeling pretty low on the "good mother" scale, I took the only step left to us and consulted a child psychologist. It was only the third session when she mentioned "Asperger's syndrome."

We then started down the long road of formal procedures and diagnoses during the summer before Joey's kindergarten year. I read anything I could get my hands on about Asperger's syndrome (AS), autism, the autism spectrum, and Pervasive Developmental Disorder (PDD). I did a lot of talking, a lot of questioning. I spoke with pediatricians, nurses, teachers, and the school board's Committee on Special Education.

One of the first things I learned is how little information anyone had to offer. I expected to be able to rely on doctors and educators, but mostly all I received were "warm fuzzies" and "feel-good-about-yourself" messages. Some people even tried to convince me that I was looking for something wrong with my child to make up for my own insecurities. But I stayed focused on my research, probably to the point of being a bit obsessed. And, as I was reading and learning, I found that I understood more than my son's possible diagnosis. I was beginning to understand my own life.

After reading a series of authors—Tony Attwood, Liane Holliday Willey, and especially Temple Grandin—I had to ask, "Could this be me too?" After all, why did I understand my son so well, when no one else could? The questions kept pouring in. Is this why I get strange looks when I try to explain my son's behavior? How is it these authors describe exactly how things are for me? And what does everyone mean, "not typical"? This is not the typical way of thinking?

I did not reveal my thoughts about myself right away. I was nervous about being exposed. On the one hand, it felt good to finally know who I am—something I'd struggled with since I was a kid. But the idea of everyone knowing really scared me. Life has always been a struggle—to act correctly, to do the "right" thing, to sort out the contradictions between my perceptions and the perceptions of others. With Asperger's syndrome, would I ever be able to get it right? If people can see it in Joey, they must be able to see it in me. All I kept thinking was *how do I get out of this?*

With my thoughts closing in, I submitted to the inevitable. My mother accompanied me to the doctor's office, and this time, out loud, I asked, "Could this be me, too?" They each let out a sigh. I guess they were relieved and from their perspective, I was ready to hear the answer. "We were trying to figure out how to break the news to you," the doctor replied. My mother nodded, "I was hoping you'd figure it out for yourself before I had to tell you." I felt totally mixed up about this for a while. If they knew, why didn't they tell me? But then again, they couldn't know how I'd react.

Everything changed. I sat there thinking so many things. Will I be treated differently? Will life get better or worse? It's one thing to read about Asperger's in a book, it's another to realize that you live it.

Since my mother and I live together, I had the opportunity to confide in and consult with her daily on issues and answers I was searching for. I am a person with AS, she is a person who is neurotypical, and these two worlds are sometimes very conflicting. With the diagnosis of Asperger's syndrome, I have gone from being seen as having been a rebellious, manipulative, defiant kid who always had to have her own way to a sensitive person with deep feelings who has been misunderstood.

Throughout my own self-discovery, my son continued through the diagnostic process. It was during the middle of his kindergarten year that he received the formal label of autism/Asperger's syndrome with all the paperwork that goes with it. I also fit the criteria and received the same diagnosis.

It took some time for life to settle down. The idea of having what people call a "disability" seemed so strange. Were we now supposed to call ourselves disabled? What makes my son and me so different?

Over time, I've been able to assemble pieces of my puzzle. I came to understand two characteristics of Asperger's syndrome that have made the world of difference for me: mind-blindness and thinking in pictures. Mind-blindness, in which people on the spectrum are unable to read non-verbal expression, was very hard for me to grasp. I kept asking, "What am I not seeing?" At one point my mother told me that the face is capable of thousands of expressions and a person's expression constantly changes. I was amazed. It was unimaginable. Throughout life, I had tried to memorize people's expressions for the sole purpose of not saying the wrong thing at the wrong time. I could see happy (a smile), sad (tears), or angry (a lowered pointy brow). I thought all human interaction was based on these three. But there were thousands? What I had really discovered was that there was a lot for me to learn.

The second characteristic, "thinking in pictures"—so brilliantly described in Temple Grandin's book—finally convinced me that I did belong somewhere on the spectrum. I have asked others, "If you don't think in pictures, then how do you think?" This has created some very interesting conversations for me (but only, as I've learned, with people I really trust). Up until this point, I assumed that everyone thought in the same way. For me, thinking is seeing. In conversation, a word or group of words will bring up a set of pictures that logically lead to another set of pictures, like a "domino effect." If too many words lead to too many pictures, then my mind can, and usually will, shut down. I've equated this to my tendency to "over-talk" a specific subject, not letting anyone else speak. What I didn't know is that, socially, this is viewed as unacceptable, as appearing narrow-minded. Realizing this has helped me a great deal.

Finally, there was a way for me to understand. Learning has become my greatest tool. Knowing what I need to understand and why I need to understand it has given my life direction, a sense of how to grow. Sure, I can read all about my diagnosis and discover step-by-step how to "act properly," but learning "why" has given it all meaning and purpose. Otherwise, I am left standing there, frustrated, and asking, "What am I doing this for? Why is it this way?" Most of my life has been spent sorting out thoughts that way. How do I convince the people around me that I am trying to understand how to understand them? I want to know the difference in the way our minds work—because sometimes it's the difference that makes the difference.

For typical people who want to learn about people on the autism spectrum, there are books that describe us, describe our minds. For me, on the spectrum, I would like to learn about typical people. Why do you say one thing when you really mean something else? If I am "mind-blind," then what is the opposite? If you have mind-sight, tell me what it is that you are seeing.

Understanding has been crucial for me in communicating. As a good friend once told me, "You can't shut the whole world out. You'll always keep running into people." Taking this learning approach has made life for me, and for my son, a more positive experience. Through the diagnosis of Asperger's syndrome, my son and I are now recognized as people with real feelings, who have been misunderstood and looked at in the wrong ways. I have been able to grieve what I have lost, make amends where possible, and accept myself for who and what I am, including all the mistakes I've made. I have been able to grow by accepting the challenges I'm faced with—above all, by trying to provide a better, more comfortable life for my son.

Heidi Kunisch is a single mother living with her son, Joseph, in Rochester, New York. Heidi attended an out of state college after high school but dropped out after three semesters. Social situations have always been a struggle, resulting in many conflicts with family and peers. Both Heidi and her son were diagnosed with AS in 2002, when Joseph was five years old. Currently, Heidi works in a restaurant at night and homeschools her son during the day. She relies on her skills of memory, scripting, and imitating of social scenes to be able to be successful at her job.

43. The Way We Think

Roger N. Meyer

I was diagnosed with Asperger's syndrome (AS) in the summer of 1997, at the age of 55. This essay first appeared in its original form in 1998 on an electronic mailing list for parents of children with AS. After having left the cabinetmaking trade in March 1998, I commenced my trek towards a completely new set of careers. This piece reflects my first AHA! understanding of the impact of the way I thought about my past life as a student of ideas, and how I was now becoming a person studying and working with people, not things.

Tonight I attended a research project meeting with my employment research project co-principals, and only partway through the meeting, everyone—myself included—felt stressed not only by *what* I was saying, but *how* I was expressing myself. Suddenly, something clicked. A light went on. I'd been reading about learning disability patterns, semantic-pragmatic language issues, communication and social habits of children and adults with AS.

My colleagues were overwhelmed by my endless chatter. I, as usual, was oblivious to the signs of their distress. Someone called a halt to what we were doing, and asked how I formulated my research constructs and the project's design format. For the first time, the forest/trees issue came into focus for me. I said, "I think about concrete things in excruciating detail and then follow common threads until I arrive at my ideas." (Sound familiar, anyone?) What they were hearing in my monologues was a tangled mass of unrelated details that would then have a surprise ending. Even I would be surprised. They couldn't follow how I got to my conclusions from where I'd started. I wasn't often sure myself.

I said something like the following:
"I have trouble seeing the forest because the trees are so interesting. What I now realize is that I think 'backwards' from you guys. In college I took brilliant notes. I got so hung up with details I couldn't record the major ideas in a lecture because I just *had* to capture the lecturer's examples and details. Almost everyone else in class waited while the lecturer introduced a big idea, and then they took brief 'concept' notes. Not me.

From the moment I took my seat, I started furiously writing down everything the professor said. Intellectually, I knew there was a big picture there somewhere, but I never waited for the lecturer to roll out that big canvas before I started recording snapshots, tidbits, and what turned out to be irrelevancies or side-trips. I was hung up in the mechanics of writing. I felt driven to complete each line so that it was grammatically correct. I knew I was going through an inefficient mechanical ritual but felt powerless to stop it. At the end of a lecture, my notes were neat, but they made no sense.

My book notes were as useless as my lecture notes. When I read assigned material the first time, I'd underline the text or highlight it or do both. Two or three days later, closer to class time, I'd re-read the *whole* text all over again and print tiny notes in the margins or columns. I did this in hope of getting the big picture, but even that didn't work. I'd stumble through class, writing notes furiously in my lined paper notebooks, but then I'd have to re-read *everything*, including my incoherent notes, when cramming for exams. At the end of this Herculean effort, I wrote good exams, but at a terrific cost.

Rewards for doing things the easy and efficient way eluded me. I was a grind student. I studied all the time, but I didn't understand the first thing about how to study. Recalling that experience now, that's the reason I'm terrified of returning to graduate school. I can't face going through that whole routine again, yet I'd bet that's exactly what I'll end up doing now, 35 years later."

"The same thing's happening here," I continued explaining to my colleagues. "Just now I understand what's happening. I arrive at grand schemes and concepts by first immersing myself in detail, any and all of it, without discrimination, without using a coarse 'general idea' filter. It turns out I don't seem to have one. Out of this sand dune of minutiae, I start to see relationships between certain grains, and I make little hillocks of sand with them. Without taking the whole dune down, I start combining the small piles after sensing there are broader conceptual connections. I then return to the unsifted details, and repeat the process. Finally, the dune is dismantled after many extraction and refining exercises. Some big concepts I can already see, without completely combining all the small piles. Those meta-concepts then drive the construction of an intellectually convoluted paradigm.

This explains why I am so passionate about my ideas. Problem is, I expect you to share the excitement of each of my flashes of insight along the way. I feel driven to involve you in my thought process, not only to see how clever I am (my drive for attention), but how iron-clad is my logic. I can never remember not trying to make my point this way. When I started to speak at lectures I spoke from my own point of view, and have tried ever since to convince people to see things as I see them. At first, I didn't understand the thought processes of others. I sense the difference now, but this is an old habit, hard to break."

I explained all of this to the audience and then raised the theory-of-mind issues involved with my approach: I cannot follow the logic of others because I have a different, but not a defective, theory of mind. When left to my own devices, I cannot easily conceive of others thinking differently than I think. When in the company of others—something I've avoided in the past—I think I'm now getting the picture.

Does anyone see their "little professor" in this? Yes, eventually we come to an understanding, but it is at a terrible cost. To build the same road, others use a road grader. I use a salad fork. Others see my process as extraordinarily convoluted and very patience-testing. I can spend hours at it. In many other instances (not in this professional one, fortunately), I constantly check in with strangers, midstream, hungry for their agreement and approval. It's hard to imagine what they must feel. There I go, prattling on and on, oblivious to the slumping shoulders, the eyes glazing over, and my colleagues' subtle, polite signals of discomfort. All this until I realize, far too late, that I have "blown it" again.

Others talk of the eccentricities of bright people. Perhaps some of that applies to me. I would be the first one to raise the standard for the unappreciated geniuses as well as the appreciated ones in our midst, if not for the discomfort I feel when all too often I recognize their pain as my own.

Roger N. Meyer is an advocate, mediator, and presenter on issues concerning Asperger's syndrome and disability. He is the founder of "...of a different mind," a disability consulting and representation service. He has extensive personal, agency, and resource contacts and information regarding AS, disability advocacy, legal representation, neuropsychological evaluation, and best use of forensic specialists. He lives and works in the state of Oregon.

44. The Chains of Friendship: An Autistic Person's Perspective on Interpersonal Relationships

Alex Mont

Beware, young citizens, for you are in danger of falling prey to a totalitarian regime. This regime is more far-reaching than John Ashcroft's PATRIOT Act, and can feel more insidious than a terrorist cell. Restricting free speech is but the least of what this regime can do. It can control what you buy, it can

control what you wear, and it can control how you spend your time. It can even control what you put into your mouth. Periodically it dispatches arbitrary dictates that must be followed without question. No rationale is given, no rationale is necessary. And woe to anyone who dares to defy these regulations, for punishment is swift and extrajudicial: there is no trial, no defense, and no attorney. The deviant is simply ostracized, excluded from the group, and in some cases even worse. And by the way, teenagers: this dictatorship is not run by parents, teachers, or school administrators. It is not even run by adults at all. It is run by you. This dictatorship that I am speaking of is no other than the unwritten social class structure and relationship structure of American teenage life. That is, the need to fit in and make friends.

Although what I have said may sound extreme, it is actually quite accurate. According to the Garment Industry Development Corporation, the US fashion industry makes $172 billion a year (over $600 for every man, woman, and child in the United States), much of it from teenagers, who need to buy expensive clothes so that they can fit in. Social pressures certainly control how teenagers spend their money. If you took that $600 and brought it to a bookstore, you could buy at least one book to read every two weeks for a year. That would certainly be a much more worthwhile expenditure than spending it on clothes that go out of fashion anyway. Fashion is one of those "arbitrary dictates" that I mentioned: really, when people say they need to buy the latest clothes that are "in fashion," do they really know why they're "in fashion" or think that "fashionableness" is a reflection of some intrinsic, valuable quality of the piece of clothing itself? No: if you ask most people, they'll just say that a specific style "is cool" or "all the cool kids do it." And about controlling what you put into your mouth? Well, plenty of teenagers put lots of extremely toxic substances in their mouth so they can be friends with other teenagers who also put those same toxic substances in their mouth. They're called cigarettes.

Why all the rush to fit in? Being in a prestigious Math, Science, and Computer Science Magnet Program, I decided to take a scientific approach to this problem. The first part of my study involved background research, in this case asking my parents what they thought. Apparently, the main reason people want to fit in is so they can make friends. The next research question immediately posed itself: what is a "friend," and why is it so valuable that people are willing to engage in so many self-destructive behaviors to get one? In order to test the hypothesis that friendship is extremely valuable, I decided to conduct an experiment: get a friend, and then see what's so valuable about it. However, this line of investigation quickly ran into difficulties due to the lack of an appropriate methodology. Translation: I didn't know how to make a friend.

A couple years ago, I joined a support group for people with Asperger's who were having trouble making friends. There were three people in the group: the leader, me, and another boy, John [not his real name], who was a senior in high school. His problems with friendship made mine seem minor by comparison. John told me that he once had a friend who would constantly accuse John of breaking his stuff after he came over to his house. This "friend" would spread that information, making John a pariah among his classmates. The problem got so bad that John was forced to spend several hundred dollars on a polygraph test to clear his name, and even after that his friend didn't believe him. This whole enterprise of friendship was starting to look a little less promising than I first thought.

Given this additional data, I reconsidered my original hypothesis. If friendship was this dangerous, then why was everyone so desperate for it? I wasn't sure, so I did more research: I talked to my parents and the group leader again. I realized that my data was biased: since I was in a support group for people with social problems, of course I would hear about more problems than successes and good friendships. But they told me that the main reason was that most people have a need for social interaction, and that friendship is a way to fulfill that need. I, however, never seemed to have that need: while I do like to talk to my teachers about academic subjects or to adults about news articles and the like, I never really needed to interact with other kids and I am perfectly happy alone reading books or playing computer games.

But considering how totalitarian the regime of social structure is, I thought it was perhaps for the best that I never got a part of it, at least not until I knew what I'm doing. I never felt the urge to drink alcohol, smoke cigarettes, or skip school in order to be part of a group. I never felt the need to spend a lot on clothing: if it provides adequate thermal insulation, it's fine with me. And more importantly, the need to fit in with a group severely constrains how one can react to social situations. For example, when I was in middle school, I was bullied incessantly, with people hitting me or bumping into me in the hallways. Most people would have a very hard time with this problem, since they would not want to go to a teacher for fear of being perceived as weak. However, since I did not care how other students perceived me, I was able to work with teachers to formulate effective strategies, such as eating lunch in the main office and waiting until the halls cleared to change classes so I could avoid hallway bullying. Also, I learned from reading newspaper articles on bullying that many had it far worse than I did: many people are seriously hurt or have materials stolen from their backpacks. If that had happened in my case, I would simply have adapted my strategies: I would have had an escort in the hallways or left my books at home and used a class set. I was essentially insulated from the most serious problems precisely because I had no need to fit in: I was not artificially constrained from taking effective action by the need to maintain a façade of "toughness."

Many of the problems I faced, while severe, were actually a lot simpler than the problems most NTs (neurotypical people) face. For example, while I had problems with making friends (I couldn't make one), when I look at many of the problems NTs face I think, "Can you explain to me again why that's a problem?" Many people, for example, are distraught because their girlfriend left them. If I had a friend who left me I would certainly not be emotionally affected: I would just get a new one. Since I do not have nor need any of the deep emotional attachments that other people need, I am shielded from the emotional effects of relationship failure.

So you don't believe me when I say that I don't have any friends? Actually, I do: computer games are my friends. Computer games are my friends because they are complicated, yet simple: complicated because many computer games have sophisticated rules, tactics, and strategy, but simple because they follow specific rules: they do not get angry or make arbitrary decisions. And most importantly, when playing a computer game I am in control: if I am not having fun, I can always turn it off. However, with a human friend, that can be difficult: for example, I used to play sports with my brother, and we would make deals that said that we would play one game that he wanted to play, and one game that I wanted to play. But this took control out of my hands: many times I would be miserable 15 minutes into the game, but I couldn't stop playing because we had a deal. While everybody likes to talk about how interpersonal relationships are more valuable than anything material, for me the opposite is true: material things are normally predictable, while relationships can swing from rewarding and fulfilling to excruciatingly painful with no rhyme or reason. I just don't know why any willing person would subject themselves to that kind of torture. I guess I'll never know.

Alex Mont is a senior in the Math, Science, and Computer Science Magnet Program at Montgomery Blair High School in Maryland. He has competed in several prestigious math competitions including the USA Mathematical Olympiad and the American Regions Math League. Last summer, he worked on a research project at the National Institute of Standards and Technology. He is also a speaker for the Montgomery Exceptional Leaders Program, which is a group of high school students that gives presentations to students and teachers about issues relating to disabilities. He is a self-described "geek" and proud of it, and does not understand why anyone would consider geeks unpopular just because they like math and science.

45. Jordan's Gift

Todd J. Schmidt

Not long ago I turned 37. Some say that you get wiser with age. I don't know much about that. But I do know that I am wiser now.

No one knew. They weren't supposed to know that it was okay to be like me. They couldn't have known that their methods of teaching, parenting, teasing, and judging were just about the worst thing they could do to a kid like me. I was over-sensitive, an underachiever, odd, lazy, weird, stupid, and gullible. I didn't have autism—that was the kid who never spoke. I never shut up. It must be my fault. They simply didn't know. And how could they have?

So today, I find myself a husband and a father. I am gainfully employed. I coach little league and scoop ice cream at the PTA fundraiser. I also obsess. I overanalyze. I am compulsive, rigid, insecure and, at times, anti-social. I confuse my co-workers by turning normal conversations into oblong tangents. I frustrate my boss by being brilliant one minute and absent-minded the next. I madden my wife when I need constant reinforcement because I can't tell that she loves me. I have no faith that I can't touch, no security that doesn't scream out at me. I have learned and applied more social skills than anyone I can imagine and I know I am only a fraction there. I cannot know what I cannot taste and I muddle through life constantly feeling out for what I cannot infer. I am a man who lives with Asperger's syndrome. And this is my story.

Until I left home in my twenties, I considered myself a failure. Kids didn't get me because my thinking was so different. Teachers rode me hard because I was brilliant, but a C student (therefore seemingly lazy and not making an effort). My parents believed in negative motivation— which of course backfires on someone who takes everything literally.

As for other kids—I was a target. They preyed upon me, and I was faulted for allowing them to do it. My parents pointed at other kids and asked, "Why can't you be like them?" And that's all I really wanted to be—like them. But I couldn't and had no idea why. Again, no one knew. Least of all me.

So I had lousy self-esteem. I was awkward and socially inept. And let's make this clear—all I wanted was for people to like me. But I had no tools to accomplish that. I was handsome and could speak well so getting dates with girls who didn't know me very well was pretty easy. But maintaining any relationship past a few months was impossible. I simply didn't know the rules and would scare women by either rushing into things or ignoring them completely. Looking back it's perfectly understandable. But at the time it was painful as hell.

In college I got a perfect score on an essay in freshman English. My instructor told me that I was very good and should write more. So I did. I wrote for the school newspaper and rose (in a straight line) to editor in chief. In that job, I wrote and edited proficiently but alienated the entire staff.

I chose advertising as a career because it sounded exciting. The straight line took me not to copy writing, but to being an account executive. Forget for a minute that the job required subtlety, the ability to read between the lines, and an ability to handle people—I thought it was something I could do. Who knew I was walking into the teeth of my weaknesses?

It was about that time when I met Debbie. Again, straight lines. We met, fell in love, got pregnant, and got married. She had no idea what she was getting herself into. After the baby was born, I went through severe mood swings as I was unable to manage how the baby would change my plans. I had anxiety attacks because I couldn't control the baby. But I knew how a father should act. So I became a doting and supporting father, determined not to have an insecure, unpopular, underachieving son like me.

At this point, I was failing at my career, fumbling through my marriage, and feeling my way through fatherhood. I looked at other people and it all seemed so easy for them. For hours at a time I would ponder what was wrong with me. I would pore over self-help tomes, searching for something that would allow me to escape myself. I tried positive thinking, personal power, seven habits, and so on. I had to wait for my son, Jordan, to show me the answer.

Jordan wasn't a typical baby. Transitions made him tantrum out like nothing I had ever seen. And he wouldn't hug; he would make himself rigid and not cling back. It got more peculiar when he got older. He memorized long operettas like *Les Miserables*, and became an expert on Italian opera and the solar system by age two. The tantrums continued, endless and severe. He raged over things like finishing dinner, or leaving the house. He lashed out verbally and physically. We had no idea what was wrong. At age three he would engage adults, but not other kids. When other kids were playing together, Jordan was not. In many ways I saw that Jordan was just like me. That bothered me a lot.

It took a family friend to point out that Jordan might have a learning disability. After weeks of debating the merits and drawbacks of having him evaluated, we did. The news was startling. Pervasive Developmental Disorder—PDD. What the hell is PDD? Autism? He doesn't have autism—he never shuts up. How in the world can he have autism? But that's what the experts said, at least the first experts we saw. Then we saw more experts and they confirmed it. "Yep, he's got it," said our neurologist. "Don't treat the label—work hard to advocate for your son and get him what he needs. He's wonderful. Don't let the schools ruin him."

It was the best advice we were ever given. Debbie and I chose to learn everything we could about autism. We hit the internet, made phone calls, and in the time of one week had accumulated a small mountain of paper to sift through. We dove into the mountain and began to read. We created a pile that did not apply to Jordan—this included most of the documents. But then I came across a pamphlet about Asperger's syndrome. Slowly I read the pamphlet and then scanned the "instant diagnosis" checklist that I had come to regard as psychiatric fast food. But I read it, just looking for something, anything. As I hit each checkpoint I saw my son, but by the third I had forgotten about Jordan. I was seeing myself. I read the pamphlet ten times, read it aloud to Debbie, and then searched for more on the subject. I stayed up most of the night reading and thinking.

After all this time—this was who I was! There is a reason for this! There are other people like this! This is nothing I did, this is not my fault, I am not lazy, or crazy, or wrong—this is the way I came! The only way I can describe this feeling is to picture myself with a two-ton safe on my chest, and to have it finally removed. Almost at once I saw it: "Jordan is who he is, and I am going to help him through every rough spot I went through. I am going to guide him through every painful moment I went through. I am going to ensure he has good self-esteem. I am going to steer him toward his strengths and away from the pitfalls."

In the coming months we began working with Jordan on social skills. We also learned new parenting skills designed to manage transitions and reduce his anxiety. And it worked for me as well. I began taking anti-depressants and the change was immediate and a complete success. No longer was I doing things because there was something wrong with me. I was doing things to adapt to the way I was, to improve my reactions based on what I now knew about myself.

Over the years I began to thrive in a new career, one tailored perfectly to my ability to write and my love of sports. Debbie and I began to understand each other more and our marriage became more stable. And Jordan. Jordan has developed far beyond what we ever could have expected. He has learned social skills academically and has used his incredible ability to collect information to create a "social situations" database inside his mind. He's physically and socially awkward like me, but he gets it more and more each day. He is an incredibly positive young man with great confidence and an infectious personality. We have surrounded him with a collection of teachers, counselors, and friends who support him, teach him, and love him.

We've gotten involved in trying to find a cure for autism. Over the past three years we've chaired events that have raised over half a million dollars. The three of us are known throughout our community as spokespersons for the autism community. Jordan knows about Asperger's. He doesn't like it, but he knows that it's a part of him, and me as well. He's been taught that there's good and bad in everything and to make the best of the skills he does have and the talents he does possess.

He's in third grade now. The teasing and torture that I once received have never touched Jordan. If it has, he has never allowed it to affect him. I still worry about it though. I still see each pitfall that crippled me as a child, and I fear it also finding him.

But a funny thing I have learned: Jordan is not me. He is my son. He will have his own road, his own challenges, and his own destiny. He will need help and I will be there when he does. But I worry a lot less about him now. And I worry about me a lot less as well.

There are many times when Debbie will look at the two men in her life who have autism and shake her head in frustration. She's learning. We all are. I guess that's the best part of everything. After all, why should I be the only one who grows wiser???

Todd J. Schmidt is a New York-born, New Jersey-based writer and filmmaker. He was diagnosed with Asperger's syndrome in 1999 at the age of 32. A graduate of Temple University, he is a founding board member of the Greater Delaware Valley Chapter of the National Alliance for Autism Research: www.autismwalk.org. He and his wife, Debbie, have one son, Jordan, who also deals with Asperger's.

46. The Importance of Parents in the Success of People with Autism

Stephen Shore

After two hours of labor and a slightly faster then average developmental trajectory I was hit with the "autism bomb" at 18 months. I went from being an interactive and talkative toddler to a child who withdrew from the environment, throwing tantrums, losing verbal ability, and engaging in self-abusive behaviors. Being the early 1960s my parents were at a loss for what to do. Because my older brother was already diagnosed with mental retardation, my parents knew that this was not the challenge they faced with

me. However, unlike today, there were no supports such as conferences or books for parents and other family members of children on the autism spectrum. Discussion of autism was limited to "highly qualified" professionals who wrung their proverbial hands in hopelessness about this rare psychiatric disorder which they believed was caused by mother–child relational pathology. Bruno Bettelheim likened the child's existence to that of the extreme environment of a Nazi concentration camp with the mother as oppressor.

It took my parents an entire year to find a place for me to get diagnosed. At two and a half, I was labeled with "atypical development, strong autistic tendencies, and psychotic" and the clinic would not be able to enroll such a "sick" child as an out-patient. My parents were grimly told that for the better of both child and family, institutionalization was strongly recommended. Upon reaching public school age, I could look forward to the custodial class. If I was lucky, there was a slim chance I could reach the educable range of mental retardation.

Refusing to accept such a limited existence for their son, my parents said "no way" and convinced the diagnosing professionals to accept me into their school in a year. It was 1964 and my parents were left with providing what we now call early intervention all on their own. My father was present and involved as much as he could be, however, he spent the days and some nights working. My mother was left home with one typical daughter, and two atypical sons. It was left to her to provide what we would call today a home-based early intervention program emphasizing movement, sensory integration, music, narration, and imitation with no texts or recommendations from doctors to follow.

I was always accepted in my home as a full and complete human being with the realization that there were some challenges to be overcome. My parents accepted all three of us for who we were and left the judging to a higher power. Typically, a parent will try to get an infant to imitate facial expressions and other movements. Facial expressions had no meaning for me so why should I imitate? My mother intuitively realized that she needed to reach *in*. Since my sensory receptors made it difficult for me to make the initial contact, she did the work by imitating *me*.

I would make a sound or initiate a movement and she would follow. Imitating me made me aware of her existing within my sphere of environmental awareness. Most people have an unlimited "zone of intention" (a term used by Arnold Miller and his wife, Eileen Eller-Miller, to describe the amount of distal awareness around a person) which allows them to perceive objects and people at the far end of a room or even the distant clouds and the moon. Those with autism often have a very restricted zone of intention, explaining why a person with autism might not respond to their name, or may seem to ignore a request. That's why I wouldn't hear my mother when she called me in for lunch but suddenly would grab her hand and go into the house with her when she touched my shoulder.

Music was an important part of our lives and continues to be so. There was always a lot of humming, singing, and moving to music. The heavy involvement with music may explain why one of my focuses is teaching people with autism how to play musical instruments. Often I am mistaken for a music therapist and even introduced as such. Whereas practitioners of music therapy use their skills to focus on extra-musical goals such as developing social interaction, communication, body awareness, and other domains of development, my intention is to develop facility on one or more musical instruments. That way, in addition to the therapeutic benefits of music, students are given a productive leisure time choice and a tool for making friends and getting involved in the community. The pleasure I receive from interacting with people on the autism spectrum as I teach them music is a gift from my parents.

By age four, my speech was beginning to return and I began to relate better to my environment. At this point, I was now considered to be neurotic rather than psychotic and was granted admission to the school that initially rejected me. My parents continued to work with me and I saw a psychiatrist until my mid-teen years. Fortunately, the psychiatrist also respected who I was and rather than attempt to change me he helped me make more sense out of the world. My parents also saw to it that I knew exactly why I saw this professional and why things were different for me. They used the word "autism" around the house just like any other word. In doing so, disclosure never became an issue. I've known ever since age five or six that I had autism and that's what led to my differences in school, home, and in the community.

Proper disclosure to the person with autism of their condition is vital to building good self-awareness and esteem leading towards developing skills in appropriate self-advocacy. While it is important for people with autism to maintain our own identities as a culture and way of being, it is also important to learn how to interface with the vast majority of people who are not on the autism spectrum. Having good knowledge of one's strengths and challenges at an early age plants the seeds for developing self-determination as well as building a foundation for learning how to successfully advocate for one's needs in a way that is easy to understand by others. Realizing that my having autism is neither bad nor good but just something to take the positives from is yet another gift I have received from my parents.

I seemed to always have a need to move, climb tall trees, and spin around on lawn toys and otherwise seek activities that provided a lot of sensory input. Today an occupational therapist would diagnose me as being hypo-sensitive in the vestibular and proprioceptive senses. In other words I needed more stimulation by movement and deep pressure than most people to help find myself within the environment. It is often difficult for people on the autism spectrum to accurately determine where our body ends and the environment begins. As a result we may fuse with certain aspects of the environment and assume we are attached to them. For example, in elementary school a whistle would blow every Friday at noon. One day, I fused with that sound, howling like a dog, and only became aware of this when I heard the rest of the class and the teacher laughing. This fusion with the environment causes me to imitate people's vocal patterns and movements for long periods of time before I realize it. Often I find myself fusing to other people's emotions. My parents taught me that "people are not mind readers" and that if you have a feeling you need to state it. As a result, whenever I have an emotion that seems out of context with the environment I have to look around and verbalize it to another person. For example, if I am feeling unusually anxious I might ask my wife if *she* is having a lot of anxiety about something. Often she will say she is and we'll talk about it. I then realize that this emotion is not coming from me and I am now free to empathize with her and provide the support she needs. The only difference between my having empathy and a person not on the autism spectrum is that I have to access it cognitively whereas most other people empathize automatically.

I have much to be thankful to my parents for. They have and continue to provide a good role model for how to process my environment. Being able to accept, appreciate, and understand myself, as well as using music to interact with and help people on the autism spectrum, and being able to empathize with others as needed are just a few of the lifelong gifts my parents have given to me that have helped me lead a fulfilling and productive life.

Diagnosed with "Atypical Development with strong autistic tendencies," Stephen Shore was initially recommended for institutionalization. Nonverbal until four, he is now completing his doctoral degree in special education at Boston University. In addition to working with children and talking about life on the autism spectrum, Stephen presents and consults internationally on adult issues pertinent to education, relationships, employment, advocacy, and disclosure as discussed in his book *Beyond the Wall: Personal Experiences with Autism and Asperger Syndrome*, the recently released *Ask and Tell: Self-advocacy and Disclosure for People on the Autism Spectrum*, and numerous other writings. A board member of the Autism Society of America, Stephen serves as board president of the Asperger's Association of New England as well as for the Board of Directors for Unlocking Autism, the Autism Services Association of Massachusetts, and other programs.

47. Culture, Conditions, and Personhood: A Response to the Cure Debate on Autism

Donna Williams

I had a letter from a fellow Autie Spectrum person writing to the United Nations in the pursuit of having those with Autism Spectrum Conditions recognized as a social minority whose rights need to be protected.

I describe these people as "culturalists" meaning they tend to see Autism Spectrum Conditions as a shared culture, the largest disability of which is the inability of non-autistic culture to accommodate their differences in respectful, empowering, and constructive ways.

The "culturalists" have widely attacked pressure groups which seek to "cure" or "eradicate" Autism Spectrum Conditions, particularly through genetic screening and engineering which they see as a form of eugenics (an immoral social quest for "purity").

The "culturalists" rightly argue that many people on the autism spectrum have one or more parents with features of an Autism Spectrum Condition and that often the condition is at least partially genetic but that this does not necessarily make it an illness.

On the other side, those who seek a "cure" or eradication of autism from the planet are often traumatized by feeling deeply for the frustration and distress of some of the most severely affected individuals diagnosed with autism, some of whom actually suffer from (sometimes treatable) severe medical conditions including gut and immune disorders and/or mood, anxiety, and compulsive disorders to such severe degrees that these severely limit the expression, comfort, and capacity of those individuals.

I have been close to people in both groups and know that not all of the distresses, frustrations, or anguish of those diagnosed with autism come down to society not understanding or accommodating them. Many of those most severely affected by autism are understood and respected but suffer, nevertheless, from (often untreated) co-morbid medical conditions which can severely exacerbate the extremity of their autism. By contrast, I have met many people for whom an Autism Spectrum Condition has no associated health issues not directly attributable to the stress of being incompatible with non-autistic multi-track social systems.

I believe that there is a middle ground between the "culturalists" and the "cure seekers" in which both perspectives can be recognized and respected. Personally, I myself struggle with being mono-tracked in a multi-track world and having a solitary, idiosyncratic, and artistic personality. This combination of traits predisposes me to fixation on my own space, my own world, and my own creativity in a world that is usually more externally oriented toward socializing and inter-verbal blah. Working on my personal weaknesses and improving my processing through nutritional tracks, tinted lenses, gestural signing, and the use of objects as communication tools, and insistence on a more indirectly confrontational style of interaction and communication has helped me enormously. Yet I'd not be able to cope or relax into my "cultural differences" had I not also sought and maintained treatment for gut/immune, mood, anxiety, and compulsive disorders which have at times been so severe and distressing as to pose very real threats to my health and life. So, for me, treatment has some very real validity, as much as empowerment, respect, and accommodating diversity does.

I'd not be who I am without all that I am and have been. But sometimes we have things in such abundance and degree that it is more than our body, mind, or emotions can stand. I support anyone in this situation who chooses treatment over giving up and giving in and those who support them in that choice, either before or after they have the ability to conceive, express, or act on those choices themselves.

Thus, in reply to that letter, I asserted that I totally agree with the need for those with an Autism Spectrum Condition (ASC not ASD) to be recognized as a minority whose rights and needs need to be acknowledged and respected by the majority. But on the basis that they have a shared information processing difference to the majority of the population; they are usually receptively mono-tracked information processors in a world of majority multi-track processors who often fail to provide forms of education, communication, social activities/networks, occupation, and employment most appropriate to this form of information processing.

Those with ASCs also often share a collective of personality traits more common among minority populations than those of the majority of the population including: (1) solitary, sensitive, idiosyncratic, artistic personality traits and (2) more diverse sexual orientation. The sexual orientation of those in this group is of a different ratio to the general population with a far higher proportion of bisexual, homosexual, transgender, and asexual people than in the majority population.

This collection of traits combines in most cases to produce a distinct set of ways of relating, communicating, thinking, and behaving that are far more shared within this population than in the majority population. It is these shared ways of relating, communicating, thinking, and behaving that are currently the basis of subtle and overt social discrimination on a wide variety of levels. Furthermore a fair proportion of those with ASCs often have a higher level of sometimes disabling co-morbid treatable medical conditions such as gut and immune dysfunctions, mood, anxiety, and compulsive disorders such as Obsessive Compulsive Disorder (OCD) and Tourette's. Whilst these impact and increase the degree of one's "autism," these deserve treatment as much as any medical condition when at a level that disables the individual and should not be confused with the ASC itself.

Thus, with all of these issues in mind, I propose that the middle ground between "culturalists" and "cure seekers" can begin to be defined and understood.

Donna Williams was thought to be deaf, psychotic, and emotionally disturbed, and was finally diagnosed with autism in adulthood. She became an international best-selling author with eight published books in the field of developmental "disabilities," including her autobiography, *Nobody Nowhere*. She has written three sequels to this book as well as four textbooks and a collection of poetry. Donna has been the subject of three international television documentaries and is a specialized autism consultant to professionals, families, and people who are on the autism spectrum. In addition to being a qualified teacher and sociologist, Donna is also known as a composer, sculptor, and painter. To those who know her personally, she is, most importantly, simply Donna. After 13 years in the UK, she is now back in her homeland of Australia where she lives with her husband, Chris. Visit her on the web at www.donnawilliams.net.

Part 5: Working on the Spectrum

What children and families need from the professional community is hope and help which includes empathy for our situation and good services for our children. Without these vital ingredients, resentment and anger fester. It is rare to meet a parent who doesn't have a horror story or two about a doctor or the educational system. On the other hand, professionals who are compassionate and hopeful and who take a special interest in the family while providing help are kindly remembered and effusively praised.

This section features contributions from professionals, some of whom are also parents of children on the spectrum, who have expressed vulnerability in their essays. Clearly they share heartbreak and triumph with children and families. Not all professionals have these qualities, but many do. We counsel people to look for these traits in the professionals they choose for guidance. Of course, professionals do not have the same kind of responsibility as parents or the same emotional investment. On the other hand, their acceptance and devotion to children can be an essential inspiration.

The outcomes are best when parents and professionals work as partners with mutual respect and shared decision-making power. Parents, by virtue of their bond with their child, are true authorities in their own right, with information to contribute that no one else has access to. Professionals, on the other hand, through training and experience can offer expertise and a broad perspective that parents alone don't have. Each has only partial knowledge with neither having complete expertise.

We chose these essays as models because of how these practitioners relate to the issues and therefore to children and families. Confidence in the treatment relationship and in the professionals with whom one works is critically important. The input of good professionals transcends philosophy and methodology. Having the right professional team working together for a given family and child can be critical in offering the guidance and encouragement needed to navigate the many and complex issues along the spectrum.

48. A Sound from Kuwait

Samira Al-Saad

When I graduated from high school, I chose geology as my major at Kuwait University. My family wondered why I chose such a major and questioned my ability to work in harsh conditions in the desert of Kuwait. I took the challenge and graduated with honour.

After graduation I got married and dedicated myself to my family and children. In time I had three children. The youngest, Fatima, was crying most of the time, talking to dolls and not to us, and holding our hand to the refrigerator when she needed something. The usual tour with doctors to find out the reason for such disruptive behaviour led to more confusion and different diagnoses. Some doctors said that she might have hearing problems; others diagnosed her as mentally retarded and suggested institutionalizing her in appropriate institutions.

After a lot of frustration during which the suffering of our daughter seemed to intensify, we decided to seek professional advice in the US. It was in 1984 when we first heard the term "autism" from a child specialist in UCLA (University of California, Los Angeles) Hospital. We were devastated to learn that Fatima, our daughter, would not become a normal child. I recall that day we went home crying and frustrated about our daughter's future and our own.

The shock motivated me to read more about autism and to seek the help of professionals in Kuwait. Unfortunately we found that professional support and awareness surrounding autism was seriously lacking in our country.

One night, my husband came to me and said "That's it. If the assistance for Fatima and us is in another country, we will move there." This brought us to another challenge which was moving to the US to obtain proper assistance for our daughter. Since my husband held the position of undersecretary, he needed to get permission from the ruler of Kuwait. We all remember the wise words of our ruler: "I feel sorry that my country does not have these facilities and services, but try to make it your mission to create them when you return."

To pursue such a vision, my husband and I took Fatima and our youngest daughter to the United States. We left our two older children, who were nine and ten at that time, in Kuwait with my mother. I first attended a master's program in special education at Lesley College in Boston. Further, I did practical training in specialized schools including the famous Higashi School of Japan, also in Boston. Such experience later helped me in establishing a preliminary educational program for autism in my home.

Another challenge in the way was the station of my husband in Saudi Arabia working in a senior position in a leading international institution. We had moved back to Kuwait after my education and my husband was assigned as Vice President for Development in the Islamic Bank in Saudi Arabia. We could not move with him because I had to continue the class that I had opened in our home for Fatima and three other children with autism. We went to visit him a few months after he began his station on July 25, 1990 and the invasion of Kuwait by Iraq occurred eight days later, on August 2. Our family then stayed together in Saudi Arabia. I returned to Kuwait briefly immediately following the liberation but returned to Saudi Arabia and remained there with my family for four years.

While still in Saudi Arabia, I finished and released my first book on autism in Arabic. This book received wide interest in the region since many families were suffering with their children who had autism. Each positive move led to another one. I started a class in my home in Jeddah, Saudi Arabia, called "Friends' class" which was shifted to Al-Faisalyah Women Society, one of the leading non-government organizations (NGOs) in Jeddah, with the cooperation of its Head, Princess Fahda Bint-Soud. This marked the beginning of establishing the Jeddah Autism Center in Saudi Arabia. This was a success story that encouraged others to follow suit.

Before leaving Saudi Arabia I was contacted by the Kuwait Awqaf Public Foundation to start a school for children with autism. I accepted this new challenge without any hesitation. After returning to Kuwait I started the Center with six children and I trained ten teachers to take care of them. The teaching staff was first selected after a thorough estimation of commitment, patience, and working talent, and then given special training to understand children with autism. Currently, the Center is enrolled with 100 children and 50 teaching staff, and another 250 children benefit from facilities that the Center provides. Different services are provided throughout the year such as Morning Program, Evening Program, Thursday Club, Summer Camp, Spring Camp, Swimming Club, Youth House Program, and so on. Thus, I established an integrated educational program that included among other things a diagnosis unit, a research centre, and a training unit.

I eventually completed my Ph.D. in special needs from the University of Leicester, UK. I continued to work to promote understanding and help to children and families dealing with autism.

In the year 2000, an occupational program for people with special needs was started at our Center with the aim of investing the energy and abilities of those special people to find a suitable job and secure a better life. We launched this project by employing one young man with autism and another young lady with Down syndrome.

To achieve our goal of spreading autism awareness throughout the world, we launched different ventures. International experts in the field of special needs were invited to Kuwait to give lectures, run workshops, impart training, and speak at conferences to help and train parents and professionals. Two International Conferences for Autism were successfully organized and held in Kuwait, in 2000 and 2003.

Various research projects are under way at Kuwait University in cooperation with Harvard University in the US. The Center has a special Unit for Evaluation and Diagnosis devoted to fulfilling the needs of families and studying the main problems and difficulties with which their loveable children with autism suffer. The academic and psychological evaluations are done at the Center but the medical tests are completed with the cooperation of genetic centers.

A bimonthly newsletter in Arabic called *Silent Scream* is issued by the Center, with the purpose of enhancing autism awareness. In addition, more than 60 publications have been circulated. Since the resources for autism in the Arabic language are scarce we have translated some books, videos, and audiotapes on autism from other languages into Arabic and still continue to do so. To help spread awareness of autism among children we also write and translate children's stories.

To pull our resources together in our region, an autism union for the Gulf has been established. With the Gulf Autism Union (GAU) we are aiming to unify services, eliminate redundancy, and spread autism awareness. This Union is also doing a survey on people with autism, to offer better services to them. The Kuwait Center for Autism has become a scientific reference for all researchers, specialists, and students of institutes or universities on different sides of the Arab World, receiving great acceptance for its existence and mission.

Ours has been a long and often difficult journey, but one worth taking, which started with the cry of our daughter, Fatima, and led to the establishment of a pioneer center for autism in our region. Fatima has now joined the Youth Club Program at our Center where she is learning to be more independent in her life which is helping to make her more confident and to trust in her own abilities. We hope and expect that this will lead her to a happier life.

Samira Al-Saad, Ph.D. is the Founder and Director of the Kuwait Center for Autism in Al-Rawda, Kuwait. Dr Al-Saad received her master's degree from Lesley College in Boston and her doctorate in Special Needs from the University of Leicester, in the UK. She lives with her husband and daughter, Fatima, in Kuwait and devotes her time to helping advance autism awareness in her region and throughout the Arab World. The website for the Kuwait Center for Autism can be found at www.q8autism.com.

49. Learning from Oliver

Margaret Anderson

At our first meeting, Oliver was oblivious to having a stranger in his house and avoided all attempts from me to make any kind of contact. He was a passive little chap of two years old, who clung onto his Thomas trains (one in each hand) and moved around the furniture slowly. He leant on the sofa and chair cushions one at a time and then wandered from the room.

Although not much more than a baby, Oliver's autism was obvious. He had developed well until 16 months and then began to lose skills—the familiar story. His parents acted very quickly to put an at-home education system in place and Oliver began intensive intervention three months after diagnosis. I was supervising Oliver's program and was excited at the prospect of beginning with so young a child and the enormous potential for learning and growth before us.

Oliver is now seven years old and he has changed so much and gained so many skills over the last five years. Oliver is a seriously cool child—he is generally calm and affable, although, like all other children, he does get cross at life's perceived injustices (such as having to do something someone else wants him to do rather than hang out in the garden or watch a video). He has a good communication system and can express his needs and wants. His self-care skills are fairly good, although washing and choosing clothes hold about as much interest for him as these activities do for most seven-year-old boys. He has broad general knowledge. He has spent the early years of his statutory education alongside his peers in regular school, but the literacy demands of the curriculum have become rather too high. He is about to transfer to a specialist unit, where the skills and talents he has can be nurtured in a positive environment.

What I learned from Oliver is about respect. Oliver is one of three brothers and (when we started work) lived in a street with lots of other children. I was very keen to work hard on the socialization aspect of Oliver's program and much effort was spent in teaching him play skills that he could use with the other children. Whilst the group of children was very happy to have Oliver around, he did not appear keen to join in and so during outdoor play, one of Oliver's tutors would be part of the group to facilitate interaction between Oliver and the other children where necessary. Intensive prompting was needed to encourage Oliver to initiate an interaction and, whilst he was always willing to do as asked, he did not generalize this behaviour or display any desire to engage others.

In order to further promote his opportunities for interaction, Oliver's parents registered him at a local nursery for a few sessions a week. This nursery provided an amazing environment for Oliver: the staff was very positive about having Oliver as part of the nursery community. They spent their lunch breaks in education sessions and meetings to learn more about autism and about Oliver's particular needs; they amended routines and practices within the nursery to give Oliver good learning opportunities; they facilitated small group work for Oliver and a few peers in order to focus on his areas of need; they were very open to suggestions and new ideas from all sources in order to help Oliver. In short, this was an ideal environment for Oliver to learn to be with and enjoy other children.

However, at the same time as Oliver was racing away in other areas of the curriculum, he continued to show no real enthusiasm for the other children. If they approached him and asked or told him to do something, he would either comply or ignore them. Despite his eye contact with known adults being good by this stage, he did not look at the other children directly and did not approach them for interaction. Again, the full panoply of techniques was used in order to interest Oliver in the other children. Games he enjoyed were set up so that he needed another child to play them. The see-saw was a favorite of Oliver's for some time, which provided a real need for a partner. In less preferred activities, the other children would share a treat with Oliver at the end of the game. The nursery staff and Oliver's tutors worked endlessly in engineering and following through on social situations and exchanges. Oliver remained unimpressed.

By the time Oliver transferred to statutory education, he was an established part of the peer group. The other children knew him and liked him. Oliver, however, continued to be indifferent to them and they accepted this. The emerging pattern seemed to be that Oliver chose to play alone and the other children respected his choice. Over the course of the day, his peers would try to interact with him in class. They worked as part of a group, or in play, encouraging Oliver to join in, which he invariably ignored—and a status quo emerged with which Oliver was comfortable.

He was continuing to learn at home, and was gaining further communication, play, and social skills. Through the first year or so of Oliver's schooling, I continued to program social interaction skills and to use every opportunity to promote interaction with his peers. However, it slowly became apparent to me that the whole 'socialization' agenda was being driven by my need, not Oliver's. At home, Oliver was happy to be with his family, enjoyed being with and near his brothers, and relished family activities. When his brothers had friends around, Oliver would always be near the other children, but not with them and attempts to integrate him into the group were not successful as Oliver just did not want this kind of contact.

In all the time I worked with Oliver I saw him approach another child for interaction only once. At this time, Oliver had been introduced to signing, rather than using Picture Exchange Communication System (PECS) as he had previously. He loved signing, and it opened a whole realm of communication to him. When looking in books, if Oliver saw something he did not know the sign for, he would ask, and, in school one day, he approached a peer to ask the sign for something. He did not repeat this.

So, what I have learned from Oliver is to respect his choices. Whilst I think that providing him with the skills he needs to interact with other children is the right approach, I have had to recognize that this is not something that he chooses to do just now. Taking Oliver to appropriate social gatherings and continuing to provide opportunities for interaction forms an important part of his 'learning week' and will do so in the future. We need to be providing real choices for Oliver—giving him the skills to choose to socialize when and if he wants to. Denying him the choice by failing to teach skills and provide opportunities for socialization would be neglectful, but trying to force a social agenda that is 'ours' rather than 'his' is not helpful, may be counter-productive, and certainly feels disrespectful. I think Oliver knows what he likes and is comfortable with and I have (at last, he might think) learned to listen to him.

Margaret Anderson, Ph.D. has worked with children and adults with learning disabilities in the UK for the last 25 years. She has published on Autism Spectrum Disorder (ASD) and has worked as part of a UK-wide autism organization for the past five years. She is currently a lecturer in the area of learning disability with a specialism in autism, and maintains a clinical practice with children on the spectrum. Dr Anderson's current research interests are in the field of consciousness and ASD and the inclusion of children with ASD in mainstream education. She lives on the East Anglian coast in southern England with her daughter and is a keen distance runner and gardener.

50. Closet Case: Finding the Way Out

Cindy N. Ariel

I can no longer imagine sitting on the shelf in a closet surrounded by a few stuffed animals and other inanimate objects for hours on end. Yet this is how I chose to spend a portion of my time as a child and adolescent. Even when I grew up and moved out on my own, I initially kept the closets clear just in case. I never did return to one though and after completing college, years of therapy, becoming a psychologist, and having children of my own, it would never occur to me to return to my shelf.

Sometimes parents of children with autism who come for help want to know if I am, myself, the biological parent of a child with autism. I am not. How can I understand them, they wonder, often out loud. While I have known and worked with many children and families touched by autism and am also the stepparent of a child with autism, these are not qualifications for the work I do. Though it is a popular belief that for one to understand and be helpful to another they should experience the same experience or trauma, this is not necessarily true. Not everyone has the kind of empathy needed in this kind of work, and sometimes we are handicapped by our experiences when they interfere with our ability to listen and respond objectively.

Some of my childhood issues included extreme shyness with tactile and auditory hypersensitivity. Family members let me know that I wasn't "bubbly enough." I was slow to articulate my thoughts. I was told in many ways, including quite directly, that I was a great disappointment—I wasn't like my female cousins; I wasn't like the daughters of family friends; I wasn't even like many of my own friends. I always did have friends and enjoyed typical activities, yet my sensitivities were hard for some adults to understand, and sometimes they would ask me why, why couldn't I be more like others? More outgoing, friendlier, bubblier?

Back then, many of my relatives and others around me seemed loud and hard to understand. Sometimes when we went to visit relatives I would stay in the car. I couldn't face the light and sound show. Other times, I'd come in, but would try to find a quiet place like the darkened living room and hope that nobody walked in. Grown-ups would encourage me to go play. I'd go to where the children were and wouldn't always know how to join in, so I'd go back to sit with grown-ups who'd admonish me for being rude to other children. So then I'd go hide—perhaps in the hallway behind a door, maybe on a stairwell.

Parties could be enjoyable, yet the combination of lights, touch, and sound contributed to my need to retreat at some time during many events for a little while, perhaps under a table, perhaps just to my room if we were in my home. Some people back then tried to reach me more than others. I appreciated the few special people who would quietly visit me in my room on the nights when I feigned sick so that I wouldn't have to go downstairs to the party. When I did join the parties, I was often very quiet. I had fun, though the social expectations of others made me uncomfortable at times. I suppose I didn't look like I was having fun; my quietness was misunderstood.

That was classic me. I loved people and always thought that if only they knew me, they would totally love me too. Of course, now I know that they probably did love me—many of them anyway—but didn't know how to reach me as I did not know how to reach them. Fortunately, I have become much more adept at relating to people and reaching out to others. It still helps when others come part of the way.

It has been mostly true, that when people get to know me, they find me likeable. But getting to know me isn't always easy and some people are put off by the effort. People are more readily drawn to those who are socially outgoing and less quiet. In college, I sometimes made friends simply by being at the top of a class. Though my lack of participation could initially be mistaken for shallowness, ignorance, or apathy, as soon as the first test or paper came back, suddenly other students wanted to be in my group. When an instructor would single me out for recognition, my passions and intelligence would be revealed and others sometimes gravitated to me for that. As always, the way to reveal the secret of my love, intelligence, and good humor, was to come and find me.

I am very fortunate to have had the neurology to overcome many of my obstacles by being motivated and finding meaning. You have to jump through a lot of hoops to get through college and become a psychologist. Maybe I wouldn't have to be bubbly, but I would have to do oral presentations (ugh), go on interviews, talk to authority figures, and even get the nerve to ask one for a recommendation or to supervise me. I would do it all, I decided. And thank goodness that I was able to do it all, even if it was excruciating at times. I remember driving to my Ph.D. oral exams belting out "Let There Be Peace on Earth" in my car. I was searching (as loudly as possible) for some peace within me to help me to get through that one defining morning.

Through the years, I have worked with people with all kinds of disabilities as well as "typical" folks in all walks of life. It was no coincidence that my first job, over 25 years ago, included working with people on the autism spectrum and that I ended up marrying someone with a son who has classic autism. Gradually, I came down from my shelf and out into the world to learn how to heal myself and others. Through my journey, I found that the gamut of human emotional experience can be found in all of us. I have worked with individuals, groups, and couples regarding many issues including depression, anxiety, sexuality, and post-traumatic stress. I can also write a true story about the personal struggles I have experienced that have led me through many such issues. Who among us has never experienced any form of trauma, fear, illness, grief, anxiety, depression, stress, anger, rage, relationship failure? It's hard to live this life without some such experiences as well as at least periods of feeling the emotionally high experiences of love, happiness, success, calm, inner peace. Somewhere inside ourselves, if we look deeply enough, we can find the empathy to relate to others on the human spectrum.

People who have shared the same experience as one another, such as other parents of children with autism, can often validate and guide each other through that experience. They can be an invaluable resource to each other in many ways. There is no substitute for the parent network for support and information regarding our family lives and our children. Being a parent, however, or even the parent of a child with autism does not automatically result in someone who can objectively help another to cope and to heal. Sharing the same experience or trauma is not necessarily helpful for helping others. Besides, no two people can possibly experience even the same event in the exact same way. In our lives, suffering is the shared experience. And compassion is the bridge from one person to another.

At difficult times in our lives, it helps to have people who care for us, have empathy for our situation, and who can help us organize our thinking and guide us through our dark days until we can find our own light. This has certainly been true for me and I see it making a difference through the eyes of others as well. Those who can help light the way for others are those people who know how to truly listen to each unique story and help guide another in her or his personal journey through it. The information is there inside all of us and those with the gift of accessing and using their deepest empathy to relate to others on the human spectrum have the ultimate ability to be effective healers. In the presence of such individuals you can feel a caring soul reaching out to yours. I look for these individuals, and I recommend for others to look for them as well. They are there for you and your children; and you will know it.

51. The Wizard of Echolalia

Gerard Costa

Catherine was a remarkable five-year-old girl whose diagnosis of Pervasive Developmental Disorder might obscure her quiet fascination with social play. Her mother, Joyce, seemed to have unbounded energy as she created art and educational materials to help Catherine become more socially engaging and to support her capacity to be included fully in her kindergarten class. Joyce was intense in her passion not to let up and like many parents of children with developmental difficulties, worked as if any moment not spent in helping her daughter's development was a moment wasted. She also carried the scars of such passion—an exhaustion that she fought with activity and an obsession that was rewarded with wonderful progress in Catherine.

I made weekly home visits, and focused on promoting engagement and social reciprocity with Catherine, following a model at the time known as Floortime, developed by Dr Stanley Greenspan and his colleagues, and now more properly described as the Developmental, Individual-difference, Relationship-based (DIR) model. During each session, I would alternate between intense play with Catherine, who could be quite dramatic, and developmental guidance with her mother. Joyce would be prepared for my visits, as was Catherine, who immediately assembled our play materials for the day—her agenda—on my arrival. In addition to Joyce's love for and commitment to Catherine, she was a fierce organizer and was the first to acknowledge that she kept a fastidious home. Catherine was already aware of the notion that clean-up followed play and that progress was no excuse for chaos. Well, herein lay the rub!

I had worked with Catherine and her family for over one year, mostly in home-based play sessions, and a familiar theme that emerged in Catherine's play was a joint re-creation of scenes from *The Wizard of Oz*. Catherine knew all of the characters and her play could be rather rigid involving almost precise re-enactments of scenes with almost identical scripting which she would direct. Much of my work involved gently, then more directly and persistently, challenging these rigid scripts so that she and I could become more spontaneous in our reciprocal interactions and less rigid in the drama—so that play was an emergent creation between us—always capable of something new each and every time.

One day as I arrived, Catherine grabbed a small play basket (for her dog Toto) and she pretended to be Dorothy. I, it turned out under the clever casting scheme of this impish director, was assigned the role of the Cowardly Lion, and I often stayed to script (at least initially) and repeated with all proper inflections, "I do believe in spooks, I do believe in spooks, I do, I do, I do, I do, I do believe in spooks!" Catherine would revel in the play and of course when the precise scene she expected to create was completed, we would sometimes repeat the scene, or move on to another activity that she (then eventually I) would choose.

Catherine's frequent repetition of words and phrases is quite common in children with language processing difficulties. Referred to as immediate (when it occurs right after the word or phrase has been heard) or delayed (when repeated at a later time as Catherine did in her play) echolalia, I have come to regard this practice not as a problem but as a way children struggle to adapt and overcome processing problems. By repeating the words or phrase (like an echo), a child may hold on to the language and underlying idea for a while, allowing further processing and understanding. This is much the same way we might repeat a telephone number until we dial it. Catherine also showed me that sometimes repeating just the right words or phrase can be a way of letting me and others know exactly how she feels!

On this particular day, it seemed that Catherine and I made a real mess of the large play area in the living room. As the session was ending, I prepared Catherine for the end by announcing that we had ten minutes remaining. Joyce, the ever dutiful and observing mother also characteristically told Catherine that this meant that she had to clean up the area. Now here was the moment when Catherine became the *Wizard of Echolalia*! Catherine looked down, began to pick up her toys and in a soft voice, as if to herself, grumbled, "Wicked Witch of the West." I was speechless! One might argue that since Catherine was often echolalic, this utterance might just be a random repetition of a familiar phrase from the movie. But this seemed much too focused to me and I offered Joyce an interpretation. I thought that Catherine was enjoying our play today and when clean-up time came, signaling the end of our session, she was rightly angry and saddened but had not yet found the words or social resources to say so. She could however tap into an available affective domain from our recent play that matched the affect she had when clean-up time was imposed on her—anger and sadness—and who better represented the source of these feelings than the nasty Wicked Witch of the West? Catherine did not repeat a meaningless, random utterance. She was clear in her implication—and much more purposeful than we might have given her credit for.

Her mother took great pleasure in this insight and our work with Catherine often entailed a continuing effort to ensure that whenever Catherine made an echolalic statement (as she did when she uttered the "Wicked Witch" comment), her mother and all others would let Catherine know that they understood (if they did) what she was communicating, so that private associations and meanings could become shared affective experiences. When Joyce and I spoke about Catherine's likely feelings of anger and sadness at clean-up time, Catherine could only smile. Ah, to be understood!

It has been nearly ten years since Catherine was Dorothy and I was the Cowardly Lion, and eight years since my formal work with the family ended. I have often reflected on my time with Catherine and her family, and I have realized that they gave me much more than I gave them. Joyce taught me that a mother's conviction and commitment can often prove the expert predictions wrong. Catherine taught me that we each have a way of connecting, and that for those who come to relationships with some difficulties we must begin on their terms and turf. Lastly, I have learned that pathologizing is for the birds! We must see problems and "symptoms" as messages that are telling us about unmet needs and sensitivities, that each child must find a way to connect, and that rarely are behavior and language meaningless.

While I would suspect that Catherine will always have her unique way of responding to people and experiences these must be seen as part of the fabric that make each of us so unique. Every Christmas, the family has sent me a card letting me know how Catherine is doing. Until last year, when Catherine herself wrote me a letter to tell me she remembered playing with me—especially with the trains at Christmas time. She is fully included in school and was top student in her eighth grade class.

But while I do remember the play with trains, what I remember most is the time that Catherine became the Wizard of Echolalia.

Gerard Costa received his Ph.D. from Temple University and received specialized training in infant mental health. He is the founding director of the YCS Institute for Infant and Preschool Mental Health, a clinical service and research program concerned with optimal child development, birth to six years. He is a Clinical Assistant Professor in the Department of Psychiatry at the University of Medicine and Dentistry of New Jersey (UMDNJ) and is the pro-tem Chair of the newly forming NJ Chapter of ICDL (Interdisciplinary Council on Developmental and Learning Disorders). Dr Costa is also part of a national consultation team with the Early Head Start National Resource Center (EHS-NRC) of Zero to Three. He serves on the adjunct faculties of Fairleigh Dickinson, Rutgers, and Seton Hall Universities.

Dr Costa has a special interest in relationship-based approaches to Autism Spectrum Disorders. He has practiced as a psychotherapist for over 22 years, and is a licensed psychologist residing in Bergen County, New Jersey, where he has a small private practice specializing in program trainings and consultations.

52. Two Autistic Children— A World of Difference

Pim Donkersloot (translated by Jill Adler-Donkersloot)

A little over four years ago it felt as if the ground beneath our feet had suddenly given way. Since then, we have regained our footing little by little, bit by bit. Our growing fear that there was something wrong with our daughter Julia, who at two years old seemed to be withdrawing more and more into her own world, and avoiding contact with the other children at daycare, was confirmed by a child psychologist. Her findings were damning: our daughter had a Pervasive Developmental Disorder (PDD).

Julia is overwhelmed by the stimuli with which she is constantly bombarded, and which she is unable to regulate, or process. She has difficulty communicating and interacting. Imagine our distress as parents as we looked helplessly on while our little toddler, our beautiful daughter, slipped away into another world, a place where she could feel safe, but which shut her off from us and our world. I knew this feeling all too well.

Johan

Twenty-four years ago my son, Johan, was born. He was an unusually beautiful child. During his baby and toddler years he seemed to be developing normally, except for a deep fear of certain noises (particularly motors and motorcycles), which didn't seem to be cause for concern. But when at the age of 18 months Johan started to withdraw, the alarm began to sound. His twinkling eyes and inviting face were at odds with his increasingly bizarre behavior. When test results conducted by the Emma Children's Hospital in Amsterdam confirmed no physical abnormalities, my professional expertise (at the time, I was completing my doctorate in child psychology) led me to suspect that Johan had a developmental disorder.

This began what was to become a long and troubled journey of visits to child psychologists and psychiatrists and other specialists. To put it mildly, we did not get much out of all the advice we received. Fortunately the understanding and treatment of autism has improved dramatically since the 1980s, but back then there was not much in the way of a road map to guide us. When Johan was ten, we decided to put him in residential care. We did this to ensure that his little brother Erik would have a chance to grow up in a less stressful setting, and to give Johan a chance to develop in an environment that suited his needs and encouraged his abilities.

It's hard to imagine how difficult it is to have a child that withdraws when you want to hug him, and only allows contact on his terms; to have a child with whom you can't exchange a single word—not then and not ever—because he can't speak and never will. To have a child who rocks back and forth for a half hour with an empty box in his hands, while his toys remain untouched. As a parent, it cuts to the core of your being. But that was then.

Johan is now a young man. He is a cheerful soul who to my great relief is in his element in Bronlaak, a residential home in the south of Holland for adults with disabilities. He visits his mother and stepfather every other weekend and during vacations, and I spend time with him as much as possible on outings in the surroundings where he lives. He has learned to use a wheelbarrow and can sit on a horse while it is led around a ring. But he still has severe autism and experiences the world around him as chaotic.

Johan is like a bee that goes from flower to flower in search of honey. His attention for people in particular lasts no more than a few seconds. He is like a television which can potentially receive 50 stations but because of a faulty antenna receives all the stations with heavy distortion. Thankfully knowledge about his differences, not to mention Johan himself, has helped us to learn throughout the years to separate our drama from his. We keep looking at the world with optimism and a half smile. And I believe that Johan does too, in his own, inimitable way.

Julia

Julia's story is a very different one. There is no need to describe here her differences from a to z. This has already been done by the psychologists, psychiatrists, neurologists, speech pathologists, and floor-time therapists who have examined and/or worked with her. Julia has also been evaluated by the world-renowned child psychiatrist Stanley Greenspan in Washington, D.C. It is clear that Julia has a Pervasive Developmental Disorder, which manifests itself, among other things, in problems with social interaction, communication, and imagination. She falls under the classification PDD-NOS (Pervasive Developmental Disorder – Not Otherwise Specified).

The two consultations we had with Dr Greenspan (co-author of, among others, the groundbreaking book, *The Child with Special Needs*) helped us to better understand our daughter's challenges and showed us how we could turn stumbling blocks into stepping stones. Dr Greenspan told us to put all of the diagnoses on the shelf for a year because it was impossible to predict the limits of her potential. The most important thing to do, he advised, was to get Julia to relate. The central goal was to get her to communicate, because he believes that when there is a connection to another, there is no room for isolation and self-absorption. Dr Greenspan taught us that we as parents bore the greatest responsibility for Julia's development, not therapists or teachers; that *variation* is the operative word, not *repetition*; that all behavior, including avoidance, is "part of the game" and doesn't amount to a personal rejection; that each child needs a unique and tailor-made approach; and that it is critically important to understand the ways in which your child processes sensory input.

It has taken an enormous amount of time and effort to build a good, strong, cooperative support team for Julia. In five years' time we probably won't remember all the efforts we made, but we will never forget what these professionals have done for Julia and for us. The team, which has included a family therapist, a child psychologist, a sensory integration therapist, a play therapist, a speech-language therapist, and a music therapist, all work closely along the lines articulated and taught to us by Stanley Greenspan and Serena Wieder. We have also set up The ChildCenter, which provides access to a multi-disciplinary team that shares a common belief: that as a child (with special needs) develops, everything he or she does or thinks is emotion-based. The ChildCenter provides family therapy, sensory integration therapy, play therapy, music therapy, speech-language therapy, and assessments.

Julia reacted positively to her overfull agenda of therapy, which during most of her waking hours was filled with Floortime (where the adult follows the child's lead and tries with affection, positive obstruction, and drama to create circles of interaction with the child), three days at a special needs daycare facility, music therapy, speech, and sensory integration therapy. Because she was so young, and her system was still being hard-wired, we put all of our energy into getting her circuits going and trying to connect her to our world. We limited television and computer time, because it was an easy way to avoid contact with people. We pushed for interaction, interaction, and more interaction, with adults and increasingly with children her own age. Her and our intensive program, which required major adjustments at home, has worked. We believe in her and respect her and let her know it in every possible way. Two steps forward, one step back, slowly but surely, we navigate the road ahead together.

The Julia of today is a different child than she was when she was diagnosed four years ago. The withdrawn, defensive toddler has blossomed into a joyful little girl who is growing increasingly self-confident, discovering her musical talents, venturing out of her shell, seeking more eye contact, seeking out other children, speaking in the "I" form, playing dress up, taking the steps two at a time, standing in line for her turn on the slide at the swimming pool—in short, slowly but surely discovering the world around her. Recently, after I returned from a three-day bike trip, Julia suddenly approached me and said "Papa, I am happy; no, I am very happy…because you are back." It brought tears to my eyes. Our hard work had paid off: she could finally understand the abstract, the doorway to flexibility, because she was starting to understand her own emotions.

Pim Donkersloot is a child psychologist, specializing in autism. In 1990, his book *Autism: a Problem for the Whole Family* was published. The book combines scientific findings with his experience as a father of a child with autism. He is trained in Floortime, and is helping to educate parents and therapists in the Developmental, Individual-difference, Relationship-based (DIR) model. He has also co-translated Stanley Greenspan and Serena Wieder's book *The Child with Special Needs* into Dutch. Pim and his wife, Jill, live together with Julia in Amsterdam, The Netherlands, where The ChildCenter is also located.

53. Life as a Cooking Pot

Anne Marie Gallagher

"Watch out everyone, Mum's cleaning the bathroom again."

This phrase was heard often throughout my childhood. It was spoken usually between me and my sisters and it was a phrase to which we all instinctively knew how to respond. I can't remember asking my older sisters the reasons why we had to give Mum some space, we all just did. On these occasions there were no "buts" or "whys"—we just all busied our-

selves away, quietly, out of sight. The end of these episodes was marked with my mum coming downstairs and putting the kettle on to make herself a cup of tea. Once the tea was made and she was sitting with her feet up having a well-deserved rest then we knew it was safe to start hassling her again, as any young family does whenever Mum looks like she has nothing to do. She would turn and smile, attend to our needs, enter into some chit chat or indulge us all in one big cuddle.

The penny has now dropped. This behavior of my neurotypical mother was ritualistic, idiosyncratic, and once initiated required to be completed irrespective of what else was going on in the world. The activity would sometimes be carried out when it didn't even need to be done and the successful completion required splendid isolation. This behavior was functionally adaptive, it worked, it served its purpose well, and its purpose was the following:

To release some pent up energies.

To bring about some thinking time.

To allow escape into her own world.

To ultimately de-stress.

Now I see it everywhere in the "typical" world, people de-stressing by indulging in idiosyncratic, ritualistic repetitive behavior. Examples that I come across in everyday life involving friends and family, all of whom do not have autism, are:

Buying another handbag.

Cleaning a cupboard and taking a trip to the dump (municipal garbage area).

Cutting the grass.

Going to the gym.

Baking a cake.

Taking the dog for a walk.

As you read this you may be able to identify your own idiosyncratic, ritualistic behavior that works for you. People with autism are no different.

The notion of de-stressing for me meant "to let off steam" and I began looking at life as a cooking pot. On gathering information about the types of behaviors ordinary people indulge in when levels of stress become intolerable I began to realize that these behaviors often fell into at least one of three categories. The first, *energy release*, includes shouting, swearing, banging doors, and going to the gym. The second, *isolation*, includes walking out, going to the toilet to cry, going for a drive, and the third, *routines*, includes buying shoes and cleaning the bathroom.

These categories of de-stressing behavior represent the steam escaping from the cooking pot.

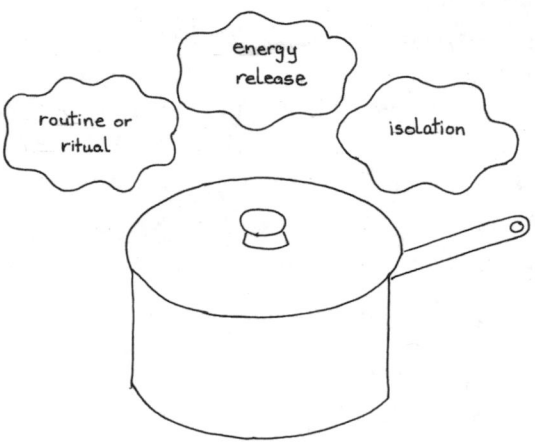

Some de-stressing behavior satisfies all three categories. Going to the gym for example satisfies energy release, usually satisfies isolation (even though there are others at the gym you can refrain from social contact), and many people have a routine programme which they prefer to follow. If you go to the gym in a state of increased stress and there is someone on the first piece of equipment that you prefer to start with, then this will increase your level of agitation. Being prevented from indulging in your de-stressing behavior increases your level of stress. Think of the mother who has had a very difficult day at home with her children, who plans that when their father comes home she will take a bike ride. Just as she's about to leave she either discovers a puncture, or worse still, the father suggests a family bike ride and they all join her on the trip.

When we look at the categories of natural de-stressing behavior they bear an uncanny resemblance to the idiosyncratic behavior, seen with autism. People with autism seem driven to carry out idiosyncratic ritualistic behavior, they frequently can be seen to indulge in isolation behavior and they regularly display energy release behaviors such as rocking, spinning, pacing, hitting, and banging. I believe it's reasonable to assume that at least some of this behavior should be viewed as de-stressing behavior.

The more de-stressing behavior that a person indulges in, the more stress they are experiencing in their lives. One of the most important properties of de-stressing behavior is that it works to serve its purpose. As caregivers we must recognize when there is a need for our clients to de-stress. We must ensure that opportunities exist within daily programs which allow them to safely indulge in de-stressing behavior that works for them. When preferred methods of de-stressing behavior cause risk of harm or personal injury, in the interest of safety these should be prevented from occurring. In this instance, it is imperative that alternative opportunities for de-stressing behavior are offered. We must begin to identify that some behavior described as "just autistic behavior" could be considered as a preferred method of de-stressing behavior.

To improve quality of life and overall well-being of people with autism we must turn our attention to the "heat" beneath the cooking pot.

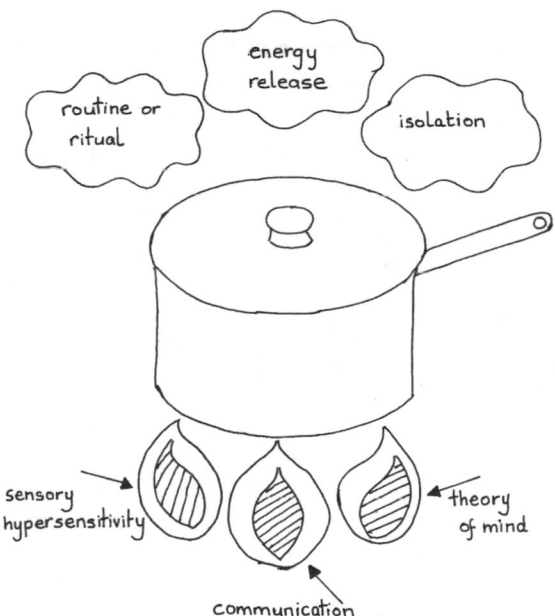

People with autism experience heat in their lives in the same way as everyone else. We all become agitated and stressed when things don't go to plan. Or rather, when things don't go to *our* plan. An example would be planning to sit down for ten minutes' rest in the middle of a busy day. You boil the kettle and prepare yourself a lovely mug of hot coffee. You go to the fridge but discover that there is no cream left. You now have to jump into the car to make the very short trip to the local shop for cream. Easily sorted, but we can all identify with the level of stress caused by the discovery that there is no cream.

Difficulties with theory of mind often lead people with autism to inaccurately predict the actions of others. Their plans for the day are often based on false data about the future of the world around them and therefore the plans are prone to unexpected change. As caregivers we have to develop systems which allow a greater degree of predictability in the lives of people with autism.

When stressed, little annoyances or "niggles" become huge. They can begin to take over one's whole mind and body and cause increases in levels of stress. Think about the dripping tap. It's alright when you're calm; in fact sometimes you don't even hear it. When you're highly stressed it appears to become louder and more intrusive. The truth is we, at the point of high stress, are less able to filter out these little annoyances. People with autism are reported to be hypersensitive to sensory stimulus in their environments and therefore are more prone to the increase in arousal brought about by these "little annoyances". As caregivers we must begin to recognize hypersensitivities and reduce the impact these have on the lives of people with autism by managing the environment in a person-centred manner. Experience has shown me that this simple analogy of behavior has enabled caregivers to develop more insight into the world of autism and has enabled them to begin to see the world through the eyes of the individual. Ironically, the key to successful support can sometimes be found in the development of skills of theory of mind not only of the person with autism but of the caregivers themselves.

Anne Marie Gallagher (39), married with two sons, earned her Batchelor of Science degree in speech pathology and therapeutics at the University of Glasgow in 1986. She is, as well as being a wife, a mother, and a 10km runner, currently involved in developing a new service for adults with ASD in central Scotland. The service will offer clinical diagnosis with pre- and post-diagnostic support and intervention. Prior to this new development she worked for ten years providing advice to caregivers supporting adults with learning disabilities who had severe and enduring challenging behavior, including Autism Spectrum Disorders, and it was here that it proved necessary to develop and trial alternative approaches to support.

54. Moving to the Heart of the Matter

Gayle Gates

What does it mean to truly relate to another human being? What is that shared moment when we truly connect to one another? How do we know that we have spanned that interpersonal space to see and be seen?

During the last 27 years as a dance/movement therapist and an educator, I have confronted these questions over and over again. They have been no more highlighted or profound than in my work with children who fall within the diagnostic category of Autism Spectrum Disorders. My clinical work has included children whose symptoms range from severe to mild and verbal to nonverbal. It is in my work with these children that many of my most poignant and memorable relationships have occurred, and I have, as a consequence, been most deeply affected and changed as a person and therapist.

No matter what the individual's diagnosis or the theoretical orientation of the therapist, it is my belief that it is the relationship between people which is at the core of change. Our relationships allow us the opportunity to experience ourselves in new ways; they help us to make sense of the world and define what things we share as human beings. Yet relationships are probably the most complicated and demanding aspects of our lives.

Our interpersonal life both enriches us and continually demands our energy and understanding on levels cognitive and emotional, verbal and nonverbal. Relationships allow us to see the world through another's point of view while helping us clarify our sense of self and our awareness of others. From birth throughout early development, it is the child's relationships with caregivers that help structure and facilitate his or her emotional experiences and all aspects of learning and development. For children with autism there may be numerous difficulties including neuropsychological, cognitive, and language problems, that interfere with and influence development and social bonds. While acknowledging the complexity and interrelationship of all aspects of our development, I view the difficulty with social relatedness, reciprocity, and interactions as the most profound. This often debilitating deficit greatly impacts the child and those individuals who love and hope for him or her.

As a dance/movement therapist, I begin therapy relationships from a nonverbal body level using my own body and nonverbal expression as a way to engage, interact, play with, and understand my clients. Whether mirroring or responding, I always use that nonverbal bodily self and kinesthetic empathy as a place to start. This approach is guided by the child's cues and what they are trying in their own way to communicate, even if the intention doesn't seem to be a shared dialogue. Nowhere are my skills more put to the test. I am challenged to put my whole "self" into the shared time and space with the hope, for perhaps only brief moments, of acknowledgement and relatedness. My hope has been that I am setting the stage for each child's greater response to the overtures of teachers, parents, peers, and all who might later come into his or her life.

Over the years, I have experienced extreme frustration. Do I know anything about autism and treatment; and more importantly do I know anything about this unique child? Do I make a difference? I still struggle with these questions. And yet there have been pivotal instances across the therapy space where I have been spontaneously recognized and acknowledged both verbally and nonverbally. The initiation of eye contact or an unprompted, "Hi Miss Gayle, time for movement," from across the room from a child usually self-involved and nonverbal have made my heart soar. I have experienced the joy of tiny almost imperceptible steps towards an expanded awareness, a shared movement moment where I realized that something nascent and full of possibilities was occurring.

There were special instances where, after periods of seemingly little connectedness, I became aware of each child's unique capacity for true play, mutuality, imitation, humor, a sustained connection, resistance, and feelings. I knew by reactions, initiations, and sometimes words that they were motivated towards me not as an object but as someone to play with and enjoy. One memorable moment occurred after having worked with one little boy for several years. As we walked hand in hand to therapy, I was talking, singing, skipping and marching, and swinging my arms. I became aware that he was intently observing my behavior and movements, and with direct eye contact and a smile, he began to spontaneously imitate me. What fun we had all the way to the therapy room! I remember the tears that welled up and sense of awe I felt knowing what it took for this boy to make that direct and active choice to join me. How honored I felt to have this partner in play and interaction, to be recognized, to be imitated, and to truly share the pleasure of movement and play together. I have experienced many such moments even with the frustrating, fluctuating, and slow nature of change and progress that occurs when working with a child with autism. There is a continual need to adjust my expectations to accept each child's strengths and weaknesses without assuming any preconceived limitations to possibilities. Each child will progress to whatever degree he or she is capable and I must accept this while rejoicing in each individual's accomplishments.

Part of my professional work involves teaching graduate students in a creative arts in therapy program. I teach a year-long class on disorders of childhood, and I begin the year with autism. In class we discuss diagnostic criteria, issues in treatment and research, assessment, and therapy techniques, and review videos. Students also have the opportunity to take a fieldtrip to observe real children. Invariably they return surprised to realize the great heterogeneity within this population and the uniqueness of each child. It has struck me that the children with autism, probably more than any other group of individuals I have worked with, have taught me a great deal about not prejudging people but instead valuing each individual. I continually encourage these future therapists, my students, to acknowledge and appreciate the unique gifts and personality of each of their young clients.

Children with autism have taught me the true meaning of patience. I better understand the careful and gradual therapy process I must enter and accept in order to work with these children. Not surprisingly, this understanding has expanded to my work with all of my clients. I have had to examine my own capacity for being flexible and accepting change, both personally and professionally. I have been humbled by what I do not know. Yet I have experienced sheer joy during moments of real engagement, mutuality, and play where I have felt hope and been reaffirmed in my belief that the relationships between people allow for the possibility of change.

My hope is that I have made a difference in the lives of the children with whom I have worked but most definitely each has made a great difference in mine. All human beings need a shared space where we can communicate and connect with one another. I have learned to respect each child's courage when I have realized how much has been required of that young person to reach those moments of interconnection with me. What a struggle and risk it is to accommodate to others! These children have helped me to see that many of the issues that they struggle with are not just unique to them. They are simply the same ones with which all human beings, including myself, struggle: forming meaningful relationships, accommodating to others, finding mutuality and acceptance, clarifying our sense of self while understanding others. These are part of everyone's life including mine. My work has taught me a great deal—especially to cherish and appreciate all the wonderful relationships that enrich my life.

Gayle Gates is a dance/movement therapist who resides in Philadelphia, Pennsylvania, with her 15-year-old daughter, Miranda. She has teaching and clinical expertise in the field of child development and the treatment of childhood and adolescent disorders. She is Clinical Assistant Professor and Associate Director of Dance/Movement Therapy Education in the Hahnemann Creative Arts in Therapy Program at Drexel University. Gayle is also a therapist at the Green Tree School in Philadelphia, working with school-age children who have Autism Spectrum Disorders. She has consulted and presented regionally and nationally on various clinical issues related to children.

55. Circle of Devotion

Trish Miron

Aspect: What aspects of myself do I need to effectively work with the uniqueness of this child?

Understanding: What do I need to understand about myself and this child in order to make a connection?

Typical: If this were a typically developing child, how would he or she and I feel about what we are doing?

Integrate: How do I help the child integrate our shared experiences into something functional and meaningful for him or her?

Sameness: What do we share that makes us the same and how can I connect with this sameness?

Motivation: How do I create the conditions in which the child is motivated to connect with the world around him or her?

For over 20 years, I have been devoted to seeking connection with children within the autistic spectrum. Yet my own journey to feel connected began long before that. In order to help you to understand my commitment to this work, it is important that I share with you some aspects of my life experience.

My family history was one of intense conflict and emotional cutoff. Life was unpredictable. We moved frequently and I had no comforting alliances amongst my family members or community. In an attempt to understand my unpredictable and chaotic home life, I learned to watch and observe as events unfolded. I was attempting to understand the patterns in the world around me, to make life more predictable and therefore safer.

My relationship with my father was defined by frequent, intense clashing. He was controlling. I felt relationships were about dealing with being controlled, one person having power over another. I was happiest when I was alone, a place where no one could intrude into my world. I viewed intrusions into my world as an attempt to take something away from me. I would walk the streets for hours to be freed from the chaos of my family home.

During my teenage years, I stopped striving to please others. My teachers expected little from me and gave me little in return. My parents expected a lot and were constantly frustrated with my behavior. I was out of synch with the demands and expectations that were placed upon me. When I thought I had done enough, they would tell me I could do better. No one was paying attention.

I first began to connect with myself when I studied karate at the age of 20. When I was training, I was able to find myself in the movement and to let my worries disappear. After two years of training, I decided to go to college, study to be a therapist and "be there" for children who, like me, struggled with connecting to their world. At social occasions, I sought comfort and safety with children. Among children, I could enter their world and be accepted for who I was and give of myself without judgment. I could suspend my own judgment of who I was and just be me. Soon after graduating with my master's degree in dance/movement therapy I began to work with children with developmental delays.

My journey of self-discovery continued as I began my work with children within the autism spectrum. I had little understanding of this disorder and didn't know at the beginning of this journey that in addition to learning about autism, I would learn so much about myself. My ability to observe, richly developed as a child, became a valuable tool. Armed with these powers of observation and my need to establish relationships, I learned how to "mirror" children as a way to establish a connection.

I learned that it was important to place myself outside the child's pattern and observe. I also learned to ask myself many questions. How does the child use the environmental space and the objects in the space? How is the child using his own body in relationship to objects and space? If I step into the child's pattern, how does the child react? Does the child react differently depending on where or how I enter the pattern? If I introduce a novel movement, will the child immediately imitate my movement or does he imitate the movement later? How long is the child able to sustain an interaction? Does the child need time to regain his inner balance or recover somehow, as a result of our interactions?

I saw that I could engage with the child by joining with his movement and following his lead. In order to foster spontaneous communication of any form, I learned to stress the nonverbal aspects of our relationship and establish a common rhythm of motion. Through the child's observation of my mirroring of his movements, he began to see that his behavior could affect others. Repetition of this activity over time was an important element in the development of our relationship. As we related, we began to feel a sense of connectedness with all that was around us. Together we could create a shared focus and a sense of having an effect on one another.

Interactions can be gradually extended into games and become a focus of joint attention. Initiations of interactions can be shared and mutually enjoyed as shown by greeting each other with a brightening of faces or a twinkle in our eyes and a smile. Through shared experiences we are able to establish a relationship of comfort, safety, and trust from which we can grow together. We can be empowered by our ability to affect one another.

There are so many important lessons that children with autism have taught me. I have learned to tap my creative resources and ability to problem solve. I discovered how to place myself in the child's place and attempt to understand what his communicative message was. I also learned to ask myself how I could create an environment of safety and comfort for each child; to stay present in the moment and be available should he seek me out for connection. If I maintain a predictable and low-key manner, I am better prepared to help the child make sense of the world. I learned it was okay to take "time out" in a relationship to recuperate and become re-centered. I learned to respond in a predictable, low-key fashion that would create an environment where each child would feel safe, secure, and connected. I learned to use my capacity to be patient and to simply watch events unfold.

Finally, I found my own strength in my connections with these children. Through being able to feel successful at reaching these hard-to-connect-with children, I began to learn to respect my capabilities. I found the courage to accept myself for who I was and the strength to begin to face the sense of isolation and withdrawal I experienced when I was growing up. I found that relationships could replenish and sustain me through some of life's difficult moments. As I became competent and comfortable in connecting and forming relationships with the children, I became more competent and comfortable in my professional and personal relationships. Each child with whose world I was able to connect and share helped me open doors and broaden my ability to form other relationships in my life.

Throughout these experiences, I learned the value of acceptance and the meaning of devotion. That was my real journey. Children with autism have helped me learn to accept myself and as I did so I learned to accept others. Acceptance is openness to myself and to all that another person brings to the world. It is not an overstatement to say that this work has led me to discover devotion—to self, to family, and to the human process.

Trish Miron, MCAT, ADTR, NCC, LPC is the Principal at The Nexus School in Huntingdon Valley, Pennsylvania. She is an Adjunct Senior Instructor at the Hahnemann Creative Arts in Therapy program at Drexel University College of Nursing and Health Professions. She maintains an independent practice as a therapist and behavioral/educational consultant for children with special needs. Trish worked for 21 years at the Center for Autistic Children in Philadelphia and was Clinical Director for 14 years. She is currently working towards her Doctoral Degree in clinical psychology at Chestnut Hill College. She lives with her husband, Art, and has two children. In her free time she enjoys reading and gardening.

56. Playing with Hudson

Eric R. Mitchell

I remember. Sitting across from Hudson on the living room floor, facing him. Right in front of him. Hudson faced my father's chair, which was directly behind me. I was in front of him, but I don't know if he noticed. I remember switching places, our mothers placing us together to play on the floor, and how, over time, I was playing and Hudson was staring. I'm not sure how old I was, but I remember. I remember that feeling of losing my friend as he drifted inside himself, into a cozy, quiet box, right there in front of me.

Our families were close friends, and Hudson and I were born about the same time. Our mothers got us together for play dates, which I now understand as a parent myself, were also times to support each other. I don't remember how many times we tried to play together, but I do remember that as I grew older and passed various milestones, Hudson did not. And I missed him. I still do.

Our families eventually stopped getting together for play dates, and Hudson's family became invested in seeking out treatment for him. They moved away, and I'm not exactly sure where they are now, what has become of Hudson, or how his family has coped with the challenges they faced. But I remember.

I've often wondered why I've always been drawn to working with children...the most challenging I could find at times. Whenever a tough case has come along, when it seems like there is no clear path to success, there's something inside me that wants to step up and take a shot. I'm not sure of all the reasons why, but I think it has something to do with that feeling of losing my friend. Trying to get him back somehow. Never wanting to let that light go out. Always wanting to keep playing with Hudson.

I think that everyone who works with children diagnosed on the autism spectrum, and keeps working with them, must have some kind of calling. We all have some connection, something inside us that calls us back to these kids. Many times, we could be working for better pay, and easier cases. But we don't. We keep coming back somehow. These children see the world in a different light. Sometimes that light tortures them, while for others, it puts them at peace. Perhaps I keep coming back because of the peace I feel within some of these children, wanting to experience a piece of that peace myself.

I learned, sadly through the death of one of the children I worked with, about the gifts all of these children bring to us. Everyone who had truly dedicated themselves to spending therapeutic time with that little girl was molded into a better person for experiencing her worldview, and the peace she maintained inside, even through behavioral patterns that left all others around her completely and utterly drained. What these children can teach us will spread far beyond our own lives to countless individuals, families, communities, and so on, well beyond our lives. It is with this realization that professionals, as well as families, can find some peace in the diagnosis and pursuant turmoil surrounding autism spectrum diagnoses.

With all of this solidarity brewing, I sometimes wonder where the line is to be drawn between the professional and the family. When this line is crossed, what can be done to reconstitute it? Does the professional working with a client with a toilet training protocol refuse to change diapers, since this is a caretaking responsibility? Should we share meals? What about birthdays? The lines are often blurred. And yet, for the best interest of the child, each boundary dilemma needs to be examined individually. It is not always easy to set those boundaries, as our hearts may beg us to disregard the line between professional and family, but we still need to have some clarity. Otherwise, what happens when the professional needs to move on, and the family is left feeling abandoned? Boundaries are essential.

Sometimes however, it can be therapeutic and necessary for families and professionals to share bonding activities in the spirit of building team solidarity. I've worked with two families who actually provided t-shirts for all the staff with tongue-in-cheek slogans about the kids we love on them, such as, "If you're happy and you know it, flap your hands." One family made a tradition of having a meal to recognize the work of professionals once they left the team. And back we came to recognize our work around the table, sharing stories of frustrations and triumphs, reminding us of why we do what we do, and how important the team approach is. This family also drew the team together at a Memorial Day barbecue where professionals stopped by with a few of their own children. There I was, celebrating our team's efforts, watching my own three-year-old son learning how to play with a child with autism, reminding me of myself at that age, playing with Hudson.

Did these gestures promote solidarity? Yes. Appreciation? Yes. Cohesion? Yes. Blurred boundaries? Sometimes. This is the nature of working on the autism spectrum. Working in the grays, and trying to re-establish boundaries so that families can eventually move on without the professional.

There is a kind of sacred society enveloping those affected by autism, personally and professionally. Although we have all been affected in drastically different ways, there are some common threads that tie those in the autism community together. Some of my work has been in the area of cultural competence development, and I have been fortunate enough to work with countless professionals over time in developing self-awareness, openness to knowledge, and communication skills related to cultural competence in service delivery. I have realized that in many ways, cultural identity also encompasses connections to certain diagnoses, such as Autism Spectrum Disorder (ASD). Families and professionals affected learn to connect with each other over time to build solidarity in politics, education, mental health, and a host of other domains. In navigating political landscapes, key players who understand some of the struggles associated with the autism spectrum are absolutely crucial. When speaking with politicians, funding entities, and so on, I can quickly recognize those who identify in a profound way with autism. These are the individuals with whom partnerships and collaborations can be formed with long-lasting effectiveness. Over time, when alliances formed with those who attend to the autism spectrum only because of its buzzword status begin to dissipate, the alliances with those who are a part of the autism community will be carried on.

We have cultivated grassroots programming in the community. We have brought school districts together at the table with the mental health system. We have been on the front cover of *Time* and *Newsweek*. National newscasters have told our stories at prime time. But we have just begun. Every day, we wake up and autism is staring back at us, never backing down. The need is overwhelming. Most of the time, I feel guilty that I can't do more for every child on the spectrum. Even though I know what it takes to promote progress in most of these children, there is too much to be done. Ironically, taking time out to recognize how far we have come, and the strides we have made, is absolutely essential. Not to be caught up in the daily disappointments, but to look back over the past month, the year, the decade, the lifetime, and to embrace the changes we have made. This is the key: to forgive ourselves for falling short of what our children deserve, and then to move forward. The downs, the ups, and then there's another day starting tomorrow. The drum beats on. And I'm still learning how to play with Hudson.

Eric R. Mitchell, Ph.D. grew up in rural Vermont and began working with children through the Vermont Association of Mental Health as a teenager. After graduating from the University of Vermont, he moved on to Rutgers University, where he began research in cultural competence. He then continued this research at the University of Pennsylvania during his doctoral studies. He accepted a post-doctoral position specializing in ASD in Hawaii. He then relocated back to Philadelphia to be closer to his family, especially his son, Dylan. Dr Mitchell is currently active as a consulting psychologist around the Philadelphia area. He has designed curricula, evaluated children, supervised intervention programs, and provided professional training within the autism community. His most recent accomplishments include the design of several programs for children on the autism spectrum in Philadelphia, such as a model after-school program.

57. The Path of Acceptance for Families

Robert A. Naseef

It's been a difficult path indeed. There are times when I still wonder who my son might have been, without the autism, and who might I have been as well. Sometimes it seems like only yesterday when I held Tariq for the first time, and yet it is over 25 years. My heart pounded with excitement as I held his soft body next to my heart and our eyes met in the delivery room. Magically he made me a father. Visions of playing baseball and building model airplanes together and having a warm, close relationship danced in my mind. It still warms my heart when I talk to people and recall how his life flowed smoothly through those first 18 months—rolling over, raising his head, creeping, crawling, cruising, triumphantly walking and then even talking.

Then everything changed as the "autism bomb" hit and he stopped talking and began an endless sequence of repetitive activities. He stopped relating by sharing his joy and interest in life. A few years later he was diagnosed with autism and mental retardation. The impact sent his development and family life veering sharply from the course we were on. That I would lose my perfect baby was beyond anything I could fathom. It is so much easier to tell this story in hindsight. How could it be that he would grow to adulthood and not read or write or speak?

I thought I could change him and make him the boy I wanted him to be, frantically and persistently following various treatment approaches: behavioral, educational, dietary, and developmental. Despite intensive treatment, he did not make dramatic progress. Instead he has been a catalyst to transform me, and help me to become the man I needed to be. He taught me the meaning of unconditional love—to honor his sacred right to be loved for who he is, not what he has achieved lately, how he looks or how much money he will earn. Without words, he continues to teach me a priceless lesson.

Now I know what Kahlil Gibran meant when he wrote about moments of joy and sorrow being inextricably woven together, for sorrow opens our hearts for the experience of joy in everyday life. Accepting that my son's condition would be enduring was imponderable. Nonetheless I learned the developmental approach of celebrating what he *could do*. This made a huge difference for our relationship. He became a happy child, and I learned to enjoy him and accept him as he was. But the autism which I hated with a vengeance refused to go away. My son twisted and turned to get away, and preferred to be alone most of the time.

Today I am blessed with a family who loves me and a job that I love going to every day. As a psychologist, I help families who are struggling with the special needs of their children. I try to help them enjoy life with their children by first accepting and embracing their pain. Long before I researched how families cope and got my Ph.D., I was learning about overwhelmed, stressed-out parents, for I am the oldest of my parents' eight children. I undertook my profession to help myself as well as others. What I started learning in the family I originated in, I continued learning in the family I procreated and polished those lessons in my professional development.

A book that helped me was *When Bad Things Happen to Good People?* by Rabbi Harold Kushner. Autism seems so unjust and this evokes our anger. The emotional ups and downs create a landscape around us as families that can be treacherous and threatening. Any disaster from the personal to the epic can trigger a spiritual crisis such as occurred with the Indian Ocean tsunami of December 26, 2004. Is God punishing innocent people for sins of past generations or reminding the world of his omniscient power as some people believe? Or is God found in the healing and compassion that is evoked around the globe in how we respond? Indeed such an event of nature places the individual diagnosis of autism in a perspective that can calm and enlighten.

In my everyday life, some of the issues you would hear in my office if you were invisible would include mothers obsessed with their child's needs and barely able to think about anything else and feeling guilty about that. Fathers are feeling left out and powerless to rescue their families or cheer up their spouses. Children are trying to cheer up their overwhelmed parents. I see families split in two, one parent with the "special" child and the other with the "typical" children. Children are struggling to make friends, as are their parents who want to fit in with the community of mothers and fathers. They grow weary of being a therapy mom or dad instead of a soccer mom or dad.

This is only the tip of the iceberg. When people get more comfortable talking about how life really is, they often reveal signs and symptoms of clinical depression, anxiety, traumatic stress, anger management issues, sexual dysfunction, etc. All the while love makes giving up unthinkable. Helping people to regain their balance, taking care of everybody's needs, and rejoining the current of their lives involves endurance, courage, and accepting whatever remains unchangeable.

First, I try to help people look at their grief. It doesn't help to pretend to be positive when underneath you may be lonely, afraid, or sad. I learned we don't have to lie to ourselves. You can grieve. You can complain. You can mourn. This helps you to go on, make the best of the situation, and enjoy life. Our life force is resilient, but the longing for the healthy child or a typical existence may endure. You have to learn to live with that yearning, but you don't have to lie to yourself about how hard this can be.

I have observed the tendency that women shed their tears openly while men cry on the inside. Some individuals cry a lot; some cry a little; some never cry. Everyone's heart breaks and it takes time to heal. In the ninth century, the Persian poet Rumi told us to pay attention to the wounded and bandaged place for that is where the light enters. The grief can be because our lives are not as expected. As D. W. Winnicott said in his book *Talking to Parents,* "Mothers are helped by being able to voice their agonies at the time they are experiencing them. Bottled up resentment spoils the loving which is at the back of it all" (p.75). Winnicott was talking about the mothers of typical children. I have come to realize that in some measure this is the journey of all families. Feeling our experience is the first step to handling it wisely.

Second, I try to help people accept themselves just as they are. This is key in accepting our children with an open, kind, and loving heart. Of course this is far easier said than done. A perfectly lovely child or adult on the spectrum can be very hard to be with because of their behavioral, social, or communication issues. *But when you love someone, you expect yourself to love to be with them.* When you don't feel that and think you should, the guilt can be unbearable, and your heart aches. This is an inner conflict that any parent can relate to, but when a child has autism, this can happen much more frequently.

You cannot accept yourself or any experience without seeing it clearly and with compassion in a tender sympathetic way. What Tariq has taught me besides accepting him is to accept myself. I think the challenges in our children radiate inwardly to our own imperfections. I had to begin accepting my own flaws, warts, and blemishes. As Carl Rogers taught, when we accept ourselves, only then can we change.

Finally, accepting our pain and ourselves leads to accepting and enjoying our child and our family life. That awareness is the gateway to love and wholeness. Ultimately Tariq is not "damaged." Along with other children and adults on the autism spectrum, he bears witness to the diversity of the human condition and the resilience of our soul. We are all so perfectly imperfect. That deep connection that a parent feels with a newborn, or a child's first steps, or first words, can be felt at any moment when we are truly aware and attuned to our child.

This awareness keeps the heart open and the mind as clear as possible. Yearning for what we don't have blocks knowing and loving the child we do have. Seeing our child for who she is and giving what she needs from us to whatever extent that is possible. This is the path of acceptance for families.

Tariq is still my little boy. He still puts his head on my shoulder, and I have never stopped wanting to hear the sound of his voice. He has brought many kind people into my life and helped me to understand myself and others. He made me a better father and a better man. His greatest gift to me is a glimpse into the human heart, where it is not who you know or what you know or what you have—but who you are.

58. The Challenges of Autism: An Introspection

Bertram A. Ruttenberg

There is a family story that I cried for the first six months of my life and that the more my mother tried to comfort me, hold me, rock me, sing to me—the more I cried. My distress finally lessened when she followed her older sister's sage advice. Lower the shades, stay by him, talk to him softly, and don't try to pick him up or rock him. T. Berry Brazelton, "Dr Pediatrics," many years later described to me a type of infant—long, skinny, hard to console, hypersensitive to sound or touch, some of whom are eventually diagnosed with autism by one to one and a half years of age.

Was I headed for autism? Does it explain my developing an interest in autism in the mid-1940s and in feeling challenged by child patients with certain characteristics even before I had heard the name "autism"?

I am still tactile defensive although I manage to control and hide my reaction beyond tensing up. I love music; it helps me focus, but that's right brain mediated. I'm very right-handed which is left brain mediated. I'm both visually and auditorily attuned. Looking and listening are both distinct sensory functions as opposed to the tactile and temperature which are interdependent. My sense of smell is also keenly developed, I detect lingering odors of cooking and perfumes.

So do I fit into the autistic spectrum? Do I have the traits but not the functional syndrome? Have I managed to adapt and adjust to some innate traits, learning to sustain eye contact, and even developing reasonably good relationships including with my wife and kids who are liberal activists? I did have the habit of introspective drifting off at the dinner table, at which point a good humored "Earth to Bert" would bring me back to interaction with my family.

Though I have no problem reading the expressions and innuendo of others, I do sometimes take seriously what someone is saying in jest. As far as humor, I am mostly a punner, with play on words. These are fine and subtle deviations from the norm but they are there. When I'm reminded by my wife of a lapse in social graciousness, towards her or others, I'm immediately aware of it and quickly correct or make up for the lapse. So it's not that I don't understand what to do, rather that the correct behavior did not come spontaneously.

I wonder how many individuals like me, with a "touch" of autism, are walking around, doing good things for others, perhaps as a compensatory stance learned early on, for their "touch" of autistic traits. I know that by kindergarten others brought their worries and problems to me. I read well by age three and I helped others. Looking back perhaps it was a way of relating, yet keeping a bit apart from the others; my global love affair with the world as Phyllis Greenacre described artists and entertainers as having. So I loved everyone. (But I also had one or two good friends still sustained since grade school.)

I'm quite comfortable with children who have autism. Perhaps the adage "It takes one to know one" applies here and explains why I seem to know what to do for children and infants with autism, and just do it instinctively. It's after I've intuitively handled a situation with a child that I then look back at what I've done and put it into words and concepts. It may explain why I don't do much formal paper or book chapter writing unless

I'm talked into the state of being obligated. I am happier as a clinician and a direct supervisor.

How many of us are out there at the far end of the autistic spectrum? Perhaps Asperger's syndrome is closer to the middle of the spectrum. People with Asperger's talk and learn intelligently and want to relate but more or less don't know how to go about it. Attention Deficit Disorder comes closer to what I've described about myself, but the problem is not an attention deficit. *Au contraire*, it's a global attention to everything that needs discipline and comes close to distractibility, too many things to notice and take in. As I write this non-stop I think I am on the road to differentiating an as-yet-undefined or unnamed syndrome, as a modal point on the autistic spectrum line and extending the line.

In summary I have moved in an almost free-associating way toward defining myself and how and why I became involved with autism, and why from my full spectrum of medical, child development, psychiatric, and psychoanalytic training I have arrived at this area of work and expertise. The study of individual vocational choice and evolution, or why we end up doing what we do with such passion and also dispassionate certitude is a fascinating subject and a challenging topic for one or more future Ph.D. theses.

Bertram A. Ruttenberg, M.D. is a child psychiatrist and Founder and Director Emeritus of the Center for Autistic Children in Philadelphia, Pennsylvania. This was one of the first facilities, begun in 1955, devoted exclusively to the treatment of children with autism. Dr Ruttenberg is one of the early pioneers in the developmental approach of meeting children on the spectrum where they are and helping them reach for the next developmental steps. He "retired" in 2004 after 49 years of service to children with autism and their families. He is dear to the hearts of countless children and adults and their families.

59. No Looking Back

Fiona J. Scott

I came to an interest in autism during one of my undergraduate developmental psychology lectures in the 1980s. Our professor was talking about "theory of mind," the naturally developing ability to understand that people's behaviors are driven more by what they are thinking, what goes on

in their heads (beliefs, desires, wishes, hopes, etc.), than by the reality of the world around them. Thus, for example, if Sally believes that her toy is in the cupboard she will go there to look for it, even if it is really under her bed. This ability to understand and to predict people's behavior according to their "mental states" typically develops by the age of four years. However, in the lecture I learned that a then recent study had been published ("Does the autistic child have a theory of mind?", by Simon Baron-Cohen and colleagues) that showed 80 percent of individuals with autism could not do this. I had never heard of autism before, but my mind swam with attempting to imagine what it would be like not to be able to do something that comes so naturally to us that we don't even think about it. I left that lecture and went straight to the library to read everything I could find on autism, and I have never looked back.

Since that day, over 15 years ago, I have had the fortune to work not only with the world's leading clinicians and authorities on autism and the autism spectrum, but also with many individuals and families affected by autism and Asperger's syndrome. The opportunities I have had through work, training, and freedom of professional choice have put me in the position of being involved at the forefront of research into the autism spectrum whilst at the same time doing clinical work with families, providing training for other multi-disciplinary professionals through conferences and through training courses for diagnostic instruments, and being involved in educational assessment and recommendations. Having my fingers in so many cross-disciplinary pies, and having continued links with families and individuals, has taught me more about autism and Asperger's syndrome than I would ever have learned from textbooks and manuals.

My first and perhaps most vehement point is *listen to the parents!* Parents know more about their children than any professional can ever hope to understand. If a parent is concerned about their child's development or behavior this should never be dismissed simply because the reported difficulties are not seen by the professional during a one-hour observation, or in a different context. The classic situation I come across is parents explaining how their son or daughter shows school refusal, anxiety, frustration, aggression, destruction of their room or belongings, depression, and other associated behavioral difficulties at home, and the school responds that he or she does not show such behaviors in school. Therefore it is concluded that there is either (a) no problem at all and the parents are neurotic, or (b) any problem is somehow due to parental neglect, incompetence, or worse.

It is very common for children and adolescents with Asperger's syndrome in particular to expend vast amounts of energy and effort trying to fit in and appear "normal" in the school setting, and as soon as they cross the threshold into the comfortable, safe home environment to "explode" from the exhaustion, frustration, distress, and stress of trying to do this. The fact that the difficult behaviors are not observed in the classroom is a measure of the child's ability to mask their difficulties, not evidence of a lack of any difficulties.

I have also learned over the years that the "secondary" difficulties often associated with Asperger's syndrome and the autism spectrum are equally if not more important in the understanding and support of individuals than the core "triad" areas of social difficulties, communication difficulties, and restricted, stereotyped or repetitive interests or behaviors. The majority of individuals that I have worked with have sensory processing differences that impact hugely on their lives. This can range from the young boy with such an extreme aversion to the smell of tomatoes that he would scream, rage, and lash out in terror if anyone approached him having eaten or handled a tomato beforehand; to the child who developed school phobia because the sound of the school bell hurt his ears every time it rang and left him cowering on the floor with his arms over his head; to the adult who could not concentrate at work because she was too distracted by the worry that someone might come up from behind and touch her unexpectedly. The ranges of heightened or reduced sensory processing in all areas—smell, sight, hearing, touch, and taste—that are seen in individuals with an Autism Spectrum Disorder should not be underestimated. It is most likely that behaviors seen by us as inexplicable and bizarre are in fact reactions to stimuli that are, for them, extreme.

In addition to sensory processing differences other areas where there are common differences in the autism spectrum include attention, motor coordination, organization, planning, and short-term memory. An individual with autism can at one time be so absorbed in an area of interest that you cannot get their attention at all and they may remain thus absorbed for hours on end. At other times the same child may be so distracted by surrounding stimuli that they cannot focus at all. Common motor coordination difficulties include handwriting problems. A child may be able to produce neat handwriting but only with great effort, only being able to write a small amount if neat and when asked to write a large amount of work their handwriting is illegible. For these children, scolding or suggesting that they could write neatly if only they try is ineffective at best as their difficulty is real and due to neurological problems in the link between brain and hand movements, not lack of effort. Instead, allow them to audio-tape their work on a dictaphone perhaps, or to word process it if they are capable with computers. Many individuals are unable to recall what books they need for what lesson, to remember a string of instructions, or to work out in advance what they must do and how to do it. Individuals with a diagnosis on the autism spectrum often find it almost impossible to "multitask."

As professionals, any of us working with children or adults on the autism spectrum must ensure that we are up to date with our understanding, and this means attending specialized training courses or conferences. Professional awareness is still inconsistent. We should be aiming to improve consistency and awareness throughout education, adult services, psychology and psychiatry, general practice and elsewhere. However, the learning experience that has had the greatest impact for me as a professional working with families affected by autism and Asperger's syndrome, is to be in awe of the dedication, commitment, persistence, faith, and overwhelming love that parents and partners demonstrate. I have been lucky to meet so many families who have never given up despite their concerns and beliefs being dismissed by educational or health services. It is because of these personal experiences and my contacts with these families that my drive to further understand the causes and the psychology of autism and to be able to educate other professionals in this area continues. It is humbling to see the psychological and emotional resources possessed by these families, often in the face of overwhelming adversity. They have encouraged autism to become my vocation and not just a career, and for this I will be eternally grateful.

Fiona J. Scott, Ph.D. is a chartered psychologist and Senior Research Associate with the Autism Research Centre, University of Cambridge, UK (www.autism-researchcentre.com). She also has an independent practice offering professional training, diagnostic assessment, consultation, and expert reports relating to Autism Spectrum Disorder, Asperger's syndrome and developmental psychopathology. Dr Scott has over 12 years' experience in researching and assessing children and adults with Autism Spectrum Disorders. She has been involved with a Department of Health workshop and policy drafting on Asperger's syndrome; the All Party Parliamentary Group on Autism; the National Initiative for Autism Screening and Assessment (NIASA); and the Medical Research Council Review of Autism Research. Dr Scott lives in Suffolk, UK, with her family. She spends her spare time riding her Harley-Davidson motorcycle around the UK and Europe with her partner and friends from the Fenlanders Chapter of the Harley Owners Group.

60. Spiderman at Mini-Camp

Lillian N. Stiegler

Today Spiderman kicked me in the leg. It really hurt, but it was my own fault—I'm the one who picked the battle. Spiderman was angry with me because I was stubbornly blocking the elevator door. He loved the elevator and longed to press the lighted buttons, to feel the slow-motion movement from first to second floor, and second back to first. He craved hearing the mechanical hum during the ride and the little ding each time the elevator reached its predictable destination. He adored watching the doors open momentarily, and then lazily close. Spiderman was prepared to defend this wondrous elevator as his rightful turf, but I was thinking, "Come on Spidey, you didn't come to this mini-camp just to ride up and down the whole time, did you? Be part of us, be one of us, just for a while..."

I teach an intensive summer course on Autism Spectrum Disorders to graduate students in speech-language pathology. As part of the class, we invite local, school-age youngsters with autism (and their siblings) to participate, free of charge, in a three-day mini-camp, which consists of a daily progression through four activity centers. I tell my students that the best way to discover the culture of autism is to meet a lot of different people with that diagnosis, just as one would visit a foreign country to learn more about customs, languages, and ways of life. The purpose is not to attempt to change the campers, but to *know* them to some degree. So we turn our academic building inside out for a few days: the conference room becomes our art studio, the speech-science lab is transformed into a station for technology play, an unused classroom becomes a venue for rowdy or graceful movement games, and the faculty lounge is converted into a sunny, creative, recreational kitchen.

The graduate students are apprehensive, but curious and filled with expectancy. The day before camp begins, someone asks, "What if one of the kids freaks out?" Before I can open my mouth to offer some sort of professorial response, another student tells her, "We'll try to figure it out. We'll handle it." They work in teams, diligently, thoughtfully, to prepare all sorts of wonderful activities, knowing they will always need a range of quick Plan Bs. Based on a small bit of advance information, they try their best to accommodate each camper's individual needs and interests: no peanut butter activities because of one camper's allergy, a geography game for a map buff, a Spiderman CD-ROM for you-know-who. I ask my students to simply engage the campers—to start conversations and try to keep them going.

Each day, campers are enthusiastically greeted at the front door with a visual schedule to show them what comes first, and where they're going second, third, and last. Bright yellow tape on the floors runs the length of the hallways and up the stairs to show the way from one room to another. Within the centers, there are visual supports: recipes, instructions, choice menus. A volunteer floats around, capturing the proceedings with video and still cameras. Each rotation is about 22 minutes long, with a minute's worth of transition time in between. That's the plan, anyway. We hope for smooth changeovers; sometimes they happen and sometimes they don't. I literally jog from room to room, peeking in, offering quick words of encouragement, advice, and praise to students and campers alike. Sometimes I just stick my hand through a crack in the door and hold up some fingers, indicating the number of minutes until the switch to the next center. The whole thing lasts an hour and a half.

Our mini-camp works on several levels. For the campers, it's a bonus opportunity to have some new experiences in a nurturing environment. They get to practice skills, and they are challenged to interact and communicate with diverse partners in novel environments. The graduate students are accorded a singular chance to compare their preconceived notions about autism to a whole range of real-life individuals with diagnoses that are "on the spectrum." They can feel relaxed because they're being graded only on their participation, planning, collaboration, and flexibility—their skills as interventionists are not, for once, being scrutinized. They witness full-blown tantrums and stereotypical behaviors in a way that videotape fails to reveal, and they also get to see that eventually, tantrums resolve and stereotypes wane. They hear varieties of echolalia, incessant questioning, unusual vocal patterns…and they can practice interpreting and responding to these unconventional communication strategies. From the parents' perspective, the mini-camp is one more source of recreation for their children during the long summer. They use the time as a sort of three-day support summit, where they sit together in the lobby, commune, and share stories of horrors and successes. They swap wisdom on all manner of topics: medications, traveling, navigating the public school systems. It is difficult to gauge who benefits most, but it very well might be me… I am taught by everyone involved. I even indulge myself by imagining what it would be like if my students' high levels of joy and energy could be preserved throughout their professional careers…or even if it could be bottled and lavishly poured onto interventionists and teachers who have, sadly, lost that priceless spark.

As the grad students return the campers to the lobby, I get brief snapshots. An adolescent girl asks me my age, my birthday, and whether or not I like chives, umbrellas, grape-flavored snowballs. Someone whispers that today a certain child ate an index card. A boy vigorously waves his "bubba"—that's what his mom calls it—a thick strip of rubber band that he frequently holds and chews to decrease his anxiety in this, or any, foreign place. Mothers exchange telephone numbers and email addresses, promising to keep in touch. There is a deliciously sweet, citrus smell emanating from the kitchen, where four different groups made fresh-squeezed lemonade. Some of my students have tears in their eyes as the parents thank them. Spiderman looks happy. He is an eight-year-old boy in a body-hugging costume. He talks to his caregiver, contentedly showing her a piece of artwork on their way to the car.

I feel a trace of guilt. Several parents tell me they wish the camp lasted a whole week, or better yet, the whole summer. One mom of two high-functioning sons talks about the critical need for a year-round teen social group in our area, and she's right. I think about how I might do more, considering the limited resources of my small, public university. Maybe I can. Perhaps some of my students, with their incredible gusto, will turn out to be change-agents within their own communities, advocating, planning, and working hard to provide the neighborhood support services that families truly need. I tell myself that this mini-camp is, at least, a start…a small contribution…and then the last child to leave, a veteran camper, uses her interrogative forms to communicate her hope for the future: "Fun activities next year? In July? Monday, Tuesday, Wednesday?" I smile, and nod, and answer yes, that's the plan.

The bruises on my shin are already healing.

Lillian N. Stiegler, Ph.D. is a certified speech-language pathologist with over 20 years of experience. She is an associate professor of communication sciences and disorders at Southeastern Louisiana University. As a consultant to the Louisiana Department of Education, Division of Special Populations, she provides annual training workshops on communication strategies for individuals with autism and other developmental disabilities. In addition to her course on Autism Spectrum Disorders, Dr Stiegler teaches university coursework on the neurophysiology of communication, neuropathology of communication, and language intervention. Dr Stiegler lives near a shady old oak tree in Covington, Louisiana. She is married to a hard-headed man and has three wonderful grown-up sons.

Appendix: Further Reading and Internet Resources

Further Reading

Attwood, T. (1998) *Asperger's Syndrome: A Guide for Parents and Professionals.* London: Jessica Kingsley Publishers.

Baker, J. (2003) *Social Skills Training for Children and Adolescents with Asperger Syndrome and Social-Communications Problems.* Shawnee Mission, KS: Autism Asperger Publishing Company.

Baron-Cohen, S., Leslie, A. and Frith, U. (1985) "Does the autistic child have a theory of mind?" *Cognition 21,* 37–46.

Bashe, P. Romanowski and Kirby, B. L. (2001) *The OASIS Guide to Asperger Syndrome: Advice, Support, Insight, and Inspiration.* New York: Crown.

Bleach, F. (2002) *Everybody Is Different: A Book for Young People Who Have Brothers or Sisters With Autism.* Shawnee Mission, KS: Autism Asperger Publishing Company.

Durand, V. D. (1998) *Sleep Better: A Guide to Improving Sleep for Children with Special Needs.* Baltimore, MD: Paul Brookes Publishing.

Grandin, T. (1996) *Thinking In Pictures: and Other Reports from My Life with Autism.* New York: Vintage.

Grandin, T. (1996) *Emergence : Labeled Autistic.* New York: Warner Books.

Gray, C. (2000) *The New Social Story Book : Illustrated Edition.* Arlington, TX: Future Horizons.

Greenfeld, J. (1970) *A Child Called Noah.* New York: Washington Square.

Greenspan, S. I. and Wieder, S. with Simons, R. (1998) *The Child with Special Needs: Encouraging Intellectual and Emotional Growth.* Reading, MA: Addison Wesley.

Gutstein, S. (2001) *Autism/Aspergers: Solving the Relationship Puzzle.* Arlington, TX: Future Horizons.

Haddon, M. (2004) *The Curious Incident of the Dog in the Nighttime.* New York: Vintage.

Hall, K. (2000) *Asperger Syndrome, the Universe and Everything: Kenneth's Book.* London: Jessica Kingsley Publishers.

Jackson, L. (2002) *Freaks, Geeks and Asperger Syndrome: A User Guide to Adolescence.* London: Jessica Kingsley Publishers.

Jacobs, B. (2003) *Loving Mr. Spock—Understanding an Aloof Lover—Could it be Asperger's Syndrome?* Arlington, TX: Future Horizons, Inc.

Kephart. B. (1999) *A Slant of Sun: One Child's Courage.* New York: Norton.

Kluth, P. (2003) *You're Going to Love this Kid!: Teaching Students with Autism in the Inclusive Classroom.* Baltimore, MD: Paul Brookes Publishing.

Kranowitz, C. S. (1998) *The Out-of-Sync Child: Recognizing and Coping with Sensory Integration Dysfunction.* New York: Berkeley.

Kushner, H. S. (1981) *When Bad Things Happen to Good People.* New York: Avon.

Leaf, R. and McEachin, J. (1999) *A Work in Progress: Behavior Management Strategies and a Curriculum for Intensive Behavioral Treatment of Autism.* New York: DRL Books.

Lewis, L. (1998) *Special Diets for Special Kids.* Arlington, TX: Future Horizons.

Lovaas, O. I. (1981) *The ME Book: Teaching Developmentally Disabled Children.* Austin, TX: Pro-Ed.

Maurice, C. (ed.) (1996) *Behavioral Intervention for Young Children With Autism: A Manual for Parents and Professionals.* Austin, TX: Pro-Ed Publishing.

May, J. (1991) *Fathers of Children with Special Needs: New Horizons.* Bethesda, MD: Association for the Care of Children's Health.

McHugh, M. (1999) *Special Siblings: Growing Up with Someone with a Disability.* New York: Hyperion.

McKean, T. (1994) *Soon Will Come the Light: A View from Inside the Autism Puzzle.* Arlington, TX: Future Horizons.

Meyer, D. (ed.) (1995) *Uncommon Fathers: Reflections on Raising a Child with a Disability.* Bethesda, MD: Woodbine House.

Meyer, D. (ed.) (1997) *Views from Our Shoes: Growing Up with a Brother or a Sister with Special Needs.* Bethesda, MD: Woodbine House.

Miller, N. B. and Sammons, C. C. (1999) *Everybody's Different: Understanding and Changing Our Reactions to Disabilities.* Baltimore, MD: Paul Brookes Publishing.

Mont, D. (2001) *A Different Kind of Boy: A Father's Memoir about Raising a Gifted Child with Autism.* London: Jessica Kingsley Publishers.

Myles, B., Trautman, M. and Schelvan, R. (2004) *The Hidden Curriculum: Practical Solutions for Understanding Unstated Rules in Social Situations.* Shawnee Mission, KS: Autism Asperger Publishing Company.

Naseef, R. (2001) *Special Children, Challenged Parents: The Struggles and Rewards of Raising a Child with a Disability.* Baltimore, MD: Paul Brookes Publishing.

Paradi , V. (2005)*Elijah's Cup: A Family's Journey into the Community and Culture of High-Functioning Autism and Asperger's Syndrome* (Revised edition). London: Jessica Kingsley Publishers.

Seligman, M. and Darling, R. B. (1997) *Ordinary Families, Special Children: A Systems Approach to Childhood Disability.* New York: Guilford.

Shaw, W. (2001) *Biological Treatments for Autism and PDD.* London: Sunflower Books.

Shore, S. (2003) *Beyond the Wall: Personal Experiences with Autism and Asperger Syndrome.* Shawnee Mission, KS: Autism Asperger Publishing Company.

Shore, S. (2004) *Ask and Tell: Self-advocacy and Disclosure for People on the Autism Spectrum.* Shawnee Mission, KS: Autism Asperger Publishing Company.

Siegel, B. (1998) *The World of the Autistic Child: Understanding and Treating Autistic Spectrum Disorders.* London: Oxford University Press.

Stern, D. N. and Bruschweiler-Stern, N. with Freeland, A. (1998) *The Birth of a Mother: How the Motherhood Experience Changes You Forever.* New York: Basic Books.

Stone, D., Patton, B. and Heen, S. (1999) *Difficult Conversations—How to Discuss What Matters Most.* New York: Viking/Penguin-Putnam, Inc.

Thompson, T. (1996) *Andy and His Yellow Frisbee.* Bethesda, MD: Woodbine House.

Vermeulen, P. (2000) *I Am Special: Introducing Children and Young People to their Autistic Spectrum Disorder.* London: Jessica Kingsley Publishers.

Wheeler, M. (1998) *Toilet Training for Individuals with Autism and Related Disorders.* Arlington, TX: Future Horizons.

Willey, L. H. (1999) *Pretending to be Normal: Living with Asperger's Syndrome.* London: Jessica Kingsley Publishers.

Williams, D. (1998) *Nobody Nowhere: The Remarkable Autobiography of an Autistic Girl.* London: Jessica Kingsley Publishers.

Winnicott, D. W. (1993) *Talking to Parents.* New York: Addison Wesley.

Internet resources

About Autism – www.autism.about.com
American Academy of Child and Adolescent Psychiatry – www.aacap.org
American Psychological Association – www.apa.org
Asperger Syndrome Education Network (ASPEN) – www.aspennj.org
ASPIRES (Asperger Syndrome Partners & Individuals Resources, Encouragement & Support) – www.aspires-relationships.com
Autism One Radio – www.autismone.org/radio
Autism Organizations World Wide – www.autism-india.org/worldorgs.htm
Autism and PDD Support Network – www.autism-pdd.net
Autism Research Institute – www.autism.com/ari
Autism Resources – www.autism-resources.com
Autism Society of America – www.autism-society.org
Autism Today – www.autismtoday.com
Cure Autism Now – www.cureautismnow.org
Developmental Delay Resources – www.devdelay.org
Families for Early Autism Treatment (FEAT) – www.feat.org
Fathers Network – www.fathersnetwork.org
Federation for Children with Special Needs – www.fcsn.org
First Signs – www.firstsigns.org
Floortime Foundation – www.floortime.org
Inclusion Press International – www.inclusion.com
Inclusive Education – www.uni.edu/coe/inclusion
MAAP Services – www.maapservices.org
Medscape – www.medscape.com
MIND Institute – www.ucdmc.ucdavis.edu/mindinstitute
National Alliance for Autism Research – www.naar.org
National Autistic Society – www.nas.org.uk

National Dissemination Center for Children and Youth with Disabilities –
   www.nichcy.org
National Institutes of Health (autism page) – www.nichd.nih.gov/autism
Nonverbal Learning Disorders Association – www.nlda.org
Online Asperger Syndrome Information and Support (OASIS) –
   www.udel.edu/bkirby/asperger
Parents Helping Parents – www.php.com
Pediatric Dentistry – www.aapd.org
Picture Exchange Communication System – www.pecs.com
Psych Central – www.psychcentral.com
Schafer Autism Report – www.sarnet.org
Sensory Integration Network – www.sensoryintegration.org.uk
Sensory Processing Disorder Network – www.sinetwork.org
Sibling Support Project – www.thearc.org/siblingsupport
talkAutism – www.talkautism.org
TEACCH (Treatment and Education of Autistic and Related Communication Handi-
   capped Children) – www.unc.edu/depts/teacch
Toys and Play – www.lekotek.org
Unlocking Autism – www.unlockingautism.com
World Autism Organization – www.worldautism.org

About the editors

Cindy N. Ariel, Ph.D. is a licensed psychologist specializing in women's issues particularly around physical/emotional health and relationship concerns. She received her master's degree from Hahnemann University and her doctorate from Temple. Dr. Ariel provides short- and long-term psychotherapy for individuals dealing with anxiety and depression as well as guidance for couples in both traditional and alternative family arrangements. She has worked with individuals with disabilities in various settings for over 25 years. Her current psychotherapy practice also includes individuals, couples, and other family members who are living with a loved one who has special needs. Dr. Ariel brings these experiences to bear as an editor in this volume, her first collection of essays.

Robert Naseef, Ph.D. has practiced for over 15 years as a psychologist and as a consultant to numerous schools and human service organizations. He is a graduate of Temple University and has a special interest in the psychology of men. He specializes in families of children with disabilities. He has lectured internationally and made numerous appearances on radio and television. Rabbi Harold Kushner, the author of *When Bad Things Happen to Good People*, endorsed his book, *Special Children, Challenged Parents*— "Writing with the wisdom of a mental health professional and the compassion of a loving father, Dr. Naseef has given us a book that will instruct and inspire us all."

Together Cindy Ariel and Robert Naseef are the founders of Alternative Choices, an independent practice in psychotherapy (see www.alternativechoices.com). Their practice offers an alternative to managed care and large impersonal mental health settings and provides a personal and confidential approach to treatment and evaluation. It includes the Special Families Resource Center. Doctors Ariel and Naseef live and work in the Philadelphia, Pennsylvania area with their two daughters, Kara and Zoë. They are interested in your reactions to this collection of essays. Readers can contact them at voices@alternativechoices.com.